S0-AHA-171

UNSECURITY

Information security is **failing**. Breaches are **epidemic**. How can we fix this **broken industry?**

EVAN FRANCEN

— Beaver's Pond Press —
Minneapolis, MN

Unsecurity: Information security is failing. Breaches are epidemic. How can we fix this broken industry? © copyright 2019 Evan Francen.

All rights reserved. No part of this book may be reproduced in any form whatsoever, by photography or xerography or by any other means, by broadcast or transmission, by translation into any kind of language, nor by recording electronically or otherwise, without permission in writing from the author, except by a reviewer, who may quote brief passages in critical articles or reviews.

Edited by Steve LeBeau and Christine Zuchora-Walske

ISBN: 978-1-64343-974-7
Library of Congress Catalog Number: 2018913784
Printed in the United States of America
First Printing: 2018
23 22 21 20 19   5 4 3 2 1

Book design by Athena Currier

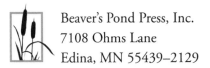 Beaver's Pond Press, Inc.
7108 Ohms Lane
Edina, MN 55439–2129

(952) 829-8818
www.BeaversPondPress.com

To order, visit www.ItascaBooks.com or call
1-800-901-3480 ext. 118. Reseller discounts available.

This book is dedicated to my best friend, my wife.

—E.F.

Author's Note

Confession: I'm an information security guy. I'm not the best information security guy who ever lived, but I'm probably better than average. Here are four things you should know about me right away:

1. **I've been an information security professional for more than twenty-five years.** I've done a lot of things and seen a lot of things. Some good and some bad. This is sort of important, because experience matters. Here are some highlights from my experience:

    - I founded FRSecure, a leading information security consulting company with more than one thousand clients, in 2008.

    - In 2017, I founded SecurityStudio, a software-as-a-service (SaaS) company dedicated to building a community of information security practitioners who speak the same security language.

    - I coinvented the FISASCORE, the information security risk translation and assessment tool for companies.

    - I coinvented the myFISASCORE, the information security risk translation and assessment tool for consumers.

- I developed the FRSecure Certified Information Systems Security Professional (CISSP®) Mentor Program. The Mentor Program was established in 2010 with 6 students and has grown to more than 350 students in 2018.

- I advised legal counsel in high-profile breaches, including Target and Blue Cross Blue Shield:

  - 2014/2015—Consultant to the Special Litigation Committee of the Board of Directors of Target Corporation; derivative action related to the Target breach.

  - 2015/2016—Consultant to legal counsel and Blue Cross Blue Shield related to remediation efforts (postbreach).

- I served as an expert witness in several federal criminal cases.

- I've served hundreds of companies, big (Wells Fargo, Target, US Bank, UnitedHealth) and small.

- I've made dozens of television and radio appearances; topics included the Target breach, vendor risk management, and artificial intelligence.

- I've delivered hundreds of information security talks at dozens of conferences to audiences ranging from fewer than ten people to more than one thousand.

- I've written more than 750 published articles about a variety of information security topics.

2. **I'm more comfortable in the background.** My favorite place to be is in my office, solving a problem or helping someone else solve a problem. Never heard of me? That's not surprising, because I probably didn't want you to.

3. **I take my work very seriously.** I take my work seriously because people are affected by my performance, or lack thereof.

4. **I'm blunt and honest.** People get offended, but I call it how I see it. Besides, I don't get paid to tell people what they want to hear. I get paid to tell the truth.

These things, and a few others, lead to a mission. The mission is to fix the *broken information security industry*. Not by myself. Lord no! I'm not nearly capable of significantly impacting an entire industry by myself. This is a mission that requires the help of many like-minded people coming together as one. This cooperation is a central theme of this book.

This is the first book I've ever written. Writing a book is a bitch.

Introduction

Information Security Is a Game, and We're Losing

This is a game that we play every day, and you have no choice but to play. It doesn't matter whether you're a chief information security officer (CISO) at a Fortune 100 company or a full-time student. Here's the game:

- Our game is played on a field that is both intangible and tangible.

- There are two teams: the good and the bad. The good are morally and ethically good. The bad are morally and ethically corrupt.

- There are no rules. Well, that's not entirely true. There are rules; they are mandatory for the good team and optional for the bad team.

- The good team defends a goal of variable width, but it's always significantly larger than the bad team's goal.

- The object of the game is to score goals; each goal results in a significant money or asset exchange and/or lives that are negatively or positively impacted.

- There is no scoreboard, and we don't know what the score is exactly. We just know who's winning. If we really knew the score, maybe we'd take our game more seriously.

The game we play is a losing proposition. It's rigged against us. Add the fact that members of the good team don't have any viable winning strategy or method to work together, and what are we left with? The status quo is a guaranteed loss.

I hate losing. I especially hate losing to morally and ethically corrupt people. We need change.

Fight Fear and Breach Fatigue

Fear comes from a perceived danger or threat. Fear is exacerbated by ignorance, or the inability to put the perceived threat into its proper context. Fear is an intense emotion, and it gets tiring quickly. Maybe this is why we've grown weary of breaches. We've got breach fatigue, and some of us have just accepted fate; whatever that may be. We're defeated, or at least we have a defeatist attitude.

We can win this game though! Before we go too far, we need to take stock of where we're at now. We don't know the exact score, but we do have some indicators of what the score might be:

- We suffered an estimated 160,000 successful online attacks in 2017, including five megabreaches—the most significant being the Equifax breach, in which sensitive financial data for 145 million people was stolen. That's half the US population. (Source: https://www.darkreading.com/attacks-breaches/2017-smashed-worlds-records-for-most-data-breaches-exposed-information/d/d-id/1330987)

- More than 60 percent of Americans are willing to pay a ransom for internet extortion, almost twice as much as the global 34 percent. (Source: https://www.symantec.com/security-center/threat-report)

- Seventy-eight percent of people claim to be aware of the risks of unknown links in emails, yet somewhere between 25 and 45 percent of the same people click on the links anyway. (Source: https://blog.barkly.com/cyber-security-statistics-2017)

- The financial costs of breaches are unfathomable—an estimated $2 trillion for 2019 and as much as $6 trillion by 2021. That's more than the illegal drug trade for the whole world! (Source: https://www.juniperresearch.com/press/press-releases/cybercrime-cost-businesses-over-2trillion)

- Ginni Rometty, IBM's chairman, president, and chief executive officer (CEO), says, "Cybercrime . . . is the greatest threat to every profession, every industry, every company in the world." (Source: https://www.csoonline.com/article/3210912/security/is-cybercrime-the-greatest-threat-to-every-company-in-the-world.html)

- Microsoft CEO Satya Nadella stated $3 trillion of market value was destroyed in 2015 due to cybercrime. (Source: http://www.smartcompany.com.au/technology/49457-complacency-over-cybercrime-cost-3-trillion-in-2015/)

- Only 33 percent of small and midmarket businesses (SMBs) think their organization can prevent a cyber-attack. (Source: https://csrps.com/Media/Default/2017%20Reports/2017-Ponemon-State-of-Cybersecurity-in-Small-and-Medium-Sized-Businesses-SMB.pdf) Comment: this is harsh, but the other 67 percent are ignorant.

It's hard to make a case that the information security industry isn't broken. We used to be shocked by these headlines, but those days are gone. In a few cases, the shock has turned to anger, but where do we vent our anger? Maybe we give the mob someone's head. We can force a few retirements and launch a few lawsuits. After the anger (or memory) subsides, we just start over again. Memories fade, but nothing fundamentally changes. The cycle plays over and over.

It's Up to Us to Fix Our Problems

The primary audience for this book are my peers, the other eight hundred thousand-ish people in the United States who have carved out careers as information security professionals, and hundreds of thousands more across the globe. Why us? Because we are the ones who understand the game we play better than anyone else. We are the professionals, we are the experts, we are the team captains.

There's a difference between information security professionals and the rest of the world. We don't represent the norm. We think we do, but we don't. According to CyberSeek (http://cyberseek.org/heatmap.html), we are part of a cybersecurity workforce, an elite group cybersecurity engineers, cybersecurity analysts, cybersecurity managers, chief information security officers, researchers, and penetration testers. We hold cool certifications like the Offensive Security Certified Professional (OSCP), Certified Information Privacy Professional (CIPP), Global Information Assurance Certification (GIAC), and Certified Information Systems Security Professional (CISSP).

We really are an elite force of awesome people with all sorts of different backgrounds, but one thing binds us together: we are all on the good team. We are all in this together, and it is time to pick ourselves up, look in the mirror, and get honest with ourselves. Together, we must sort through the problems facing our team. Each chapter in this book focuses on different challenges we must address, and offers ideas for solutions:

- **Chapter 1: We're Not Speaking the Same Language**—*The information security industry is broken because we don't speak the same language.*

- **Chapter 2: Bad Foundations**—*The information security industry is broken because we build on bad foundations, or worse, without a foundation at all.*

- **Chapter 3: Lipstick on a Pig**—*The information security industry is broken because we don't get real with ourselves.*

- **Chapter 4: Pipe Dreams**—*The information security industry is broken because reality is a hard pill to swallow.*

- **Chapter 5: The Blame Game**—*The information security industry is broken because people don't want to own it.*

- **Chapter 6: The Herd Mentality**—*The information security industry is broken because people focus on others instead of themselves.*

- **Chapter 7: Because I Said So**—*The information security industry is broken because people don't want to do the right thing.*

- **Chapter 8: Empty Promises**—*The information security industry is broken because we don't commit and keep our word.*

- **Chapter 9: The Money Grab**—*The information security industry is broken because money is more important than your security.*

- **Chapter 10: Too ~~Many~~ Few Experts**—*The information security industry is broken because we have too many "experts" but not enough experts.*

My Motivators

I care for people and hate cheating. I love winning and hate losing.

People are woven into fabric of everything we do. This may sound corny, but it's the truth. If you love people, it makes you a better information security professional. We don't protect data just for the sake of data. Behind every health record there's a patient. Behind every social security number there's a grandparent, parent, son, or daughter.

Deep down, I hate seeing people taken advantage of and I hate cheating. In our industry, there's plenty of both.

Throughout this book I will refer to the information security industry as "our" industry. My foundational belief is that we're all in this together.

We must get started now, because we can't afford to wait any longer.

Why We Must Fix the System

I don't have a majestic Braveheart speech to rally the troops, but I do have several stories that illustrate why I care.

Mom-and-Pop Printing Company (M&P)

This story shows that when a large company flexes its security muscles without thinking it through, it can hurt good people.

M&P was a small, family-owned printing company in Phoenix with about sixty employees. It printed all sorts of materials for large companies, and one extrabig company—we'll call it EBC—accounted for about 60 percent of M&P's business.

One of the struggles facing this small company was that each of the large companies it served had its own specific information security requirements. You see, ever since the big Target breach of 2013—which accessed the retailer via its HVAC vendor—companies have made more of a point to do vendor risk assessments.

Some of M&P's clients wanted an SOC 2 report, some companies developed their own assessments or questionnaires, and at least one large company wanted ISO 27001 certification. These requirements were an increasing burden for M&P, which was already struggling with being profitable due to razor-thin margins. The printer had to comply or risk losing business.

Everything came to a head when EBC changed the way it handled information security for its vendors. This company decided that instead of assessing risk, it would simply require all its vendors to install the same security controls that EBC used. Now, EBC had a multimillion-dollar budget for information security, and the number of its security staff alone exceeded the number of employees at M&P.

This put M&P in an impossible position, and the results were catastrophic. Because this small company could not afford to secure information the same way that the large company did—regardless of risk—the small company lost the business. The last I heard, M&P was forced to lay off more than half of its workforce.

M&P didn't pose a greater risk to EBC; you could even argue that it posed a lesser risk. The small company simply couldn't comply with the unreasonable requirements of the large company. I can only imagine the heartbreak felt by the owners of M&P when they were forced to hand out the layoff and termination notices.

Don't be fooled into thinking that this sad story is an isolated incident. This type of thing happens more often than we'd admit.

Long-Term Care Organization (LTC)

The information isn't yours, but it is.

LTC was a fast-growth company with a real track record of success as defined by market share and revenue. Management had a "growth at all costs" mentality, and information security was but an afterthought, or simply a box that needed to be checked. LTC had grown primarily through innovation and acquisitions.

Occasionally, a business partner or board member would inquire about information security. After all, LTC held millions of sensitive health records belonging to various downstream customers. To satisfy the occasional requests, LTC decided to do periodic Information security assessments. To the outsider, LTC appeared to run a tight ship.

Things were not as they appeared, however. Information security was treated as an IT issue, not a business issue. When LTC's information security personnel reported that the company's risk assessment was ranked "very poor"—450 on a scale of 300 to 850—the executives failed to take it seriously. The attitude among executive management was that the information security team was composed of paranoid people who continually said no. They were the "no" people and didn't understand how LTC's business operated. You'd think that a "very poor" risk assessment would be enough to motivate executive management to put better practices in place. You'd be wrong.

The motivation of LTC was never to be more secure. Its motivation was to do the least amount of work and spend the least amount of money possible to appease anyone who asked about its security. The common question was "Do you do periodic information security assessments?" The answer was "Yes." Nobody asked if the company improved security as a result of any assessment. Did they do an information security risk assessment? Yep. Done.

The company handled millions of sensitive health records for people living in long-term care facilities. If the company suffered a breach, who suffered? The information belonged to the people living in LTC's facilities, yet they had no say in how their information was protected.

This is BS.

Large Distribution Company (LDC)

Ignorance is no excuse, and it's not defensible.

LDC never gave a second thought to information security beyond a firewall and some passwords. The only reason passwords were a thing is because the computers came with them. LDC never thought it'd be a victim of an attack. Its logic was that it had nothing that an attacker would want, so why bother? It didn't have any credit card data. It didn't have any health data. Security wasn't a concern whatsoever.

Information security wasn't an afterthought for LDC; information security wasn't a thought at all.

One day, weird things started to happen. Whatever. Then a few weirder things happened. Whatever. For the next month, weird things continued to happen—things like unexplained network and server performance fluctuations, missing files, new user directories, and user accounts that nobody recognized or claimed to have created. No matter. Whatever.

One Saturday, the CIO got a text from the company's president. Saturday? That was odd. The text said, "Just got a call from the president of Big Customer. They're claiming that we're sending them phishing emails. Do you know anything about this?"

Big Customer (BC) was LDC's largest customer. BC decided to block all emails from LDC because of the high volume of phishing attempts.

This time LDC decided to act, because it had no real choice in the matter. LDC called an information security consultant to investigate. Within fifteen minutes the consultant found a remote access Trojan (RAT) on a domain controller. A closer look revealed an active reverse shell to a source in the Czech Republic. Ugh!

Then the consultant found six additional RATs, other malware installed in countless places, compromised user accounts, and unexplained files everywhere. I guess that explained the weirdness. Oh, and it looked like the bad team made off with nearly a million dollars stolen through a series of unauthorized ACH transfers. ACH is short for automated clearing house, an electronic funds-transfer system run by the National Automated Clearing House Association (NACHA).

We shake our heads. Stories like this one tick us off. Some jerk took off with almost a million dollars that could have been spent to grow the business, pay employee bonuses, or whatever. Instead, the money is gone, and the bad team can reinvest a portion of it to enable better future attacks on others.

Could LDC have made this any easier?

This was a case where nobody was responsible for information security. Would you believe after this breach that executive management and ownership still debated the value of information security? They did, and it's sad.

The Prognosis

Depending upon how deep we want to go, we can find millions of flaws in our industry. We should not get bogged down in the minutiae, though. One of the telltale signs of an experienced information security analyst is the inability to put things into perspective.

We also need to keep our pride in check, look at ourselves honestly, and fight our biases. Introspection sets good security people apart from great security people. Great security people are introspective geniuses. They look for solutions to their problems within themselves first, before they point fingers at others.

Some truth and encouragement before we move on: Not all is doom and gloom. There are many good things about our industry. Unfortunately, due to the nature of our work, it's easier to find the broken things because they stick out. But we have thousands of smart, dedicated, and talented people working in our field. We spend millions of tireless, thankless, and selfless hours protecting people we will never meet. Some of us are innovative, selfless, and passionate. This core of strength and integrity gives us the courage to address our problems and to improve our industry for the sake of everyone.

Contents

1. We're Not Speaking the Same Language 1

Problem #1: We Don't Have a Common Language 4

Solution #1: Agree on Our Common Language 6

Problem #2: We Lack a Common
Understanding with Normal People 14

Solution #2: Find Our Common Ground 19

Problem #3: Foolish Conversations
Occur between Organizations 32

Solution #3: Translate Security between Organizations 35

2. Bad Foundations .51

Problem #1: Building without Blueprints 52

Solution #1: Starting with Blueprints 53

Problem #2: Building without Permits. 59

Solution #2: Building with Permits 59

Problem #3: Weak or Absent Foundations. 61

Solution #3: Establishing a Solid Foundation 67

Problem #4: Overengineered Foundations. 76

Solution #4: Simplification 77

3. Lipstick on a Pig 79

Problem #1: Lipstick Makes Us Appear
More Attractive Than We Really Are 80

Solution #1: We Need to Get Real. 84

Problem #2: Lipstick Makes Us Feel Better about Ourselves 86

Solution #2: We Need to Be Honest
with Ourselves and One Another 91

Problem #3: Technology Is the Most Common Lipstick. 96

Solution #3: We Should Use Technology
Only When and Where It's Needed 98

Problem #4: Layering on Lipstick Makes Things Worse 99

Solution #4: We Need to Simplify. 100

4. Pipe Dreams 101

Problem #1: Ignorance Is No Excuse
for Poor Information Security 103

Solution #1: Understand What
We Should Know and Learn It 106

Problem #2: Panic and Anxiety Stem
from Our Lack of Understanding 109

Solution #2: Plan for the Worst and
Hope for the Best, a Sense of Calm 110

Problem #3: Fantasies Make for Bad Decision Making 112

Solution #3: Expect Reality Using Logic and Facts 117

5. The Blame Game 127

Problem #1: There's No Shortage of People
or Things to Blame for Our Shortcomings. 129

Solution #1: Define Roles and Responsibilities 131

Problem #2: We All Live in Glass Houses 137

Solution #2: Accept That We All Have Our Problems 138

Problem #3: We Fear Blame and Reprimand 139

Solution #3: Cultivate Transparency and Incentives 141

Problem #4: We're Not Good
at or Ready for Attribution 142

Solution #4: Plan for Attribution 142

Problem #5: There's No Recourse
for Faulty Products and Services. 143

Solution #5: Hold People Accountable 145

6. The Herd Mentality 147

Problem #1: There's a False Sense of Safety in the Herd 149

Solution #1: Use the Herd to Your Advantage 154

Problem #2: Herd Mentality Leads to Poor Choices. 157

Solution #2: Take the Time to Research 162

Problem #3: Even If the Herd Is Right, Its Still Won't Fit Us . . . 164

Solution #3: Focus on You and What You Can Control 165

7. Because I Said So 168

Problem #1: We Have so Many Laws, but So Little Direction 171

Solution #1: The Intent of the Law Is Key. 175

Problem #2: We Have No Choice, but to Comply 177

Solution #2: How We Comply Is Where We Find Our Choices. . . . 179

Problem #3: Compliance Makes a Crappy Foundation 180

Solution #3: Focus on the Foundation. 182

8. Empty Promises 183

Problem #1: Troubles with Commitments. 184

Solution #1: Making Commitments Carefully. 191

Problem #2: Money as a Demonstration of Commitment. . . . 198

Solution #2: Putting Our Money Where Our Mouth Is 201

Problem #3: Thinking Obscurity Makes Us Secure 202

Solution #3: Taking Our Head Out of the Sand. 204

9. The Money Grab 205

Problem #1: There's Plenty of Snake Oil for Sale 207

Solution #1: Do Your Homework 213

Problem #2: Fear and Sex Sell Lots of Stuff 217

Solution #2: Fight FUD and Be a Little Less Sexy 221

Problem #3: Money Spent Poorly Is Bad Money 223

Solution #3: Buy What You Need 228

10. Too ~~Many~~ Few Experts 232

Problem #1: We Need More Good People,
but We Don't Know Who 233

Solution #1: Define What Makes a Good Security Person 236

Problem #2: The Severe Talent Shortage
Is Painful and Getting Worse 240

Solution #2: Commit to the Cause 256

Acknowledgments 263

About the Author 266

1

We're Not Speaking the Same Language

The information security industry is broken because we don't speak the same language. Like a shattered pane of glass, the information security industry is broken into many pieces, large and small. It is the purpose of this book to rally our tribe of information security professionals to put the pieces together into a coherent and functional whole.

This is a noble and challenging undertaking, and it is also an unselfish one. We need to work together in an organized fashion to get this done, and we must forget for a moment that we are competitors. Seriously, there's plenty of business for everyone anyway! One thing we'll notice shortly after we start cooperating (as an industry) is that we are not speaking the same language.

Isolation from one another and the adoption of various methodologies and systems have given us different vocabularies and different languages. Trying to communicate with one another is like being in a foreign country—if you can't translate the foreign words, then you can't get anything done. Even worse, failures in translation lend themselves to assumptions, misconceptions, and conflict.

The primary communication gap in our industry is our inability to agree on and consistently use the same language. However, we have two more communication gaps as well: translation problems between us and normal people, and translation problems between organizations.

Along with language gaps among information security professionals, there is a virtual Grand Canyon between us and all other people who do not work in our field. That metaphor may seem rather dramatic, but it is apt. Normal people—mainstream regular men and women—greatly struggle to understand what it is that we do. We can rarely figure out a clear way to explain it to them. There's always some anxiety when we try to explain ourselves, and it's because we're not very good at it.

The important aspect of this "us versus normal people" language translation gap is that it applies to all the normal people who run the businesses that we serve, as well as to all their employees, whom we depend upon. Speaking different languages causes dysfunction. We urgently need to call in a team of translators, because we can't work together if we don't understand each other. Confusion will reign and mistakes will be made.

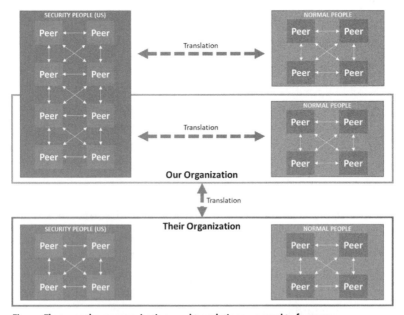

Figure: These are the communications and translations we need to focus on.

Finally, we need to examine the language gaps that exist between different organizations. There are so many different approaches to information security that any two businesses are likely to have made different choices. The different choices and different systems mean different vocabularies with different meanings—and therefore, different languages. An organization-to-organization language gap rears its ugly head in third-party (or vendor) risk-management activities. It presents another serious need for translation.

So, we have a triple set of communication gaps in our industry:

1. **Within our own tribe.** Information security professionals do not share a common language.

2. **Between us and normal people.** We don't speak the same language that normal people do.

3. **Between organizations.** Organizations often speak different security languages.

In this chapter we will examine these language problems, and then I'll propose some ideas that may help us find solutions.

Problems covered in this chapter include:

- Problem #1: We don't have a common language.
- Problem #2: We lack a common understanding with normal people.
- Problem #3: Foolish conversations occur between organizations.

Some of the potential solutions we'll explore include:

- Solution #1: Agree on our common language.
- Solution #2: Find our common ground.
- Solution #3: Translate security between organizations.

We are severely limited by our industry's language and translation problems. It will be very difficult to mature into other areas of information security with any consistency until we figure out our fundamental communications problems.

PROBLEM #1: WE DON'T HAVE A COMMON LANGUAGE

Developmentally speaking, the information security industry is still in the Wild West. We have not civilized with a single set of common standards, policies, or guidelines as other professions have done. Instead we have dozens—or thousands—of sets. We have no information security association to which everyone belongs. Attorneys have the American Bar Association, and accountants have the American Institute of Certified Public Accountants. We have a couple of dozen organizations, including some that are excellent, but none has evolved into a single governing body for us. (See the sidebar "Annotated List of Information Security Associations" on page 46.) Maybe the closest are the International Information Systems Security Certification Consortium (ISC)² or the Information Systems Audit and Control Association (ISACA). But so far, we have no single authoritative voice for how our industry should operate.

Instead of a sense of professional unity and order, we all like to think we have better ways of doing things. We miss the basics, while looking for our "easy buttons." We each do our own thing, thinking that we can outsmart one another. We create complex, sleek-looking solutions to minor problems. We create thousands of different solutions for the same result, each one trying to outdo the other. Which standard should I use? ISO 27001, NIST SP 800-53, COBIT, CIS? Should I use a framework like NIST CSF? We'll all argue for different approaches, frameworks, and standards, but we'll

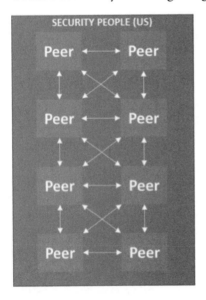

SECURITY PEOPLE (US)

Peer ←——→ Peer

Peer ←——→ Peer

Peer ←——→ Peer

Peer ←——→ Peer

rarely agree. We can't reach a consensus, that's for sure.

And then we have lone rangers who refuse to collaborate with others in the industry, and who compete by bashing others instead of trying to drive innovation. They are in this for themselves and try

> The information security industry needs a **single** professional organization to create unity, define our profession, establish standards, and work for the greater good.

to get as much out of the rest of us as possible. There's no place for them in our industry, not anymore. Get the chip off your shoulder, learn some humility, and serve your colleagues in making things better. Don't serve to make a name for yourself, serve to help someone. Too many times we've witnessed people in our industry who aren't in it to help people; they're in it to make a name for themselves and to dominate others. I'd like to think that these people are outliers and do not represent the rank and file in our profession, but I'm not so sure.

> Compete to help and drive innovation. Don't compete by putting others down. Putting others down is part of the bad team's game plan.

One very popular and well-respected expert in our industry, Dave Kennedy, posted this troubling series of tweets to his more than 75,000 followers:

> *"I try to live my life based on family, friends, and positivity. I see people tearing each other down in the most vicious ways. Even close friends. It's alarming and it's sad. (4/15)"*

> *"Complete disregard without any thought on the emotional, reputational, or personal impact towards the people they go after. In our industry it's running rampant. (5/15)"*

> *"I see people trying to amplify their voice and status in security by destroying other people or attacking their personal belief, religion, lifestyle, their looks, family, and more. (6/15)"*

"Instead of doing research, contributing, learning off of one another, it's a side-step method to gain more credibility or followers. Even running a conference for "fun" has spiraled into a chore and dealing with elevated volumes of social and behavioral problems. (7/15)"

"I see what was once a community driven on knowledge, sharing, or working together to make a positive difference, regardless of who you were or where you were from, completely shift towards going after one another. (8/15)"

"Not saying that there isn't a ton of positive out there in this industry. It's (for me) being drowned by the negativity against one another and destroying individuals without facts or conversation. I understand that this negative voice is that of the few, but it's growing. (9/15)"

(Source: https://twitter.com/hackingdave/
status/1056921028868268032?s=12)

There is absolutely no place for this in our industry, or any other industry for that matter. In Chapter 10 we explore our talent shortage problem, and I can't help but wonder who would ever want to subject themselves to this behavior. Who wants to take a risk, stick their neck out, and suggest solutions when they'll just get kicked in the privates by their peers and "friends"? We can't afford to be this way. If you're one of the people that Dave is referring to, you are part of the problem, and you won't be part of the solution unless you change.

SOLUTION #1: AGREE ON OUR COMMON LANGUAGE

Perhaps what bothers me the most about our fragmented industry is that we do not even have common agreement on the words we use to communicate with one another. We have no common definitions for some of our most important concepts. We speak different languages. The immediate solution to this is to find agreement on some fundamental definitions.

Find consensus on basic definitions among information security professionals and use them consistently.

The Definition of *Information Security*

We need to use the same phrases and words to mean the same things consistently. The words we use have meaning, but only if we use common definitions. Here's a simple question to ask your colleagues and friends: what is your definition of *information security*? This is an important and fundamental question, and I've asked it of more than a thousand people over my career. Some of the answers are downright embarrassing, and it's very rare to get two answers that are exactly the same. How can our tribe even function as a whole if our members don't agree on what it is we do? This is pretty basic stuff for any industry.

I've critically examined a lot of definitions of our industry—both formal and informal—and I've reflected a lot on my twenty-five years in the business. This is the definition that I use religiously:

Information security is managing risks to the confidentiality, integrity, and availability of information using administrative, physical, and technical controls.

Information security is *not* the same as *cybersecurity, internet security,* or *IT security*, although many people use the terms interchangeably. *Cyber, internet,* and *IT* all relate closely to technology, and information security is *not* a technology issue. Information security is a business issue. This may seem a little "potayto, potahto" to you, but it's not. The more we deviate in our basic definition of such things, the more room we leave for confusion.

Our definition of the term *information security* forms the foundation for everything else we do. It doesn't matter if you're a researcher, a pentester, a compliance manager, or a CISO. It's a definition that applies and keeps us honest. Of course, to understand this definition, we must first understand the definitions of its component words and phrases. The important components are as follows:

- managing risk
- confidentiality
- integrity
- availability
- administrative controls
- physical controls
- technical controls

Define *Managing Risk*

The very concept of managing risk means that we will always have some risk; you can never be 100 percent free of risk in information security, just as you are never free of risk in aspects of your daily life. There are varying amounts of risk whenever you are walking in your neighborhood, driving your car, or taking a shower in your own bathroom. Risk is relative, and that means information security is relative, too.

Information security is relative, and the state of information security is represented by a risk assessment.

Risk definition:

Risk is the likelihood of something bad happening, and the impact it would have if it did.

In the simplest sense, *managing risk* has two elements:

- risk assessment
- risk treatment

Risk assessment definition:

Risk assessment is the evaluation or estimation of, and the nature of, risk.

A risk assessment provides the current state of your information security program and gives you a baseline to create a road map for improvement. There are numerous challenges to address, and one of them is choosing from the various methodologies and types of information security risk assessments. You'll need to choose a method and type that suits your particular organization and purpose. Different organizations call for different approaches.

Choosing a Risk Assessment

Risk assessment must produce credible information that allows for sound decision making. Executives make significant business decisions based upon the results of our risk assessments, so we need to choose one that allows for decision making, measurable actions, and repeatability, and of course it must translate well into the language of normal people. We need an assessment that can be easily understood by executive management, the board of directors, important customers, and other stakeholders.

Credible information comes in the form of objective criteria and factual data whenever possible. If the assessment is straightforward and efficient, it will more easily integrate into the business. If we choose a risk assessment that's too cumbersome and time-consuming, we waste significant resources. While measuring threats and weaknesses, risk assessment must also account for administrative, physical, and technical controls in relation to confidentiality, integrity, and availability. While there is no perfect risk assessment, we do need a standardized method of measuring information security risk in our industry.

Risk treatment definition:

> *Risk treatment is the process of risk decision making and the actions that result.*

Once risks are assessed, they must be handled, or treated. Unfortunately, many companies conduct a risk assessment, and then don't act on it. They pay a large sum of money to do one, and once it's complete, they put the report on the shelf, never to be seen again. This is a waste of money; good risk assessments must lay the groundwork for risk treatment.

Every risk requires an action, or a treatment. Inaction, or lack of treatment, defaults to risk acceptance. Risk ignorance, or claiming to not know, is not defensible.

There are four, and only four, options for treatment:

1. acceptance
2. mitigation (remediation)
3. transference
4. avoidance

Every risk that's discovered and assessed calls for one of these responses, and the decisions must be made by executive management, the board of directors, or the information owner (assuming one exists). Risk decisions must *not* be made by us. We're information security experts; we provide the information, not the decisions. Even if we don't agree with a risk decision, we respect the decision and live with it. Over the course of my career there have been thousands (maybe hundreds of thousands) of risk decisions that I didn't agree with. Document the decision, including who made it, and move on.

- **Acceptance:** Risk acceptance is a legitimate business decision. Just because a risk is cited doesn't mean that we must mitigate it.

- **Mitigation:** The organization (or the information owner) may decide to adjust or implement controls to reduce risk.

- **Transference:** Transferring risk means that another organization or person will assume the risk on our behalf. The most common method for transferring risk is to obtain insurance.

- **Avoidance:** Avoiding risk means that we will stop doing whatever it was that led to the risk in the first place.

Mitigation, transference, and avoidance require action. The actions require planning, resource allocation, and execution. The execution strategy becomes the information security road map to follow between assessments. Once a period (a year or a quarter, for example) has passed, it's time to conduct the next assessment, and the cycle continues.

The definition of **compliance** is *not* the same as the definition of *information security*.

Compliance definition:

> *Compliance is the act or process of complying to a desire, demand, proposal, regimen, or coercion; it is conformity in fulfilling official requirements.*

Compliance is not information security, but if we do this right, it can be built into information security.

Many of us confuse information security with compliance. In fact, complying with various requirements is the primary driver for information security programs in most organizations.

Regulatory (and industry) requirements such as the Health Insurance Portability and Accountability Act (HIPAA) and the Gramm-Leach-Bliley Act (GLB Act or GLBA) are not prescriptive enough to mandate what specific controls must be applied or in what manner. For instance, HIPAA does not mandate any specific technologies or a specific training vendor. It can't, because even within the health-care industry there are vast differences among organizations. Instead, regulatory requirements are written (letter of the law) for the intent of the law.

The trick is interpreting what the intent of the law versus the letter of the law is. In the case of HIPAA, the Security Rule requires that covered entities perform a risk analysis (or assessment) and manage risk. The intent is to manage information security well, and our definition of information security includes managing risk; therefore, an information security program built on our definition automatically ensures compliance. GLBA and other information security–related laws are no different in this respect.

Knowing that the intent of the law (or compliance requirement) is to manage risk, we must build compliance into our information security programs and not the other way around. This also makes sense from a risk perspective: What's the likelihood that we'll be found noncompliant with whatever requirement, and what will the impact be? If the resulting risk is unacceptable (which it probably would be), then we choose mitigation and proceed.

Balancing Confidentiality, Integrity, and Availability

According to our definition of *information security*, the three characteristics of information that require protection are confidentiality, integrity, and availability (CIA). Any textbook on information security discusses the challenge of balancing this CIA triad. We tend to either overemphasize confidentiality at the expense of availability (remember, a business is in business to make money, not to secure information) or allow the quest for availability to run wild while we take a half-assed approach to protecting confidentiality.

Confidentiality definition:

> *Confidentiality is keeping information secret, allowing only authorized disclosure. The opposite of confidentiality is disclosure.*

Integrity definition:

> *Integrity is ensuring that the information is accurate. Accurate information is critical to us in making sound decisions. The opposite of integrity is (unauthorized) alteration.*

Availability definition:

> *Availability is ensuring that information is accessible in an authorized manner, when it's required. The opposite of availability is destruction.*

These three variables all play off one another, but especially confidentiality and availability. In general, when we increase our protection for the sake of confidentiality, we lessen our protection of availability—and vice versa. If you require a more complex password to improve confidentiality, then you make the information a little more difficult to access (availability).

When we ask people for their definition of *information security*, they usually overemphasize the *C* in the CIA triad. But when we review what they *actually* do, they overemphasize the *A*.

If we go to either extreme, it gets in the way of the company's primary purpose: to make money.

Controls: Administrative, Physical, and Technical

Our definition of *information security* refers to three types of controls: **administrative, physical,** and **technical**. We tend to spend most of our precious resources on technical controls, treating information security as if it were a purely technical issue. It's no wonder why we have trouble translating what we do to people who aren't technical, and why normal people have trouble relating to us. We've been fighting for years to get face time with the board of directors, touting that information security is a business issue. We shoot ourselves in the foot when we treat security as if it's a technical issue—more reason to use terms like *cybersecurity* and *IT security* carefully.

Administrative Controls

Administrative controls are used to manage personnel behavior using things like policies, standards, procedures, and training. These things may not be exciting or sexy, but they are critical to good information security management.

In too many cases, we've neglected administrative controls. We prefer technical controls because they are easier and sexier. Perhaps our definition of *information security* can help put this into perspective.

Physical Controls

The physical aspects of information security should not be overlooked. Physical controls can typically be touched, and they manage physical access to information. They include things like door locks, alarm systems, and camera surveillance. My favorite saying about physical controls is: *It doesn't matter how good your firewall works, if someone steals your server.* That's usually worth a few chuckles.

Physical controls are easy to relate to, but harder to assess.

Technical Controls

This is the IT part of security. Notice that it is only one part of information security and not all of it. The technical, automated, computerized systems, or portions of systems, are designed to protect digital information. These controls include things like firewalls, antivirus software, passwords, and permissions. An overemphasis on technical controls can make our jobs more difficult, especially in how we relate to normal people.

So, there we have it, an explanation of our definition of *information security*. It is both academically rigorous and completely practical. It's a definition that has kept me honest in my work for more than twenty-five years. If we constantly remind ourselves of the definition, we will more consistently practice our craft on all of information security, not just a part of it.

To summarize: solving our industry problems starts with us.

PROBLEM #2: WE LACK A COMMON UNDERSTANDING WITH NORMAL PEOPLE

Information security professionals aren't invited to a lot of parties, other than our own. I'm kidding. Sort of. This is just one of those not-so-subtle reminders that we are not considered to be normal people. If they just knew us better, they'd see that we're a fun bunch. They should watch how we party at hacker conferences like Black Hat or

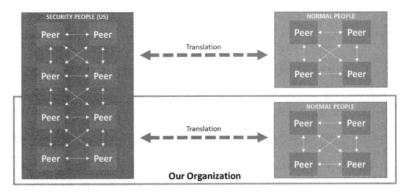

Figure: Translations between us and normal people, both within and outside our organization.

DEF CON! Then they would know how much of a blast we really are! But—alas—normal people don't go to our parties. It's not a normal thing to do.

Why are we outcasts?

We're not invited to a lot of meetings either, especially with top executives. I clearly remember the first time I was invited to a board of directors meeting. I was asked to present the results of an information security assessment, and to be frank, I was a little nervous. As I walked in, one of the directors said, "Oh, here's the IT police!" This comment led to an eruption of laughter among the directors. Everybody thought it was so funny. Except for me. I gave the obligatory smile and half-hearted chuckle, but deep down, I knew I was the odd man out.

My name is Evan, and I am not normal. Thank God!

I don't mind the ridicule so much, but their mockery revealed that they didn't really understand me or my work. At every level of a company, information security professionals can be considered to be antagonists. It's the old dichotomy of security versus freedom. Every new security measure seems to take away someone's freedom to get their work done, and they blame us for slower productivity or reduced revenue. What a bother we are!

We're the "no" people. They think that if they invite us to a meeting, we're just going to say no, or at the very least, we'll bring the mood down in the room. We're no fun, right?

We don't tell people to choose strong passwords because we like to make their lives miserable. We tell people to choose strong passwords because strong passwords are harder for the bad guys to crack. We don't tell people to change their passwords every forty-five days because we are evil dictators. We tell them to change passwords regularly because people share passwords, write them down, and use them in places where their confidentiality can't be assured—like social media sites, entertainment sites, dating sites, you name it.

We don't make people come to training because we like to sound smart in front of groups of normal people (although some of us probably do). We make people come to training because all of us pay the price for a mistake made by just one of us.

It's no wonder that people don't want to work with us. If we slow down the business and its ability to make money, then what good are we?

Here's a quick example using soft costs.

Let's say the average labor cost per employee in our organization is $35 per hour for one thousand employees. Our overall labor cost for the year is $72.8 million. If we implement a control that adds just one hour per month to each of our employees' work, then the control costs our company $420,000 in productivity, not to mention the additional frustration. Is our control worth it? Does it offset an estimated $420,000 or more in risk? Maybe. Maybe not. If it doesn't, then maybe it's the wrong control.

How often do we put a control in place only to find that our users are circumventing it? Take file sharing and remote access, for instance. If using a virtual private network (VPN) is more cumbersome for our users than Dropbox, what do you think they'll use? They have deadlines and deliverables to consider. They're likely to use Dropbox. We then block Dropbox access to find our users sending attachments to their personal email accounts. So, then we start blocking personal email account usage. Next the users start storing and transporting files on USB devices and smartphones. The cycle continues indefinitely.

This is the game we play. Do you see anything wrong with this? For starters, we're setting a tone within our organization that it's OK to bypass our controls. We're also introducing constant inefficiency. If users are bypassing our controls, there's a reason. The reason isn't because our users are difficult or ignorant. It may be because our controls are poorly designed. Usually it's because we haven't made our case clearly understood to normal people (our users). They don't get why they should do it our way.

> If users bypass our controls, it's not their problem; it's ours. We've designed our controls poorly or we've misunderstood our users.

The list of things that we make people do is lengthy. If only they saw the world the same way we do, they'd be much more secure. The problem is that they don't, and we don't spend enough energy showing them what it's like to be one of us. We don't venture out enough from our cubicles, our offices, our security conferences, our security associations, or the other groups that we form for our own protection. If we do, we're sometimes so focused on our own agenda that we don't truly hear their perspective.

This disconnect with normal people is compounded even further by the language that we use. It is virtually impossible for us to explain our profession quickly and easily to the average normal person. It is the cause for much anxiety among us.

A typical encounter of this sort occurred while I was writing this book. I went to Mexico to avoid distractions, and I sat outside to type. One day my well-intentioned American neighbor came by while I was writing.

"What are you working on?" Vicki asked pleasantly.

"I'm writing a book."

"Oh, what's it about?"

This question touched off a mild anxiety attack, because I knew what was coming.

"It's about information security and how the information security industry is broken."

Vicki gave me a confused look and a blank stare. Awkward silence followed. Meanwhile, I tried to read her reaction, so I could figure out my next few valuable words.

"Like internet security or something?" she asked.

I debated whether to correct her and have a longer discussion or to allow the conversation to end peacefully, as it does at parties.

"Sort of," I replied. "Information security is more than just the internet, though."

More blank staring. More awkward silence.

"Vicki, the fact that you seem confused is one of the problems that I'd like to fix with this book."

I could see the light bulb growing dim—and poof, she gave up.

"That sounds great, Evan. It's all over my head—but good luck with your writing!"

I could see that any further attempt at explanation was useless. It was another failed communication between a normal person and one of us. It is a challenge to discuss information security with non–information security people, whether it's on the street or in the office. We're not doing a great job, and this communication gap leads only to greater misunderstanding. We speak two different languages and we don't have a good translation.

To be blunt, we don't really understand normal people either. Ever marveled at some of the insecure things that people do, and wondered what the %$&* is wrong with them? Ever wondered if we're the problem? Not the problem in the sense of doing the insecure thing, but the problem because of the way we communicate what's obvious to us in a way that resonates with them.

Take this statistic: 78 percent of people claim to be aware of the risks of unknown links in emails, yet somewhere between 25 and 45 percent click on the links anyway. (Source: https://blog.barkly. com/cyber-security-statistics-2017) I would hate to think that 25 to 45 percent of people are just stupid. This is a scary thought if we consider that these same people share the road with us each rush hour.

Have you ever been completely flabbergasted by something that someone has done? It's unfathomable that someone could possibly think that it's OK to leave their laptop on the front seat of the car. Who would think that it's OK to divulge a password to someone who calls us on the phone? Clicking a malicious link in an email right after we trained you not to click on malicious links? Seriously, who does that?!

SOLUTION #2: FIND OUR COMMON GROUND

Understanding Normal People

Remember my conversation with Vicki? Her husband, Don, came by later the same day. He heard from Vicki that I was writing this book. Don used to work in IT.

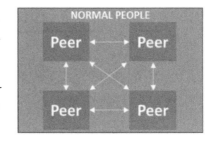

"Hi, Evan," said Don, "Vicki tells me you're writing a book. What's it about?"

"It's about the information security industry and how I think we can do things better."

It's not just them; it's us.

I would have to admit that our omnipresent jargon doesn't make it easy for normal people to understand us. We're stuck in a world of buzzwords, acronyms, and catchphrases. Some of them are useful, and some of them are cute and a little funny, but too many of them are used to make ourselves seem smarter than we really are. Much of our esoteric vocabulary is like a secret handshake; if you understand our language, you are one of us. If you don't get it, you are normal.

Here's some typical jargon of information security professionals:

APT, BaaS, BC/DR, Blockchain, CaaS, cloud computing, fog computing, DAST, DCIM, DCPM, DDoS, DevOps, DevSecOps, DLP, DLT, DRaS, FUD, hybrid hosting, IAST, IoT, IDS, IPS, MTDC, RBAC, RSAC, SAST, SDDC, SDLC, SDN, SSP, ST&E, UC, UCaaS, UCOMS, WebRTC.

He sat back in his chair with a sly grin on his face. He looked like he had something to say but was holding back.

"What was it that you used to do, Don?"

"I used to work for Cray Computers, but then Seagate bought the division I worked in. I finished my career there."

"That's cool! Cray has a big history in Minnesota, where I'm from."

"So, your book is about information security—and something about fixing it?"

"Yep, I've been working in this field for a long time and I have some ideas how to make things better."

"I can tell you a thing or two from my experience," said Don. "Where I used to work, information security was always getting in the way and making our lives much more difficult than they should have been."

"Really? That's a pretty common problem, I think."

"The worst part was that they never listened to us or got our take on things. It was just the way it was. I had deadlines that had to be met constantly," said Don, "and we could have been just as secure if they would have let me do things the way it made sense."

"I can only imagine."

"Will you be covering stuff like this in your book? Things like how security people don't listen and always think they have the best way to do things? If not, you should. We would have respected the security people a lot more if they would have listened to us."

"It'll be in the book, Don."

This was Don's perspective, and normal person's perspective. I agree with him; he was right. We don't spend enough time understanding the challenges and perspectives brought by normal people. We don't listen well enough or include them in our decision making. We tend to run security programs like dictatorships and then wonder why people don't like us. A quick win (maybe): establish an information security committee comprised of mostly normal people and include them in all major information security decisions.

The Role of Security in the Overall Business Enterprise

There is no common sense in information security, because common sense requires common understanding and a common language. What is needed is a single vision that can encompass the entirety of the business operation, including information security. The two halves, business operations and information security, must be made whole. We must do a better job of understanding the normal people who run our businesses, and they must do a better job of understanding us. The onus is on us, however, to craft an enterprise-wide point of view that encompasses both sides, the business side and the information security side.

We have to take the initiative, because normal people are never going to understand us unless we help them understand us. At the same time, we are never going to understand them unless we get off of our butts and make a real effort. That being said, we have a long way to go. One study claims that 52 percent of organizations report that their security officers lack an understanding of how business works. (Source: https://cybersecurity.isaca.org/static-assets/documents/State-of-Cybersecurity-part-2-infographic_res_eng_0517.pdf)

We know that businesses are in business to make money, not to secure information. A business makes less money if it doesn't secure information, but it also makes less money if it oversecures information. It's critical for us to understand the struggles that normal people face, especially when we need them to work together with us. Thankfully, this is all accounted for in our definition of *information security* earlier in this chapter. We manage risks, which allows us to determine what the right amount of security is for our organization; no two organizations are the same.

Get to Know Them

If we want to cater our information security efforts to our user base, we need to understand our users (the normal people) better. The better we understand how they operate, what motivates them, and what frustrates them, the better we can develop our language to resonate with them. The more we understand their language, the better they understand ours, because of our improved ability to translate.

So, how do we get to know our normal people? How do we get to understand their perspective and their language? Sit with them and listen. That's it. Don't try to teach them anything or try to preach anything to them. Listen.

> Find ways to listen to and learn from normal people. Their language is critical to the success of our translation.

Compromise Is Possible

Who in our organizations makes the decisions about how to deal with known risks? Who decides whether to accept risk, mitigate risk, transfer risk, or avoid risk? Hint: it is not us. The people who make these decisions are the CEO, executive managers, or the board of directors. It's their decision. These are the powerful normal people who are tasked with calling the shots. If we disagree, too bad.

It's not us versus them. It's us with them. We should strive to make their jobs easier whenever possible. We make their jobs easier by providing them with the best-quality information (based on facts and objectivity whenever possible) in a manner that they can easily understand. A win-win is when we can improve confidentiality or integrity while at the same time improving availability. If information security controls prohibit an organization from making money or fulfilling its mission, then the controls are likely poorly designed.

Compromise is a good thing. It shows our willingness to work with the business to find solutions together.

Strategize for Effective Communication with the Normal People in the Organization.

Boards of Directors

Recently I had lunch with a friend who has been in this business for more than twenty years. He had just left a large public company to take a new position with a well-respected, family-owned organization that was far behind the times when it came to information security. I asked how he liked his new gig, and he said he was already frustrated. He was promised the moon when he joined the company, and he was excited about the opportunity to build a solid information security program from the ground up. They told him that he would have all the resources he needed to do what needed to be done. So, why was he frustrated?

His problem was that he could not communicate his assessment and ideas directly to the decision makers. He reported to a director of technical services, who in turn reported to the CIO, who in turn reported to the president, who in turn reported to the two brothers who owned the business. The problem was that his message kept getting

5 Ideas for Getting to Know Normal People

1. Set aside time in your schedule to get out and talk to people. It doesn't matter if you start with upper management or with frontline staff. Try to listen to as many people as you can. The more you interact with normal people, the more they'll open up and share their thoughts and feelings.

2. Meet with human resources (HR) people regularly. HR people understand the culture of your organization well, and they're usually where people go to complain.

3. Hold open meetings regularly. They are an opportunity for people to come share ideas and ask questions.

4. Create a forum for people to interact. The forum can be used for people to ask questions, give input, or vent if necessary.

5. Every time you make a change (or at least major changes), ask for candid feedback. Consider anonymous surveys.

BONUS: Establish an information security committee (or similar).

13 Ways to Win Respect from Normal People

1. Say yes more often to things that make sense for the business. We can say yes while looking for ways to minimize risk.

2. When you say no, explain yourself in a professional manner. Continue to explain yourself until your gums bleed if necessary.

3. Use more facts and fewer opinions. Facts stand for themselves, and they provide clarity. Opinions are subjective, and they are more likely to lead to confusion.

4. Compromise correctly. There's a fine line between being a pushover and being an enabler. You enable business; however, you do so in line with your principles.

5. Make objective decisions whenever possible.

6. Listen until your ears bleed. Normal people aren't dumb; they have different perspectives.

7. Learn the languages spoken by the business. When you can speak normal people's native tongue, it shows how much you respect them. The best way to gain respect is to give it.

8. Be fun in a professional manner. People like fun and want to be included in fun. Things that can make security more fun include gamification and competition. Gamification is a wonderful advance in our field, and it will provide great benefits beyond a traditional dry approach.

9. Reward people for good behavior more than you punish them for bad behavior. Incentive-based security programs always work better. Using fear as a motivator leads to dangerous behaviors and poor results.

10. Be positive. A positive attitude goes a long way toward earning respect.

11. Adopt transparency as the way you do everything. People should know what you're doing, how you're doing it, when you're doing it, and how it could affect their world. Transparency also opens you up to criticism, but this is a great opportunity as well. When you handle criticism well, it increases respect.

12. Don't try to BS people. Always use the truth. I don't think there's a more significant respect-tank depletion technique than to get caught BSing someone. It can be a hard hole to dig out of.

13. Use normal words instead of smart-sounding acronyms. We tend to think that using acronyms makes us seem smart and in the know. It doesn't. Normal people think we are just out of touch and arrogant.

interpreted and reinterpreted by people who didn't really understand information security. His message got so distorted as it rose through the different layers of gatekeepers that the owners never got his (the true) story. Without proper information, the owners could not make good decisions concerning information security, and my friend was ready to quit.

He told me, "Make sure this gets in your book."

If the decision makers want to hear the real story, they should get it from the source.

For many companies, the board of directors is the governing body that has the fiduciary responsibility for protecting the organization's assets.

Boards are increasingly being held responsible for information security, and we need to look no further than the Target breach for evidence of this. In February 2014, Target shareholders filed the first of several derivative lawsuits against Target's board, alleging that it fell short in its fiduciary duties by failing to take sufficient steps to protect the company from the breach and its consequences.

This relatively new responsibility of boards is made explicit in a 2017 handbook by the National Association of Corporate Directors (NACD) called *Cyber-Risk Oversight*. (Source: NACD https://www.nacdonline. org/insights/publications.cfm?ItemNumber=10687) It contains five key principles:

1. Approach cybersecurity as an enterprise-wide risk-management issue, not just an IT issue.

2. Understand the legal implications of cyber-risks.

3. Boards should have adequate access to cybersecurity expertise; cyber-risk management should be given adequate time on board agendas.

4. Directors should set expectations that management will establish an enterprise-wide cyber-risk management framework.

5. Boards need to discuss details of cyber-risk management and risk treatment.

Except for their use of the word *cybersecurity*, I think this is great. The first principle says information security is a broad business issue, not just an IT issue. I get it. Information security began in IT, and it's traditionally been treated as an IT issue. So, if it is becoming recognized as not an IT issue, then why do boards still permit top information security leadership to report to the CIO?

> Boards of directors must stop treating information security as an IT issue. One significant way to demonstrate this is by having top information security leadership report directly to CEOs, and no longer allowing them to report to CIOs (or similar).

According to a 2018 study by the Financial Services Information Sharing and Analysis Center, only 8 percent of CISOs report directly to CEOs. (Source: http://www.fsisac.com/article/fs-isac-unveils-2018-cybersecurity-trends-according-top-financial-cisos) This kind of filtering is sure to have an impact on what actually gets reported to the board. It also violates the handbook's third principle, which is to have adequate access to security experts and that cyber-risk management should be given adequate time on board agendas.

But what is adequate access and adequate time? Board agendas are notoriously crowded, so information security experts, if they get invited, should be prepared to expect five minutes to present their report. You may get more time, but if you can do your thing in five, you're golden.

In that five minutes, we should be able to tell the board four things:

1. The **current state** of the organization's security program—expressed in terms of risk, not maturity, not vulnerability, not potential impacts

2. The planned **future state** of the organization's security program. (This gives them something specific to which they can hold us and the organization accountable.)

3. **How long** it's going to take for us to reach our future state

4. **How much** it's going to cost

Boards of directors must know:

1. the current state of information security,

2. the future state of information security,

3. when we're going to get there, and

4. how much it's going to cost.

We have five minutes to communicate this consistently.

If you can communicate these four things to your board of directors in five minutes or less, then you are winning the translation game with them, communicating your message to them in terms they can understand. Chances are good that the board will reciprocate with questions and other dialogue. This is always a good thing. Engagement is better than being ignored.

If you can't communicate these four things accurately and consistently, you've got work to do.

Current State

The current state of information security is the result of our last information security risk assessment and any progress that's been made since. A method that is becoming more popular is to state risk on a scale comparable to a credit score: 300 to 850. This numbering range resonates well with most businesspeople, because they are most comfortable in the land of quantification, not fuzzy ideas. This is also a translation that most of them have used before (FICO score), just in a different way.

Future State

An information security risk assessment requires risk treatment, usually an action. The future state is a road map extrapolated from the risk-treatment plan. For each risk that requires action (mitigation, transfer, and avoidance), there must be someone assigned to complete the task according to a timeline. Most effective milestones on road maps are plotted on a quarterly basis. The road map can be shared with the board of directors so that they can see the progress that's been planned.

When We're Going to Get There

This estimate is provided as part of the road map when determining a future state.

How Much It's Going to Cost

The cost of getting from the current state to a future state is a function of the services and products that will be required. Road mapping entails a determination of who is going to do what. During this process, we decide which things can be done in-house with our available personnel and products. A cost is assigned to those things that cannot be done in-house due to resource constraints, skill shortage, or product deficiencies.

The translation to the board of directors can be summed up like this:

Our current information security risk score is 580, and we plan to achieve a score of 660 by Q3/2019 at an estimated initial cost of $380,000.

The first time you send a message like this to the board of directors, expect some questions. Once the directors buy into this language, they start asking for updates regularly. Once they are assured you are not wasting their time, they will respond with more invitations.

Principle 4 from the *Cyber-Risk Oversight* handbook says directors should expect management to create a management framework for information security. A management framework is automatic if you're providing answers to the four questions. The NACD handbook mentions the National Institute of Standards and Technology Cybersecurity Framework (NIST CSF), so it may be wise to build your information security program accordingly and map your risk assessment to it. The NIST CSF isn't going anywhere, and it is well referenced industry-wide.

Principle 5 suggests directors should be prepared to plan how to treat various risks—which to avoid, which to accept, and which to mitigate or transfer through insurance. This can be a time-consuming task, and chances are slim that we're going to get enough time to deal with such specific questions directly with board members. Deliberations could take hours. Instead, you should recommend which risks to avoid, accept, mitigate, and/or transfer along with your specific plans during a road map exercise, which is shared with the board and updated regularly.

As much as is possible, the board must be provided with accurate and objective information. Too often, boards are told only about the things we do well—the good news. It is at least as important that the board be aware of the things we don't do so well—the rest of the story.

> Boards of directors must receive information security updates quarterly, or more often.

Executive Management

In many companies, the top executive is the CEO, who is often appointed by the board of directors and surrounded by an executive management team. The CEO reports directly to the board of directors and is responsible for the overall performance of the company.

The translations of information security for executive management are not much different than those made for the board of directors. Executive management's primary responsibility is to make money and/or build shareholder value. Ideally, senior management will do so in line with the company's mission according to ethical standards. The cold fact is that information security is not top of mind for most executive managers, and they are busy worrying about other priorities.

Here are the three most significant things that help with translations for executive management:

1. **Establish an effective reporting structure.** The top information security person within the organization should be a peer of other executive managers. Peers speak similar languages, and the information security message is communicated more effectively when it's communicated by a peer. This means that the head of information security must be at the same level as other peer executives, reporting directly to the CEO.

2. **Respect their time.** Like board members, executive management time is very valuable. Give them the pertinent facts; maybe it's the same exact message you share with the board:

    - What's our current state?
    - What's our future state?
    - When are we getting there?
    - How much is it going to cost?

3. **Understand them.** This helps when information security is viewed as a peer function, like a CFO to a CIO. Each executive has certain motivators. Tie information security to their motivators, and you'll have much better success at translation.

More and more often, executive management, including the CEO, is being held directly accountable for information security. Take one of the most recent famous breaches, Equifax, as an example. It took fewer than 20 days after the breach was announced before CEO Richard Smith stepped down. Target's CEO Gregg Steinhafel lasted for almost 140 days after the Target breach.

PROBLEM #3: FOOLISH CONVERSATIONS OCCUR BETWEEN ORGANIZATIONS

It's foolish when an organization expects other organizations to do things the same way they do (speak the same security language). Every organization is different, and forcing the same controls and processes is not going to work. What will work is figuring out a translation between the languages spoken between organizations.

When two companies do business with each other and there is some transfer of information, services, or goods, each organization's information security program automatically extends into the other. Since information security is essentially managing risks, we need to know what risks are associated with doing business with the other organization. These security risks must be shared, understood, and agreed upon. Each organization has a bona fide interest in the state of the other's security program. The amount of security (or insecurity) in one security program has a direct or indirect impact on the security (or insecurity) of the other organization's security program.

The potential danger of such a relationship was made vividly clear in December 2013. That's when Target Corporation suffered a major data breach over the holiday shopping season, and as many as 110 million customers saw hackers escape with credit card numbers, PIN

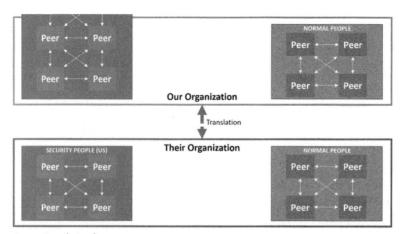

Figure: Translation between organizations.

numbers, email addresses, and more. The thieves did not enter Target's IT system directly; the initial vulnerability was in one of Target's vendors, an HVAC company. It was a vendor compromise.

The Target breach was sensational due to a number of factors, but the manner in which the breach occurred wasn't sensational at all; rather, it was very common. According to an industry survey conducted in 2017, 63 percent of all data breaches are linked, directly or indirectly, to vendors.

Vendor risk management (VRM) is a big deal, but after the Target breach it became a much bigger deal. By January 2014, after the breach, every one of our customers who were vendors to Target had received their first-ever VRM questionnaires from the organization. Prior to the events of December 2013, these Target vendors hadn't seen any before.

VRM is the process of managing the risks associated with conducting business with a supplier of goods and/or services. If the customer organization shares ideas or sensitive information or access to information in a business relationship, then it must account for the risk in such actions. Will the vendor company protect the information adequately? The answer to that question is crucial for a buyer organization that faces immense regulatory pressure or if the organization's information is extremely valuable—such as customers' credit card numbers.

Within an organization, risk-assessment results are the primary method of communicating the current state of our information security program. The same could be true between organizations if it weren't for the fact that we might end up airing our dirty laundry. The challenge is in translating the results of our risk assessment in a way that will 1) satisfy our customer, 2) will represent the facts for good risk decision making, and 3) won't air our dirty laundry. If we don't even have a risk assessment to translate to begin with, then this is, again, the place to start.

If an organization has not done a risk assessment, they don't truly have an information security program, and there isn't a viable translation to be made between organizations. We cannot effectively manage an information security program without some reasonable assessment of risk.

All organizations *must* do information security risk assessments.

While all organizations must have risk assessments, there is no official guidance on what type of assessment or how it must be conducted—yet. For the information security risk assessment to be valid, however, it needs to account for information security as we've defined it: administrative, physical, and technical controls related to the protection of confidentiality, integrity, and availability of information. The state of an information security program must account for all aspects of information security.

Requiring that organizations conduct a risk assessment isn't anything new; the US government has been mandating it for regulated industries such as health care (HIPAA) and finance (GLBA) for a while now.

If your organization hasn't done a risk assessment, do one. The next question is "Which one?" If you want your risk assessment to be useful, it must be one that will work well within the culture of your organization. Still stuck? There are dozens of risk assessment methodologies to choose from. Each one has its fans and its critics. Don't get wrapped around the axle; just choose one for now. Some common risk assessment methodologies are presented in the next sections.

Before choosing your information security risk-assessment language though, you may need to choose your information security language. Your information security language can be built off or mapped to a well-known, generally accepted information security standard like ISO/IEC 27001 or NIST SP 800-53 or a framework like NIST CSF or Secure Controls Framework. Read the standards, ask other information security professionals, and pick one that works best for you. An open standard gives you a common source of reference.

You may have a favorite, like ISO 27002, as a standard for building and managing your security program, and you may have your own method for doing risk assessments. This is your language and the one that works best with the people you need to communicate with most regularly: internal personnel, executive management, the board, and so forth. It's not better or worse than NIST SP 800-53, COBIT, or any other standard. It's just your preference. If you don't have a favorite, you will eventually.

Now we need to figure out how to translate your language to another language, and vice versa.

SOLUTION #3: TRANSLATE SECURITY BETWEEN ORGANIZATIONS

The Translation Solution

Translating risk assessments between companies is no simple task, and our industry has spent hundreds of millions of dollars trying to figure it out. Together, if we figure this out, we can save our industry a boatload of money and bring clarity to all the confusion around vendor risk management.

First, we need to figure out what we're translating—that is, what type of risk assessment we've conducted. Without a risk assessment, there should be nothing to translate.

There are dozens or well-known risk-assessment methodologies, maybe thousands when we consider all the customized approaches employed by different organizations. Here are just a few:

1. Operationally Critical Threat, Asset, and Vulnerability Evaluation (OCTAVE)

2. National Institute of Standards and Technology Risk Management Guide for Information Technology Systems (NIST SP 800-30)

3. Fiducial Information Security Assessment Score (FISASCORE)

4. ISACA RISK IT (part of COBIT)

5. Information technology—security techniques—information security risk management (ISO 27005)

6. Factor Analysis of Information Risk (FAIR)

7. Adapting NIST Cybersecurity Framework (CSF) for Risk Assessment

8. FFIEC Cybersecurity Assessment Tool

9. HHS Security Risk Assessment (SRA) Tool

A note about FISASCORE: The engineers who built this methodology specifically built it with translations between organizations in mind.

There are many more methodologies when we consider all the proprietary ones that are contained within any one of the dozens of governance, risk management, and compliance (GRC) tools. GRC tools are more commonly used by larger organizations that can afford to purchase and maintain these complex behemoths. (I'm being kind.) Seriously though, most GRC tools do a great job of translating risk within larger organizations, but don't do nearly as much for translation between organizations.

How do we translate between the commonly used risk-assessment methodologies, the custom risk-assessment methodologies, and the GRC-type tools? This is the challenge. Theoretically, it's easy to solve; practically, it's a bitch.

The information security practices and risks need to be communicated in a manner that both parties in the relationship can understand. There is no universal language for vendor risk management, and there is no universal method for translating one company's security language into another company's security language. The consequences are poor risk management by both organizations: acceptance of unacceptable risks, mitigation of risks that don't exist or that are acceptable if they are understood, wasted resources (time and money), and false assumptions.

Traditionally, the buying company would conduct a risk assessment of the vendor. This may consist of a questionnaire, an onsite audit, or a review of a SOC 2 report. There are many ways that companies assess information security risk in their business relationships. There is no single solution, and this is a problem.

Too Many Translations

Is there a single correct method of translation? Not when there is an assortment of risk-assessment tools and requirements. And if multiple companies are involved, the translation of information security and risk can quickly get complicated and potentially troublesome.

Let's take the example of a company we'll call Small Mom-and-Pop Printing Company (SMP) that reflects a real-life scenario. SMP does business with numerous other companies: Companies A, B, C, D, and E. All the companies have mature information security programs in which vendor risk management is somewhat formalized. Each year, all the companies perform their due-diligence vendor risk assessment on their relationship with SMP.

Company A sends SMP a copy of the Shared Assessments Standardized Information Gathering (SIG) questionnaire. SMP spends more than forty hours completing the questionnaire and sending it back. Company A spends as many as forty hours reviewing the completed questionnaire and formulates a dozen or so follow-up questions. A conference call is established between Company A's information security personnel and people from SMP. The call lasts an hour, and Company A requests that SMP implement some new controls and modify some others.

In all, SMP spends more than forty-five hours to complete Company A's assessment. Company A spends about the same amount of time. SMP spends another sixty hours on remediation items, because Company A requires it, but not necessarily because they are useful to SMP's risk-management practices. SMP's 105 hours plus Company A's 45 hours equals 150 hours total time related to translation. Estimating labor cost of $50 per hour, the total labor cost is roughly $7,500. This does not include any expenses related to purchases that may be required. A total of $7,500 is spent on translation.

Not that big of a deal—if the translation can be reused to satisfy another customer's language. Unfortunately, this isn't universally the case.

Company B requires that SMP obtain HITRUST certification. SMP shops around for companies that can perform such a certification and finds a list on HITRUST's website. Unfortunately, none of the companies listed on the site is a company that SMP has worked with before. SMP begins the process of determining which of the HITRUST CSF Assessors will be the best fit. SMP is confused because they've never heard of HITRUST or CSF before and have no idea what to expect from the process. They spend a total of sixteen hours just getting their heads around what HITRUST certification is and whom they should work with. Turns out that this is the easy part.

Overall, the HITRUST certification costs SMP about $50,000 in time and consulting fees. This may or may not result in the certification that Company B requires. You get the point.

In all, SMP spends about $51,000 on translation. Company B spends about $1,000 in labor cost to coach and review the process. That's a total of $52,000 spent on translation.

Company C requires that SMP undergo an on-site audit since SMP handles sensitive information. All told, the audit process takes almost sixty hours to complete. Company C also requires remediation—another forty hours of SMP personnel time and purchases totaling about $20,000. In all, SMP spends about $25,000 on translation costs, and Company C spends about $6,000, for a total of $31,000 spent on translation.

Company D sends SMP a homegrown questionnaire. It takes SMP about twenty hours to complete the questionnaire, and another forty hours to implement a requested mediation plan. SMP spends about

$3,000 on translation for Company D. Company D spends about $1,000. That's a total of $4,000 spent on the translation.

Dealing with Company E turns out to be a pain. Company E wants ISO certification and a SOC 2 report. You may think that there's no way a company would request ISO certification and a SOC 2 report, but this was a real-world issue more than once for companies that I have worked with directly. Anyway, Company E's vendor risk-management process ends up costing SMP about 350 hours and an additional $45,000 in consulting and auditor fees.

SMP spends about $63,000 in translation fees for Company E. Company E spends about $1,500 in translation fees, primarily related to communications and process management. That's a total of almost $65,000 spent on translation.

All told, due to different languages and no effective universal translation, almost $160,000 was spent on the translations between one company (SMP) and five others. The problem gets worse as the number of SMP customers increases. In the example, a significant portion of the cost is spent on only translation. Think some of this time and money would be better spent on securing stuff?

We shouldn't blame Companies A, B, C, D, and E. They are all being prudent and conducting their proper due diligence. Hard to blame SMP either: they're complying with the various requirements placed upon them. Maybe this is just a cost of doing business these days—or maybe there's a better way. Wouldn't it be better if SMP could do just one thing, run one security program that would translate well into the requirements of all their customers?

There are significant costs related to translating information security risk between organizations, and many small organizations can't afford them. This puts small organizations at a competitive disadvantage. Compounding the translation problem for small organizations is the fact that information security controls used by large organizations don't work well, or the same way, in small organizations. The security programs and risk-management practices are different. Asking a small organization to spend $50,000 or more to comply with large company requirements isn't feasible in some cases, or productive in others.

There's a significant disconnect in this translation.

The waste of time and money involved in trying to appease each of the organizations could be better spent on actual controls, or on helping the organizations make money. Isn't making money supposed to be the point of a business? There must be a better way.

> **OPTION ONE**: Force or entice all organizations to conduct risk assessments in the same manner. The risk-assessment results in one organization could then be quickly compared against the risk-assessment results in another. The point of this option is *not* to develop and implement the perfect risk assessment (one will never exist). The point is to develop and implement a risk assessment that is good enough to serve as the translation.

There are two options:

1. Get (or force) all organizations to speak the same language, meaning force all organizations to assess and manage risk the same way. The same methodology used in different organizations should produce comparable results. No translation needed.

2. Develop and implement a method to translate the different valid languages that are spoken.

There is also a third option, but it is a broken option.

The third option is to continue the same inefficient way we do vendor risk management as an industry. This option doesn't work well because there are so many different languages that organizations are forced to speak.

Translating risk assessments or information security risk between companies isn't a new idea. Enterprising businesspeople have already seen the problem and presented their solutions.

Option One: Let's Do It One Way

A chief information security officer for a company that is entertaining the idea of doing business with you could decide to ask for your ISO certification, your SOC 2 report, your HITRUST certification, your FISASCORE, your BitSight Security Rating, or any number of other things that he or she thinks will give a good indication of the risk involved in doing business with you.

Which one do you choose? Arguably, they all have their strengths and weaknesses. If you choose one, and the organization you intend to do business with doesn't have the one you chose, then what? Forcing the other organization to speak the language you understand, if it's not universal to other organizations, is wasteful. It is also rather presumptuous, like my asking the rest of the world to speak English to make it easier for me. Good luck with that.

It would be optimal if the industry could standardize on just one translation; however, this would require a lot of compromise among many people, and organizations make a ton of money off you and me in the status quo.

Option Two: A Translation of Translations

A SECOND OPTION: Develop and adopt a translation of the translations.

The second option is to develop and implement a translation of the translations. Before you call me crazy, consider the possibility.

Translate the BitSight Security Rating into a HITRUST certification, for instance. BitSight is strong at determining risks related to technical controls; especially external technical controls. Technical controls are one part of information security as we've defined it (managing risks to the confidentiality, integrity, and availability of information using administrative, physical, and technical controls). HITRUST is a rigorous and stringent certification that encompasses all parts of information security but is less technical in nature.

If a company has a BitSight Security Rating, but not a HITRUST certification, what does this say about the level of risk in doing business with the organization? It says something, but not the same thing. Without a detailed translation, we can only speculate about the overall level of risk.

Can we translate between a SOC 2 and a FICO Enterprise Security Score? Or between a FISASCORE and RiskRecon? Or between UpGuard and SecurityScorecard?

A translation of translations would require that the organizations that provide the various translations form a trade group or some other type of governing body to manage the translation of translations.

Large organizations can more easily afford to maintain the status quo; however, they could realize tremendous benefits by employing a single translation, or translation of translations. If you're a large company, you often need to staff a team of vendor risk-management professionals to run your vendor risk-management program. The costs involved in terms of people and money can be repurposed to further the organization's mission.

Translation is not as easy as it seems, and it's costly. Between validating vendor lists, classifying vendors, developing questionnaires and other documentation, communicating with vendors, following up, creating and managing remediation plans, and reporting, the hours add up quickly.

We may need a translation of the translations. One idea: create a nonprofit, inclusive of all who have created various translation solutions independently, to create the translation of translations.

Here is an annotated list of some of the organizations that translate information security risk between organizations, or try to anyway:

- **American Institute of Certified Public Accountants (AICPA)** and its certified public accountant (CPA) members: They developed the SAS 70 (back in the day) and the System and Organization Controls (SOC) internal control reports to translate risk for and between organizations. Being capitalists, they offer multiple options, including the SOC 2, SOC 2 CSA STAR Attestation, SOC for Cybersecurity, and others. Like just about anything, the SOC reports are great when they're used in the way they were intended. Some, but far from all, organizations understand the SOC language and can translate it into their own.

- **International Organization for Standardization (ISO) and the International Electrotechnical Commission (IEC)**, and the ISO/IEC 27001 certification standard: Organizations with the proper experience and credentials can certify your organization as being compliant with the standard, for a fee. It's actually one of my favorite standards to work with because of its inherent flexibility.

- **FISASCORE**: We developed this information security risk score at FRSecure in 2008 to solve the translation problem. Since then, it's caught on with one thousand or so organizations, and it's morphing into a standard. It's a fine information security risk score, but its use as a translator is directly related to the number of people who understand and accept it.

- **FICO Enterprise Security Score**: In mid-2016, Fair Isaac Corporation purchased QuadMetrics to solve the translation problem. QuadMetrics was founded in 2014 and touted its approach to managing and quantifying cybersecurity (not information security) risks.

- **BitSight Security Ratings**: This very well-known and oft-cited cybersecurity risk score was developed and is maintained by BitSight Technologies, which was founded in 2011. The ratings are derived from four categories, and all are from technical sources. If our definition of information security were purely technical, this could be an answer; however, our definition also includes administrative and physical controls.

- **SecurityScorecard**: This is another well-known security ratings system for understanding "cyberhealth." The score is calculated across ten technical risk factors. SecurityScorecard was founded in 2013.

- **UpGuard**: UpGuard claims to have the "world's first cyber resilience platform." The company was founded in 2012, and the product leverages asset discovery, security ratings, and vendor questionnaires to assess and translate risk.

- **RiskRecon**: This company developed and maintains a product with the same name. Founded in 2011, the company provides a platform for assessing and translating security risk. Like many of the others, it derives most, if not all, its intelligence from technical sources.

- **HITRUST Alliance**: This is the organization that developed and maintains the HITRUST Common Security Framework (CSF) and all its uses and supporting processes. HITRUST was founded in 2007 with the mission to "champion programs that safeguard sensitive information and manage information risk for organizations across all industries and throughout the third-party supply chain." HITRUST provides the CSF itself, as well as the CSF Assurance Program, Third Party Assurance Program, the Cyber Center (CyberAid, Cyber ThreatXChange, CTX Enhanced, CTX Deceptive), and many other services and benefits.

The vendor side of the equation is just as clumsy and costly, if not more so.

Without a translation of the translations, organizations suffer because they still must learn all the different languages and/or translations—spoken or understood—by all their business partners. The proposed solution allows us to speak the language we want within our organization and still conduct business, with less complexity and expense.

If we do this right, all the participants in the translation-of-translations nonprofit organization benefit too. It's a win-win for all translators (methodologies, commercial vendor risk-management solution providers, and GRC vendors), organizations, and individual consumers.

The translation nonprofit can handle differences in scoring systems and scope. It can also determine the criteria for determining whether or not a risk assessment is done well enough to even warrant a translation.

The Problem of No Translation

More troublesome than having too many translations is having no translation at all.

I recently had lunch with a friend of mine, Dave, who happens to have twenty years of experience in the information security business.

In the midst of a casual chat about our families, he suddenly stopped talking, and without any comfortable transition he blurted out, "Vendor risk management is a waste of time!"

"I'm sorry, what do you mean?" What I really meant was, "Where did that come from?

Dave replied, "Our internal audit department just finished their report on our information security program, and they nailed us for ineffective vendor risk management."

"How could it be a waste of time?" I asked. "Some of the best-known breaches involved vendors. Hell, some studies suggest that more than 60 percent of breaches happen through vendors."

Dave slouched a little. "I know it's important, but we spend a couple hundred thousand dollars each year just trying to keep up. Then to get nailed by our audit department?! What's the use?"

He knew I was writing this book, so he added, "Make sure that this gets into the book. It's killing us."

I can't help but wonder how many others feel the same way as Dave. The alternatives to spending so much on multiple translations is to either find just one or cease to do vendor risk management altogether. His was the voice of desperation, not one of logic or practicality.

His frustration epitomizes the choking feeling I have when I think of all the language gaps that keep our industry in pieces. We need to communicate better among ourselves, with the normal people who lead and operate businesses, and between companies that do business together. This triple effort falls on our shoulders as information security professionals. We owe it to ourselves, to our industry, and to commercial enterprises everywhere. I think our best chance for success is to accept universal definitions of our basic concepts, move toward an overarching professional governing association, and support an organization that can provide translations of translations between the information security programs of different companies.

Annotated List of Information Security Associations

You should check out these groups to learn more and to contribute to:

1. **Association for Executives in Healthcare Information Security (AEHIS)**–https://aehis.org/: "AEHIS launched in 2014 in order to provide an education and networking platform to healthcare's senior IT security leaders."

2. **Association of Information Security Professionals (AISP)**–http://www.aisp.sg/: "The Association of Information Security Professionals (AISP) was registered with the assistance of the Singapore Computer Society (SCS) and the strong support of the Infocomm Development Authority of Singapore (iDA) in February 2008."

3. **Association of IT Professionals (AITP)**–https://www.aitp.org/: AITP's vision is "to be the go-to resource for individuals seeking to start, grow, and advance careers in technology." It seeks to "fill

the pipeline with the next generation of talent, attracting and supporting the largest, most diverse, innovative and skilled workforce. As advocates for technology industry, we aspire to drive economic growth and benefit society."

4. **Australian Information Security Association (AISA)**–https://www.aisa.org.au/: "As a nationally recognised not-for-profit organisation and charity, the Australian Information Security Association (AISA) champions the development of a robust information security sector by building the capacity of professionals in Australia and advancing the cybersecurity and safety of the Australian public as well as businesses and governments in Australia."

5. **Center for Internet Security (CIS)**–http://www.cisecurity.org/: CIS is a 501(c)(3) nonprofit organization focused on enhancing the cybersecurity readiness and response of public and private sector entities.

6. **Cloud Security Alliance (CSA)**–https://cloudsecurityalliance.org/: "The Cloud Security Alliance (CSA) is the world's leading organization dedicated to defining and raising awareness of best practices to help ensure a secure cloud computing environment. CSA harnesses the subject matter expertise of industry practitioners, associations, governments, and its corporate and individual members to offer cloud security–specific research, education, certification, events, and products."

7. **Credit Union Information Security Professionals Association (CUISPA)**–http://www.cuispa.org/: Known as "the CU IT Collaborative," the CUISPA is a national association of credit union information technology professionals focused on improving security and risk management through cooperation.

8. **Cyber, Space, and Intelligence Association (CSIA)**–http://www.cyberspaceintel.org/: CSIA "was founded in early 2011 to provide

an environment for a vital flow of ideas between national security thought leaders in government, industry, and congress focused cyber, space, and intelligence challenges and opportunities."

9. **Executive Women's Forum on Information Security, Risk Management, and Privacy (EWF)**–http://www.ewf-usa.com/: Founder Joyce Brocaglia organized "the first-ever Executive Women's Forum National Conference in 2003 to provide a safe venue where women could gather, learn from each other and build trusted relationships. Today the EWF is the largest member organization serving emerging leaders as well as the most prominent and influential female executives" in our field.

10. **Federal Information Systems Security Educators' Association (FISSEA)**–http://csrc.nist.gov/organizations/fissea/home/index.shtml: "FISSEA, founded in 1987, is an organization run by and for information security professionals to assist federal agencies in strengthening their employee security training and awareness programs." You can tell by the URL that this is an organization maintained by the National Institute of Standards and Technology (NIST).

11. **Forum of Incident Response and Security Teams (FIRST)**– https://www.first.org/: FIRST is an international confederation of trusted computer incident-response teams who cooperatively handle computer security incidents and promote incident prevention programs.

12. **Information Security Forum (ISF)**–https://www.securityforum. org/: ISF is a not-for-profit organization focused on information risk management.

13. **Information Security Research Association (ISRA)**–http://www. is-ra.org/: ISRA is "a registered nonprofit organization focused on various aspects of Information Security including security research and cybersecurity awareness activities. Officially registered in the year 2010, the Information Security Research Association has established

itself as the leading security research organization in the Industry."

14. **Information Systems Audit and Control Association (ISACA)**–http://www.isaca.org/: ISACA is a pioneer organization, founded in 1967, incorporated by "individuals who recognized a need for a centralized source of information and guidance in the growing field of auditing controls for computer systems. Today, ISACA serves 140,000 professionals in 180 countries." You'll find a wealth of resources here.

15. **Information Systems Security Association (ISSA)**–https://www.issa.org/: ISSA provides local chapters through the world that meet regularly to further its mission "to promote a secure digital world."

16. **Institute of Internal Auditors (IIA)**–https://na.theiia.org/: "Established in 1941, the Institute of Internal Auditors (IIA) is an international professional association with global headquarters in Lake Mary, Florida, USA. The IIA is the internal audit profession's global voice, recognized authority, acknowledged leader, chief advocate, and principal educator."

17. **International Association for Cryptologic Research (IACR)**–http://www.iacr.org/: IACR is "a nonprofit organization devoted to supporting the promotion of the science of cryptology. Cryptology is the science of the making and breaking of encryption algorithms, but in the modern world it encompasses so much more."

18. **International Association of Security Awareness Professionals (IASAP)**–http://www.iasapgroup.org/: "Previously organized as the Security Awareness Peer Group under sponsorship of the Computer Security Institute (CSI), our core group of security awareness professionals has been meeting since 2003."

19. **International Information Systems Security Certification Consortium (ISC)²**–https://www.isc2.org/: (ISC)² is arguably the not-for-profit leader in education and certification in our industry.

20. **Internet Security Alliance (ISA)**–https://isalliance.org/: ISA was founded in 2000 in collaboration with Carnegie Mellon University. It's not my favorite because it's very expensive; however, many heavy hitters are members.

21. **Information Security and Forensics Society (ISFS)**–http://www.isfs.org.hk/: "ISFS was registered under the Hong Kong Societies Ordinance in May 2000." Its mission is "to advocate and enforce professionalism, integrity, and innovation in information security and computer forensics in Hong Kong and the surrounding region."

22. **National Council of ISACs (NCI)**–https://www.nationalisacs.org/: NCI's mission is to advance the physical security and cybersecurity of the critical infrastructures of North America. Members are the individual Information Sharing and Analysis Centers (ISACs) that represent their respective sectors.

23. **National Cyber Security Alliance (NCSA)**–https://staysafeonline.org/: NCSA's mission is "to educate and empower our global digital society to use the internet safely and securely." NCSA is a well-known information security education resource and a great place to find information for normal people.

24. **Open Web Application Security Project (OWASP)**–https://www.owasp.org/: OWASP is a 501(c)(3) worldwide not-for-profit charitable organization focused on improving the security of software.

2

Bad Foundations

The information security industry is broken because we build on bad foundations, or worse, without a foundation at all. This chapter is all about the basics. Basics are sort of boring because we're all beyond that, right? Almost every time I consult with an organization about basic information security concepts, they look at me like I'm crazy. They feel like they're way beyond the basics. If they're beyond the basics, then wouldn't we expect that they would have mastered the basics in practice? Think again.

Maybe our exceptional knowledge and superior skills have exceeded our capability to execute the basics.

Building anything worthwhile requires a solid foundation. The foundation can be physical, as in building a house, or the foundation can be conceptual, as in building a security program. The strength of any building lies in its foundation, and the strength of a security program is no different. Logic would support the assertion that:

- if building something worthwhile requires a foundation, and
- if our security program is worthwhile, then
- we need a security program with a foundation.

Seem obvious? For some, it is. For others, not so much. Too many information security professionals forge ahead in building information security programs without a good foundation. They put things together piecemeal without planning or thinking it through. Imagine a carpenter framing a house on bare ground. There will be serious problems when he or she gets to framing in windows on the second floor. The carpenter will have to tear down what has been built to compensate for the lack of foresight—a serious waste of time and resources!

Problems covered in this chapter include:

- Problem #1: building without blueprints
- Problem #2: building without permits
- Problem #3: weak or absent foundations
- Problem #4: overengineered foundations

Some of the potential solutions we'll explore include:

- Solution #1: starting with blueprints
- Solution #2: building with permits
- Solution #3: establishing a solid foundation
- Solution #4: simplification

Two of the four problems covered in this chapter are related to foundations, and two of the problems are the foundation itself. The primary focus is the foundation. In this chapter, we'll spend more time on the solutions than we do on problems.

PROBLEM #1: BUILDING WITHOUT BLUEPRINTS

"When you fail to prepare, you're preparing to fail."

–John Wooden

We wouldn't build a house without a plan, and we shouldn't be building, or maintaining, our security programs without a plan either. For a house, the plan may be the blueprints. For a security program, the plan contains things like what we're trying to accomplish and how we'll measure success. Plans may be derived from the results of a good security risk assessment, industry standards or guidelines, and we hope (perhaps most importantly) endorsement from executive management.

This first step in building the security program is a planning stage, during which the security equivalent of an architect designs a blueprint that delineates the purpose, direction, and structure of the program. This is a time for thinking, not a time for action.

Some of the prompts we often overlook when planning (or not planning) our information security programs are as follows:

- Why are we building an information security program?

- What are we trying to accomplish?

- How will we enable the organization to make more money or achieve its mission better?

- Conceptually, how will the information security program be organized and maintained?

- What is the strategy for the information security program?

- How will we determine success or failure of the program?

Once we have a plan, we need to get it approved. Then we can start laying the foundation for the security program.

As obvious and logical as this seems, there are many information security professionals who barge right into action without proper planning. Sooner or later they run into problems, just like the shortsighted carpenter who builds a room with no window.

SOLUTION #1: STARTING WITH BLUEPRINTS

Have you ever tried to build something significant and important without a plan? It can be done, but it's very unlikely that it will be done well, or as well as it could have been. I've tried it enough times to know, and some of you have too. I won't build anything of significance without these three things:

- a **plan**
- **permission**
- a solid base (**foundation**)

It just makes sense. The problem is that most of the information security programs that we come across are not well planned, are not built with buy-in from the business, and are severely lacking in foundational components that make it all work.

Maybe we don't view our information security programs as significant. Maybe we don't know how to build a security program. There is a multitude of reasons why we don't build solid, foundational information security programs. This must change if we're to stand a chance.

For a security program, the plan should address (at least) the Five *W*s:

- **Why** are we building a security program in the first place? We should never overlook the why.

- **What** are we trying to accomplish with our security program?

- **Who** is responsible for what in our information security program? High-level responsibilities may be documented in our plan, in our information security program charter, and in our enterprise information security policy. Regardless of where the who is documented, it must be documented.

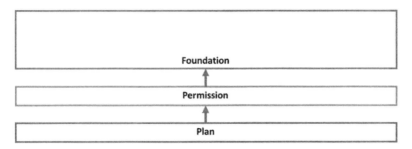

Figure: An example diagram outlining the plan, permission, and foundation.

Plan
Why we're building a security program in the first place
What we're trying to accomplish
Who is responsible
When we'll reach our planned accomplishments
Where our plan applies and where our plan does not

Figure: Don't overlook these things that may seem obvious to you. They may be obvious to you, but they're not to everyone who's involved.

- **When** will we reach our planned accomplishments? The answer to this question is often in the form of a road map or strategy.

- **Where** does our plan apply and where doesn't it apply? This is a scope document for our information security program.

There are numerous inputs into our plan, including the results of a good security risk assessment, industry standards or guidelines, and, most important, input from executive management.

Our blueprints for our information security program are our plans, our vision, our road map. What should our plans, or blueprints, look like?

Just as there are millions of different types, sizes, and shapes of houses, there are millions of different plans for security programs. Our security program must start with our why. Why are we building an information security program?

This is very important. People will get behind and support the right why before they'll get behind and support the what and the how. Don't overlook this.

From here, there are all sorts of materials, guidance, and frameworks that can help us complete our plans. Our plans contain our vision of what information should look like. Some of us use or reference a standard like ISO 27001 or NIST SP 800-53. Some of us use an information security risk assessment. Some of us start with an idea or two jotted down on a piece of paper. The point is to *start with a plan and worry less about a perfect plan.*

Our plans become our strategies, which then become our road maps. The plan is important because it's what we take to others for buy-in. Unless we're building our security program with complete autonomy, we're going to need buy-in. We'll need buy-in from the board of directors (possibly), executive management (our peers, we hope), department heads, and other influential people within the organization.

A simple plan diagram with some descriptions could suffice. Again, our plan will be unique to our culture, preferences, biases, whatever. The plan gets everyone on the same page with why we're doing what we're doing, what we're trying to accomplish, and how we're going to accomplish it. It also gives the people who will inherit what we've built some context.

Information Security and Risk

Now that we know what information security and risk are, we can build a better plan to address them.

The foundation of our information security program must be based upon our definition of the term *information security*.

Makes sense, right?

So, what's our definition of *information security* again? I know that we've already been through this multiple times. It's so important, we need to mention it again:

> *Information security is managing risks to the confidentiality, integrity, and availability of information using administrative, physical, and technical controls.*

There we go. Our plan for information security in our organization must be based on this definition. The foundation of our security program must also be based on this definition. Notice how our definition of *information security* doesn't say anything about compliance? The foundation of our information security program can't be based on HIPAA or GLBA or Financial Industry Regulatory Authority (FINRA) or anything else but our definition of information security.

We build compliance into security, not the other way around. We'll cover this more in chapter 7.

OK, let's say you're like me (God forbid), and you're going to start your plan with an information security risk assessment. What should our information security risk assessment be or look like? A good risk assessment gives stakeholders an understanding of what we're working with and provides a great place to start planning where we should go next. Here are seven criteria that a good information security risk assessment should meet:

1. It represents risk as we've defined it.

2. It's based on a combination of standards that we already know to be generally good security practices. This lends credibility to our assessment for internal and external audiences.

3. It is straightforward and efficient.

4. It translates well to normal people.

5. It uses objective criteria whenever possible. Objectivity is much closer to fact, and facts are good for foundations.

6. It accounts for administrative, physical, and technical controls in relation to confidentiality, integrity, and availability.

7. It accounts for decision making, road mapping, measurable actions, and repeatability.

We should add one more criterion while we're here and starting off our plan: our information security risk assessment must account well for the basics, or the fundamentals. If our information security risk assessment focuses too much on one type of control or one area of information security, we'll have trouble with our foundation later.

Here's a suggested approach you can use. Break your information security risk assessment into segments, based upon our definition of *information security*, like this:

- section 1— administrative controls
- section 2—physical controls
- section 3—technical controls

Maybe it makes sense to break technical controls into two sections because of the differences in the basics between internal technical controls and external technical controls. Plus, most organizations build their information security programs with a crunchy shell and a gooey center, meaning that there's too much focus on securing the perimeter and significantly less effort given to securing the internal networks and asets. So maybe our information security risk assessment gets broken into the following sections:

- section 1—administrative controls
- section 2—physical controls
- section 3—internal technical controls
- section 4—external technical controls

Now we have a structure for our information security risk assessment. Our information security risk assessment should then cover the basics in each of these sections, if we're using the assessment as a foundational part of our plan.

Remember, focus on basics and fundamentals at this level. This is our foundation for everything else we plan to do later. After we have a foundation, we can start building the first floor and eventually even tackle the sexy cool details (the trim work, counter tops, wall paint, furniture placement, and curtain colors).

Armed with the results of a good information security risk assessment, we can then devise other parts of the plan, like where we should go, when we should plan on getting there, and how much it is going to cost. Start with a plan, get permission for execution, and then lay the foundation.

We've got the plan. Now let's get the permit.

PROBLEM #2: BUILDING WITHOUT PERMITS

I don't work in construction, but I know the importance of obtaining building permits. I've heard horror stories in which the failure to obtain a building permit resulted in complete deconstruction of what was built and heavy fines.

A building permit is an official, documented approval and permission to proceed with a construction project. In information security, a "building permit" is an official, documented approval to proceed with a security program or project. The security project could be any number of things, but the most fundamental project is the establishment of the information security program itself. The agreement and permission must come from the governing body of the organization (such as executive management, the board of directors, a managing partner, or the city council) to do what it is we want to do. Usually the information security permit comes in the form of a charter or a policy.

Significant building projects always require building permits. Along the same lines, all significant information security projects require permits. If we don't have a permit where one is required, we may be forced to undo things that we've done, and we risk losing the company thousands (or millions) of dollars, not to mention our own jobs.

On the flip side; *not all* construction work requires a permit, and not all information security work requires a permit either. We do too much work that requires a permit without having one. We also do too much work getting a permit when a permit isn't required.

SOLUTION #2: BUILDING WITH PERMITS

You've heard this before, but I'll repeat it anyway: we must get buy-in for everything we do in our work. Everything? Yes, everything. We must get buy-in that's either explicit or implied. The art is in determining which things need explicit buy-in and which things do not. If we go too far to one side, that is, getting explicit buy-in on too many things, we'll be viewed as poor leaders who can't make decisions. If we go too far to the other side, we'll be viewed as renegades who are reckless and careless. If I

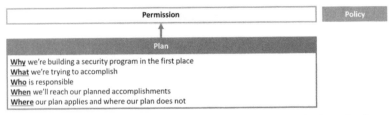

Figure: Permission is important for at least two reasons: (1) it's our authority to do what we want to do, and (2) it helps make the business leaders defensible when something bad happens.

had a choice to err on one side or the other, I would err on the side of caution, meaning I would get explicit buy-in if the decision is questionable.

Here are some common information security building permits for which we should get explicit approval:

- strategic plans

- budgets

- information security policies

- everything in which an owner is defined (This assumes we've got information systems, applications, and data ownership worked out—more on this later.)

- everything that will materially affect large portions of the user population, meaning things we're planning that could get in the way of someone or something

- everything that will affect key players in the organization (Every organization has one or more powerful, influential people whom we don't want to piss off. We need to identify these people early on and become friends.)

Here are some common information security building components that don't require explicit permits, and for which implied approval is OK:

- documentation that supports policy, guidelines, standards, and procedures

- simple changes that have minimal effect on people's work

- execution of tasks that support higher-level plans that were explicitly approved (This includes the enforcement of policy statements and requirements.)

- minor risk decisions related to things for which ownership hasn't been defined

Our job is to serve people, not to make people do things our way. Approvals (permits) give us the boundaries within which we must operate. They give us the necessary backing to get things done.

Have you ever tried going it alone before? If you have, and you've succeeded, God help your users and your organization. It's not the right way to do things.

Togetherness

Getting permits and buy-in forces us to get out of our comfort zone and among the people who are impacted the most by our decisions. Not only do we get more participation from others within our organization in this way, but we also learn other languages. It fosters a sense of togetherness. We get a sense that we, as an organization, are all in this together. Although information security is our responsibility, others are more apt to help us with our jobs when we actively include them in key decision making.

PROBLEM #3: WEAK OR ABSENT FOUNDATIONS

Think of the foundation of your home or office building. It's not exciting, it's not fun, and it's not sexy at all. Foundations are boring. We don't brag about foundations to our friends and family. Nobody cares. Foundations just do their job, and nobody takes notice. This is the sign of a good foundation.

Imagine this for a second. You just bought a new house. It's beautiful, and you can't wait to show it off to family and friends. You decide to invite everyone over to your new house. As people walk into your house and tell you how much they love the place, you reply with excitement, "You think this is great? Just come downstairs and let me show you the foundation!"

Not likely. Most people don't care about the foundation. Until it fails. Then everybody cares.

A building without a solid foundation won't stand for very long, and a security program without a solid foundation won't either. The foundation for a house is physical and tangible; it's something we can touch and feel. The foundation for a security program, however, is conceptual, intangible, and built on tenets (or principles).

In chapter 1, we established the importance of speaking the same language and using common definitions. Let's define the word *foundation* for the purpose of information security. A foundation is an underlying basis or principle for something. Synonyms include *basis, starting point, base, point of departure, beginning, premise,* **principles**, and **fundamentals**. Note the emphasis on the words *principles* and *fundamentals*.

In information security, the foundation consists of the principles and fundamentals of information security. Clearly, if we don't have a good definition of *information security* or an understanding of what the fundamentals are, then we have a problem. The problem will manifest itself in other symptomatic problems, and these problems will permeate the rest of the security program. The result is failure.

So, what are the fundamentals, and what does the foundation of a security program consist of?

The foundation of a security program must be derived from our definition of *information security*, first and foremost. Fundamental tenets of information security can then be derived from logic, if nothing else. Here's the logic: it only makes sense that *we can't secure what we don't know we have,* and *we can't secure what we can't control*. The foundations of a security program, then, would be at least *asset management, access control,* and *change control*.

The same holds true whether you're defending a multibillion-dollar company or you're defending the information managed by a three-person coffee shop. Obviously, the major difference is complexity.

People in our industry build security programs without the fundamentals, without a foundation. This is the problem.

Asset Management

We can't secure what we don't know we have.

It seems logical that we can effectively secure only the assets we know about. By luck or by chance (I believe in neither), we can still provide some security for unknown or unaccounted-for assets; however, each unknown asset is a crack in our foundation. It's far too common for organizations to have either no asset-management program or, at best, a partial and incomplete asset-management program.

An asset is *an economic resource that has value to a person or organization*. Assets can be tangible or intangible. Tangible assets are things like inventory, buildings, equipment, and computers. Intangible assets are nonphysical (they can't be physically touched). Intangible assets include things like patents, computer software (including configurations), copyrights, account balances, and data (including information).

Every organization has assets. The problem is, in most cases, organizations are not aware of and cannot account for all the assets for which they are responsible.

Here's a quick true story from a consulting engagement with a very large global enterprise. The CIO was extremely frustrated with the fact that the company was paying hundreds of thousands of dollars on a managed security operations center (SOC), and he didn't feel like the company was getting any value from the SOC. We explained that an SOC works only as well as the data it consumes. The discussion continued

> **The CISO asks "How many Windows hosts do we have?"**
>
> Antivirus Team says: 7,864
>
> Desktop Management Team says: 6,321
>
> Endpoint Detection and Response (EDR) Team says: 6,722
>
> Configuration Management Database (CMDB) Team says: 4,848
>
> SIEM Team says: 9,342
>
> Vulnerability Management Team says: 5,902

for a while, until we discussed how many Active Directory domains there were. The head of information security stated, "There are six or seven." We asked, "Six or seven—which is it?" He wasn't sure, and this was obviously a problem. We took more than half a day to track down the fact that there were actually eleven!

Which is more concerning: that there are eleven Active Directory domains or that four or five of them were completely unaccounted for by the information security team?

Want another example? How about Equifax? Equifax wasn't even aware of all its web servers or which ones were vulnerable to the Apache Struts exploit—emphasis on *wasn't even aware of all its web servers.*

Does all this seem basic, like you learned it during your CISSP studies? That's because it is basic. Get it out of your head that basic isn't cool. Basic is cool. Be basic.

Access Control

We can't secure what we can't control.

Only after we have a solid grasp of our assets can we define who and what should have access to those assets. Assuming the asset-management crack in our foundation is patched, the problems don't get easier to solve. We need to make sure that our asset inventory stays current and manageable. If we don't have adequate control over our assets, then our asset inventory is only as good as the last time we had control—assuming we *ever* had control.

Our second foundational problem is access control, both physical and technological. We, myself and my colleagues, have a saying that gets a chuckle out of some people: *It doesn't really matter how well your firewall works if someone can steal your server.* Physical and logical (or technological) access controls must work together. Logical (or technological) controls are arguably harder to manage but may be more important than physical controls because of our world is hyperconnected.

Access control is the formal (ideally) process for controlling access between people and information resources, and between information resources and other information resources.

We're broadly defining the term *information resources* as physical locations, hardware, software, and information. Examples of information resources include buildings, storage areas, server rooms, firewalls, switches, servers, cabling, operating systems, accounts (user and service), databases, file shares, and so on. Mastering the concepts of subjects and objects goes a long way toward understanding access control. Subjects are active entities and objects are passive entities. In most cases, access control

Here are some real numbers from one Active Directory domain of a large organization. This is the result of how not to do identity and access management, or access control:

- 11,463 user accounts exist in the directory.

- 4,321 user accounts in the directory are **enabled.**

- 1,079 user accounts in the directory show **no evidence of ever logging in.**

- 1,444 user accounts in the directory have passwords that **never expire.**

- 488 user accounts have **no password set.**

The organization has a foundation that is in serious disrepair.

> Arguably the most prevalent use of identification without authentication in the United States is the use of social security numbers (SSNs). Identity theft could be curbed significantly if we could figure out how to universally prohibit the use of SSNs without an accompanying strong authenticator. If we treated SSNs as we do names, things would be much different.

enforces the type(s) of access subjects have to objects. Effective access control requires planning—identifying who the subjects are (identification), how the subjects will be authenticated (password, MFA, and the like), and what they'll be permitted to do with our information resources (authorization). The concepts are well known and simple to understand. We fail in our implementation.

Entire books are written about access control. The point of this book is not to teach you all there is to know about access control. The point of this book is to describe the problem, put the problem into some context, and give you ways you can start addressing the problem.

Once you know what assets you have, then you can also tackle configuration control. Configurations of assets should be included in an asset inventory; however, the configurations are crap if access control isn't adequately considered. Configuration management, including control, is almost like rebar; it spans and strengthens our foundation between asset management, access control, and change control.

Identification and Authentication

Identification and authentication are two key components to access control. Identification is nothing more than a subject professing itself to another subject or object. Authentication is proof of the identification. A simple, easy-to-understand example is a username and password. The username is the identification; the password is the authentication. The problems arise when we try to define what is *acceptable* as *valid proof* of an identity. There are too many problems with our use of authentication in our industry to highlight each one. As an industry, we have yet to tackle the problems associated with weak authentication schemes. Some of the most prevalent problems include sharing authentication data (passwords); the failure to demand two-factor (strong) authentication on all systems, especially externally exposed applications and systems; and privileged access. The use of identification without any authentication at all is inexcusable, but we allow it every day.

One of the most common methods for network infiltration is still the use of simple usernames and passwords to secure externally exposed applications and systems. It's such a common threat vector, and still such a common vulnerability. Allowing obviously poor design and implementation in today's high-risk environments is inexcusable. I'll say it in a different way: there is *no excuse for single-factor authentication* on any externally exposed information resource, yet we still find it and permit it anyway.

Change Control

Control isn't only about access.

Change control has been the thorn in the side of many information security professionals. I've certainly had my challenges with it. Change control is another foundational component of an effective information security program. The problem is either that most organizations have no change control function or that their change control function gets in the way of doing business.

SOLUTION #3: ESTABLISHING A SOLID FOUNDATION

Now that we have the plan and the necessary permits, we can focus on our foundation. Just like everything else, our foundation is designed around our definition of *information security*, and it's built using the fundamentals, the basics. Let's start with one of the most fundamental questions: *What are we trying to secure?*

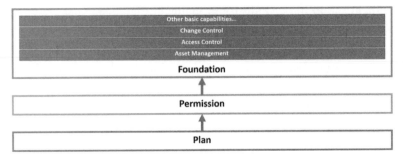

Figure: An example diagram showing a plan, permission, and a simple information security program foundation.

What Are We Trying to Secure?

Beyond understanding what security is, it's hard to get more fundamental than answering this question. It's an important question because it's very hard to secure something when we don't know we have it.

I suppose we could just rely on luck or on chance, if either exist; however, our definition of information security would change to *relying on luck or on chance to protect the confidentiality, integrity, and availability of information.*

Seems like a laughable proposition, but unfortunately too many of us use this or a similar definition.

Back to the question at hand. We need to figure out what we're trying to secure. The way we answer this question is by taking and maintaining an asset inventory.

Asset Management

Asset management is a critical component in our information security foundation. If we build other parts of our information security program, say vulnerability management, mobile-device management, or business-continuity management, without the foundational characteristics provided by asset management, then we chip away at our effectiveness and waste our time. Eventually our house, our information security program, will tumble to the ground.

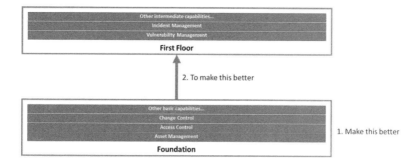

Since I mentioned vulnerability management, let's pick on this topic for a second. Most organizations appear to struggle with vulnerability management. They do a vulnerability scan using one of our industry's popular vulnerability scanning tools and find out that they've got thousands of critical-severity vulnerabilities. They're shocked because they've spent so much time and money on applying patches and deploying strong configurations. Vulnerability management is most often a by-product or symptom of good or bad asset management. Makes sense, doesn't it? How can we account for vulnerabilities (or weaknesses) in information resources if we don't know what information resources we have?

OK, you get it. Asset management is part of our foundation. What is asset management, and how do we do it better?

What Is Asset Management?

It seemed to me while I was writing this book that asset management and many of the other things covered here are common sense. The problem is that there is no such thing as common sense in information security. If there were, good security would be more common.

I'm warned to not use Wikipedia as a credible source, but the definition found there is as good as any other. Wikipedia defines the term *asset management* this way:

> Asset management, broadly defined, refers to any system that monitors and maintains things of value to an entity or group.

Now we need to define our **system** and the ***things of value***.

System

A system is *a set of principles or procedures according to which something is done; an organized scheme or method.* Our asset-management programs need to fit with this definition. Applying this to our definition of asset management, we're left with *an organized scheme or method that monitors and maintains things of value.* Got it.

> Remember: there is no common sense in information security.

The way we maintain our things of value is through an asset inventory. This is our accounting of the things of value. Things come in, things move around, things go out. This is where we need the method of monitoring. To maintain our asset inventory, we need to monitor the things that come in and the things that go out.

This is the basic system. We start with all things. Some of the things are valuable things, and these things should be included in our asset inventory. The valuable things stay in our asset inventory until they are no longer valuable things, at which time we dispose of them.

We can add more to our system if we desire, but we shouldn't lose track of this simple expression of what we're trying to accomplish. Some

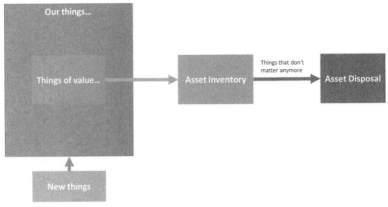

Figure: A very simple diagram of how an asset-management program should flow.

additional features we can include are asset tracking (tracking where an asset is within the organization), who the asset has been assigned to, asset or data classification (how valuable one asset is compared to another), and others.

The *things of value* are the things that we must secure.

Things of Value

What are the things of value in our organization? They come in two primary forms: tangible things and intangible things. The difference between the two is we can touch the tangible things and we can't touch (physically, anyway) the intangible things.

The tangible things are included in our asset inventory and are commonly referred to as a "physical inventory." Our physical inventory must contain all the servers, desktops, laptops, firewalls, storage area networks (SANs), switches, and everything else that has value to our organization. Most organizations have some semblance of a physical inventory.

The intangible things are much harder to account for, at least for most organizations. Intangible things include software/applications, information, and thoughts and ideas. (These are the things floating around in people's heads.) We should forget about inventorying the thoughts and ideas for now and focus on the software and information. Software and information are the intangible things that must be accounted for in our inventory.

Let's assume this logic now: if we have an asset, there must be some value in it. It may have very little value, but it has *some*, right? To determine whether or not an asset has value, we first need to account for it and evaluate its value. This is a job

> Asset management is a foundational component of every information security program that must not be neglected. A crack in this foundation will lead to deterioration in other parts of the security program.

for asset classification. Asset classification is a refinement of our asset inventory. Without a solid asset inventory, asset classification is very limited in its value to the organization. Asset classification gets applied after the inventory is compiled (and, we hope, maintained).

Phew! Now that we have that defined, we have a second question, how do we do it better?

How to Do It Better

We get better by:

- defining our system
- getting permission for our system
- formalizing our system
- automating management of our system wherever possible

We must define our system, for starters. What does our system look like? Simple diagrams like some of the ones used earlier in this book can get us started, but if we want our system to improve over time, or if we expect others to interact with our system, we'd better formalize it. Formalization, in most cases, starts with policy. Defining our asset-management policy gives us the beginning of the formalization that we're looking for, and it gives us explicit permission (assuming it's approved by the powers that be).

After permission, we can start to build out the rest of our system (or refine the system that we already have). When building out the system, keep it as simple as possible, and automate (that is, remove people from the equation) whenever possible. Manual asset-management practices won't work or scale beyond a small number of assets. Plus, people are expensive, slow, and fraught with error (some of the things that make us beautiful in the first place).

It's one thing to compile an asset inventory; it's an entirely different thing to maintain it. Again, the only way we'll accomplish this on any scale will be through automation. There are many asset-management techniques and tools that we can use to assist us. Explore their capabilities and adopt them where they make the most sense for your situation.

Your system is going to look different from my system. That's normal. The point isn't that your system looks like mine. The point is that you need and you get an asset-management program that works.

Don't take shortcuts here and expect them not to permeate into other parts of your security program. And don't just take my word for it either. There's a reason that CSC 1 and CSC 2 within the CIS Critical Security Controls (the first two controls) are dedicated to inventory:

> Asset management must be supported with asset classification, where roles and responsibilities are defined for each asset and values are determined.

CSC 1: Inventory of Authorized and Unauthorized Devices

CSC 2: Inventory of Authorized and Unauthorized Software

Once we get better at asset management, then we can begin to add the walls on top of our foundation—things like asset classification, vulnerability management, configuration management, and all sorts of other disciplines.

Practicality

One of the common objections to asset management is its practicality. There are dozens of tools on the market that are made to help us build and maintain an asset inventory. In some cases, it makes sense to use a couple of tools; this way, the output from one tool can be used to validate and/or reconcile the output from another. Take LabTech and Lansweeper for instance. One organization we know uses both of these tools to maintain their asset inventory, and they seem to work well for them. Your choice of tools should be what works best for you.

We Can't Secure What We Can't Control

Now that we've covered the foundational fact that we can't secure what we don't know we have, we can move on to the next foundational

component. How can we secure the things of value? To secure things, we must control them. This leads us to the foundational concepts of access control and change control. These are large foundational concepts that entire books have been written about. Most of the other (first-floor) concepts in building the rest of the security program are driven by one or both concepts: access control and change control, in that order.

Access Control

We need to determine who should have access to what and how much access they should have. That's a simple concept, but it's a serious challenge to implement in real life. To determine who should have access to what, we need to define who should make this determination. This is a responsibility that's best assigned to an asset owner (system, application, and/or data) as part of asset classification.

Master the concepts of access control. Access control drives permissions, privileges, identities, authentication, and authorization, among other things. Read some of the excellent books that have been written on the subject. One good book is *Identity and Access Management: Business Performance through Connected Intelligence* by Ertem Osmanoglu. It's time well spent, because access control is part of our foundation.

Change Control

Change control is as much art as it is science. The art comes from ensuring that adequate control is applied while not getting in the way of the business. Change control mandates that all significant changes require some level of approval (ideally from the asset owner), maybe some testing before and after, and proper planning (change window, step-by-step change documentation, back-out plans, and so forth).

Change control working in concert with access control and asset management ensures that the assets are maintained in a consistent and controlled manner. Change control is critical for effective configuration management, vulnerability management, firewall management, and so on.

Like access control, entire books are written about change control, and we should all master the concepts as part of our work.

Once we start getting our hands around access control and change control, other concepts come into focus more and become feasible endeavors. Things like configuration control will be possible because of its reliance on the functions of access control and change control.

We Can't Manage What We Can't Measure

This last foundation component isn't really a security program foundation component. It's more of a general management foundation component. As we're building our security programs or retrofitting established security programs, we should always keep in mind measurement. Measurement can demonstrate improvement (or, sadly, decline) in our efforts. Measurement data can be of great benefit to us for many reasons:

- It can confirm or contradict gut feelings.
- It can justify our expenses and budget.
- It can justify our existence.
- It can alert us to when something may be wrong.

As we're laying down or repairing our foundation, we should always keep measurement in mind.

You may identify other foundational components for your information security program, but the ones presented here are a good start. If we think that we don't have any cracks in our foundation, then we're probably fooling ourselves. Of the hundreds of organizations that I've worked with, both large and small, I can easily count the number of good foundations using my digits (fingers and toes; well, maybe just fingers).

Foundation Repair

If you find cracks in your foundation, should you repair the foundation or start over? In some cases, I don't think there's much of a difference.

Depending on where you're at with your information security program, you'll have to determine whether you start over or repair what you've already built (or inherited). I'm guessing that most will repair or do nothing. Doing nothing means you're doing a disservice to your organization and your organization's customers. I'm hoping that you're better than that and will act.

PROBLEM #4: OVERENGINEERED FOUNDATIONS

> Too much control is as bad as too little control, and in some cases it's even worse than no control at all.

A foundation must be right-sized for a building. It is entirely possible to overengineer a foundation and waste valuable resources. For instance, your building plan may call for an eight-inch concrete slab, but you decide to double it, just to be safe. The cost in the extra eight inches of concrete may outweigh the benefit. In the same vein, your plan for change control may include a sign-off from the system owner, but you've decided to assemble a change board consisting of various people (some of whom have no stake in most changes) just to be sure that everyone gets a voice. The decision to double the thickness of your concrete slab means that you have spent resources on the slab that you cannot spend in other places. The decision to overengineer your change control process means that you may encourage people to not follow the process because it's perceived to be cumbersome. Worse yet, you may be restricting the company's ability to make money.

We can, and sometimes do, implement overly strict access control, configuration management, and change control. An overengineered foundation can also fail when we consider two points:

1. **A business is in business to make money.** If our foundation does not permit our business to make money, or if our

foundation makes it harder for our business to make money, then we have designed the wrong foundation.

> "Security is security experts' main job; for anyone else, it's a productivity drain. Users will bend over backwards to bypass things that make their life difficult."
>
> –Angela Sasse, professor of human-centered technology at University College London

2. **People don't like when we get in the way.** If people perceive that we have put controls in place that make their jobs harder, then we have either put the wrong controls in place or we still have a language problem (See chapter 3).

The right-sized foundation requires proper planning, a lot of engineering, and some art. Thankfully, we can make foundation adjustments, but they may be a little painful or we may have to earn back some of our lost political capital.

Remember, a business is in business to make money. A business is not in business to build the most secure environment that ever existed.

SOLUTION #4: SIMPLIFICATION

We need to be careful to not overengineer or overcomplicate anything in our foundation or any other part of our security program. Whenever possible, we should err on the side of simplicity. If our building plan calls for a twelve-inch footing, use a twelve-inch footing. Too much waste can result in less security because of the complexity required in managing the program, not to mention the wasted resources that could have been spent in other important areas.

A good foundation for our information security program will be one that has only the steps necessary to accomplish a specific goal—no more and no fewer. If a process like entering a new asset into an inventory can be done in one step, don't adopt a process or product that requires five steps.

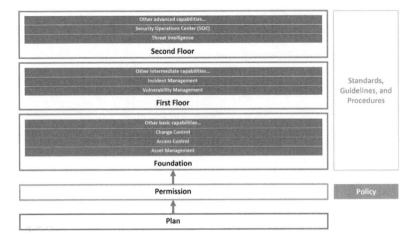

Figure: Once the foundation is laid (or repaired), then we can focus on more advanced information security program capabilities. This is a sample for illustration purposes only.

In closing

This chapter is all about the basics. There isn't anything new in this chapter for most people with intermediate information security experience.

The foundation isn't sexy. It's basic. This reality may contribute to the fact that it's sorely missing in most information security programs. Forget about the cool blinky lights that will impress your peers. Focus on the dirty work of building your foundation. It may not impress everyone, but it will be effective.

3

Lipstick on a Pig

The information security industry is broken because we don't get real with ourselves. A common saying used in politics is, "you can put lipstick on a pig, but it is still a pig." In the context of this quote, our industry is a pig, and I don't mean to offend pigs. The idea of this saying is that you may try to beautify an ugly reality, but the ugly reality remains. Our industry needs to face the ugly reality that it is broken, but instead we apply lipstick to make things appear better than they really are, and we hope that nobody notices.

The problems in our industry are not merely cosmetic. Our industry needs serious repair, and we'll need to make significant changes if we're going to fix it.

Like the other chapters in this book, this one is organized into the problems and the solutions.

Problems covered in this chapter include:

- Problem #1: Lipstick makes us appear more attractive than we really are.
- Problem #2: Lipstick makes us feel better about ourselves.
- Problem #3: Technology is the most common lipstick.
- Problem #4: Layering on lipstick makes things worse.

Some of the potential solutions we'll explore include:
- Solution #1: We need to get real.
- Solution #2: We need to be honest with ourselves and one another.
- Solution #3: We should use technology only when and where it's needed.
- Solution #4: We need to simplify.

PROBLEM #1: LIPSTICK MAKES US APPEAR MORE ATTRACTIVE THAN WE REALLY ARE

The wise woman Taylor Swift once said, "Band-Aids don't fix bullet holes." She's right. In our industry, we need to stop using surface solutions to fix deeper problems. Band-Aids are good for scratches, but they don't do a damn thing when our problems are deep below the surface. What we really need is surgery.

For example, look at the identity theft dilemma in the United States. It is a deep problem that cannot be fixed with a Band-Aid. But that doesn't stop us from trying.

Equifax and Our Identity Theft Problem

The Equifax breach that was announced in September 2017 was big news. The breach resulted in the loss or theft of personal data belonging to more than 145 million US consumers. The data included full names, social security numbers, birth dates, addresses, and in some cases, driver license numbers. Obviously, the breach caused quite a stir.

Why is the loss or theft of a social security number such a big deal in the United States? The simple answer is because someone suffers when this type of information is lost or stolen. In the wrong hands, this information can be used to steal someone's identity. With a little ingenuity, the identity theif can use it to file taxes before you do (obtaining a fraudulent refund), take a loan out in your name, and even receive medical treatment using your insurance. Imagine someone else walking around as you. (Some of us have already experienced such a thing.) This causes a significant amount of anxiety, frustration, and lost time and money.

We use our social security number for identifying who we are and for authentication (or proof) of who we are. We also allow the use of our social security number without any authentication at all, which is nearly the same thing.

Fundamentally, this is a broken identification system.

But we cover up this ugly reality with the alluring lipstick of identity theft protection services, credit monitoring, and credit freezes.

The surgical fix would be to prohibit the use of a social security number without an accompanying authenticator (password, PIN, two-factor authentication, etc.) that each individual controls. This would be a fundamental fix. However, we would rather fool ourselves into thinking that the lipstick works instead of facing reality.

Although the unauthorized use of a social security number is not the only method of identity theft, it is the most common, and arguably the most dangerous. This, in a nutshell, is what makes identity theft such a prevalent problem in the United States.

If we fixed this fundamental problem, the Equifax breach wouldn't be nearly as troublesome.

There are many other places where we use lipstick in our industry. Applying cosmetic fixes to of fundamental problems is expensive and dangerous—often more dangerous than doing nothing at all.

Our Organization

We use a lot of lipstick in our industry because we always want to put on a good face when it comes to new business, more business, or regulatory compliance. We like to convey the impression that our information security program is well designed and well run when we communicate with our board of directors, our customers, our business partners, and our regulators. We'll go to great lengths to look good, even though we may be suffering from some fundamental problems.

At least in the short term, the consequences of telling the truth seem to outweigh the consequences of putting on the lipstick.

Take Target, for instance. The security program for the retail giant looked simply beautiful (from the outside), right up until 2013, when Target suffered one of the most famous payment card breaches in history. It had all the certifications, authorizations, and shiny new security software solutions you could imagine. Target was compliant with the Payment Card Industry Data Security Standard (PCI DSS), and was certified as such by Trustwave, the market-leading PCI Qualified Security Assessor (QSA) at the time. Target had invested in some of the best tools that money could buy, including FireEye. It segmented its network to restrict lateral movement within the environment, and it was very well staffed. The list of good security things at the company was long, and it looked great!

From the outside, anyway.

Turns out, FireEye wasn't fully operational yet, and security warnings were either ignored or mishandled. The segmentation was ineffective at preventing lateral movement, which led to clarifications by the PCI Security Standards Council (PCI SSC) on what the word *segmentation* really meant. Vendor risk management was hardly a thing for Target until afterward. The breach of 2013 exposed some serious shortcomings on the inside.

As details emerged about the breach, it was evident that Target's information security was not all that it first appeared to be. There were things that Target did well, like acquire some of the best technology that money could buy, and there were embarrassing things that happened to Target, like having to be told by the US Secret Service that it had been breached. It's embarrassing (or it should be) when you don't detect the breach and someone else does.

Once it became clear that the breach came through the compromised system (or credentials) belonging to an HVAC vendor, questions quickly mounted. How could compromised HVAC vendor credentials lead to the loss of millions of credit and debit card numbers? According to Brian Krebs, "Once inside Target's network, there was nothing to stop attackers from gaining direct and complete access to every single cash register in every Target store." (Source: https://krebsonsecurity.com/2015/09/inside-target-corp-days-after-2013-breach/) So, there was a lack of network segmentation? Turns out that there are multiple definitions of *network segmentation*. The industry didn't have a standard definition of segmentation, at least as it related to PCI, so we were speaking different languages.

In the same article, Krebs cites findings from a Verizon investigation into the breach: "The Verizon security consultants identified several systems that were using misconfigured services, such as several Microsoft SQL servers that had a weak administrator password, and Apache Tomcat servers using the default administrator password." Apparently, underneath all that lipstick was a certifiable Target pig.

Since 2013, Target has fundamentally changed its approach to information security; however, in the industry as a whole, there's still plenty of pork and too much lipstick. The most common application of lipstick is to cover up our lack of a solid foundation. This cosmetic overload leads us to a serious false sense of security.

Other examples of superficial beautification include organizations that get a certification or obtain some sort of compliance certificate. A certification such as ISO 27001 or HITRUST, compliance such as PCI, or a report such as a SOC 2 doesn't always indicate good (or bad) security. Every certification, compliance achievement, and report has its benefits, but it also has its shortcomings. Truly the devil is in the details. The lipstick itself may be the best lipstick that's ever been made, so we're not talking about whether an ISO 27001 certification, a HITRUST certification, PCI compliance, or a SOC 2 report is good or bad. Each one can be used correctly by an organization, or it can be used as lipstick to dress up a pig.

This is one of the ways we apply lipstick to organization security programs.

Our Credentials

We also apply lipstick to our own professional careers. Ever come across someone with certifications that you wouldn't trust with your pencil, let alone your security program?

Certifications and education are great, and I'm not minimizing their importance at all. Education and the resulting certification are important, but they're no replacement for experience. It takes a tremendous amount of dedication and hard work to obtain certain qualifications, such as a master's degree in information security, CISSP, Offensive Security Certified Professional (OSCP), Certified Information Security Auditor (CISA), Certified Information Security Manager (CISM), Global Information Assurance Certification (GIAC), and so on. Education and certification are great ways to obtain book smarts. But book smarts don't always translate into street smarts. Street smarts come only through experience.

> Certifications and education can easily become lipstick when we put too much stock into their value.

Information security education and certification is a multimillion-dollar industry, and too many people believe that education and certification are all you need to be a great information security professional. The fact is that education and certification (combined) are only one component of what makes a good security professional. We'll cover some solutions here, but we'll get more specifics about this topic in chapter 10.

SOLUTION #1: WE NEED TO GET REAL

I hope you agree by now that the question is no longer whether our industry is a pig, but rather how ugly the pig is. For a quick trip to unblemished reality, let's scrub off the lipstick and come clean with a few barefaced facts. Here are some more real information security statistics to get us started:

- **Spending on information security is predicted to reach $93 billion in 2018.** How much of this $93 billion will be well spent, and how much of it will be spent applying lipstick to pigs? (https://www.forbes.com/sites/tonybradley/2017/08/17/gartner-predicts-information-security-spending-to-reach-93-billion-in-2018/#b5bed353e7f1)

- **87 percent of CIOs believe their security controls are failing to protect their business.** (Source: https://www.venafi.com/assets/pdf/wp/Venafi_2016CIO_SurveyReport.pdf)

- **The median number of days that an attacker resides within a network before detection is 146 days.** (Source: https://www.microsoft.com/en-us/cloud-platform/advanced-threat-analytics)

- **There may be 3.5 million unfilled cybersecurity jobs by 2021.** (Source: https://cybersecurityventures.com/jobs/)

- **Almost half of US consumers (49 percent) believe that their security habits make them vulnerable,** and I would argue that most US consumers don't even know what security habits they should follow. (Source: https://betanews.com/2018/11/06/password-reuse-despite-risks/)

- **72 percent of people globally believe that connected home devices offer hackers new ways to steal data.** Yet, we continue to deploy a network of devices, or internet of things (IoT), everywhere in our homes, sacrificing our privacy and our safety. (Source: https://www.symantec.com/security-center/threat-report)

- **41 percent of people globally cannot properly identify a phishing email** and often guess as to an email's legitimacy. (Source: https://www.symantec.com/security-center/threat-report)

- **Around 39 percent of US residents were victims of cybercrime, compared to 31 percent globally.** (Source: https://www.symantec.com/security-center/threat-report)

- **In the past year, nearly seven hundred million people in twenty-one countries experienced some form of cybercrime.** I can't help but wonder how many additional people there are who (1) don't even know it or (2) never reported it. (Source: https://www.symantec.com/security-center/threat-report)

- **$2.1 trillion is the expected total global annual cost of all data breaches by 2019.** (Source: https://www.juniperresearch.com/press/press-releases/cybercrime-cost-businesses-over-2trillion)

- **The US government is considering allowing the use of nuclear weapons in the fight against cybercrime.** This is scary as hell, and I hope it's not true. (Source: https://www.nytimes.com/2018/01/16/us/politics/pentagon-nuclear-review-cyber-attack-trump.html)

There's no shortage of depressing statistics. You may think that there isn't anything positive to say. That's not true though. We're more aware as a society than we've ever been, we're spending more money than we ever have, boards of directors are getting more involved, and our job market is awesome (from a job seeker's point of view).

Despite these positive signs, we're working with a pig, and we put a lot of lipstick on it to make it look better than it is. There's no other industry where we could point to similar statistics and conclude otherwise. Without more serious intervention, the gap between those trying to protect and those trying to exploit will only continue to get worse.

PROBLEM #2: LIPSTICK MAKES US FEEL BETTER ABOUT OURSELVES

There is no doubt that when we think we look better, we feel better. Our self-esteem goes up, our egos are flattered, and we become quite pleased with ourselves. That feeling flames up when people compliment us and praise our looks. It makes us smile to think that we are so accepted, so loved, and yes—so superior.

Much of our behavior is motivated by the pursuit of these ego-driven feelings. To a certain extent that is a good thing, because we need a strong sense of self-worth to go out and stake a place for ourselves in the world. We must be confident to compete in our business or career. Feeling good about ourselves is by and large a positive virtue. Aren't we all in it for the pursuit of happiness?

But we must be careful when feelings are involved, because it is easy to lose our common sense and reason. We go too far when our good appearances quit representing our actual reality. There are many modes of misrepresenting ourselves, and they range from over-the-top to unethical.

First there's bragging and boasting, where we magnify our good points, and that slides into a sly deception of presenting the good points while concealing the bad ones. This puts us on the road to hypocrisy, a growing disconnect between what we say and what we do. And it need not be deliberate.

In the early days of my information security firm, FRSecure, we came to the realization that we gave advice to our clients that we weren't following ourselves. Roughly six years into our existence, one of our analysts was presenting a client's FISASCORE to their executive management team. The score wasn't good, and there was a lot of remediation work to do. One of the executives asked our analyst, "What's the FISASCORE at your company?"

At the time, we had delivered more than three hundred FISASCOREs, and this was the first time we'd been asked this rather obvious question. Our analyst didn't know the answer. He didn't know the answer because there was no answer. We'd never done an assessment of ourselves.

This was an eye-opener for us, which is sort of crazy, because we are information security experts, right? How could we have been preaching information security to hundreds of clients, yet neglecting to check our own with the same rigor? Since then we've made it our policy to apply to ourselves all of what we preach before we preach it. We do assessments and reassessments multiple times per year now, we track all progress in our information security program, and we're all regularly briefed on our status and security future. It was only a matter of time before we were going to eat our own dog food, but we're thankful for the executive who pushed the matter.

Hypocrisy can be a slippery slope, so be on the lookout for it.

OK, Google, Make Me an Expert!

We want to be accepted so badly that we'll overinflate our ego. We all want to fit in and to belong. This is normal. When we cross the line into being fake or misleading, then we have a problem. If the behavior progresses unchecked, we may convince ourselves that we are someone that we're not.

I had a recent ego-inflating experience when I was asked to give a keynote speech on a topic that was not quite in my wheelhouse. As a devoted adherent to Google and Wikipedia, I did my homework and prepared my talk. When I delivered the speech, I actually sounded like I knew what I was talking about.

After the talk, more than one person came up to me and called me a "thought leader." One person was amazed by how much I knew about these things.

My overinflated ego wanted to say, "Yes, I am a thought leader on these topics. I am great. I can give all sorts of awesome advice and elevate my status with these people. Hell, I might even build a name for myself here!"

My no-lipstick ego wanted to say, "Thank you," and explain what I did to prepare for my presentation. I would admit that I'm not a thought leader in these subjects. I would admit that I Googled each of the topics, did a little research, put together a slide deck, and practiced a few times.

Any guesses as to which ego won out here? The overinflated one did.

This is an example of where my own need (or want) to be accepted by the audience led to me acting like someone I'm not.

The Expert Exposed

It's unseemly for a Google aficionado to masquerade as an expert, but it is downright embarrassing for a company that bills itself as the top IT security consultancy to be caught wearing no clothes. That's what happened to Deloitte in 2017.

The firm had been crowned the world's best information security consultancy by Gartner for five years in a row. This stellar image was brought down to earth by a series of revelations.

- A collection of corporate VPN passwords, usernames, and other operational details were discovered in a public-facing GitHub repository.

- An employee uploaded company proxy login credentials to his public Google+ page.

- Multiple critical systems were exposed to the public internet with Remote Desktop Protocol (RDP) enabled and weak authentication (username and password). Dan Tentler, founder of Phobos Group, claimed to have found "7,000 to 12,000 open hosts for the firm spread across the globe." (Source: https://www.theregister.co.uk/2017/09/26/deloitte_leak_github_and_google/)

Almost immediately, there were accusations that Deloitte was a hypocrite. After all, the firm makes millions selling its tech guru services to others for a hefty price—and yet it seemed to ignore gaping holes in its own IT infrastructure.

Was Deloitte a hypocrite? Yes, it was. We all are.

In General

Another wise person once said, "You better check yo self before you wreck yo self." That was Ice Cube.

There are obvious consequences for wearing lipstick to hide our blemishes. Our friends and colleagues never get to know the real us. A false sense of security that is personal and career limiting can set in. In severe cases, our lipstick can be career ending.

Unfortunately, there exists a class of information security elitists in our industry whose true motivation is only to make a name for themselves. They sit in high places and exploit others for their own gain. Perhaps they think they're helping, but they're not. They're making a name for themselves first and foremost. Their lipstick hides their true motivation.

It's when we brag at the expense of others that it's lipstick. Lipstick on a pig is when we strive to make ourselves look better, and someone else suffers because of it. Putting down the hard work of another person is lipstick. Trash-talking the competition because we can't figure out how to convey the superiority of our solution is lipstick. This happens too often in our industry, and it's a problem.

Have you ever gone to an information security conference and listened to what people said? I mean really listened? I try to stay away from the sales booths, because the lipstick is applied way too thick there. But you'll also find lipstick in the speaking sessions, the breakouts, and the casual conversations. Not everyone at the gatherings knows enough to distinguish between what's real and what's lipstick. Bad advice is given, and worse yet, people new to our industry can be steered in the wrong direction.

The false sense of pride in our work can result in an attitude of, "I'm great at my job, but I can't say the same thing about the rest of you."

If we are so great at our jobs, then why do the facts say otherwise? We can come up with plenty of excuses, but have you ever thought that we're not as good—at least collectively—as we think we are?

If we were honest, we would ditch the lipstick and acknowledge our blemishes.

SOLUTION #2: WE NEED TO BE HONEST WITH OURSELVES AND ONE ANOTHER

Let's be honest with ourselves. The place to begin, as in a twelve-step program, is to admit we have a problem. We are not always honest with ourselves, and we need to address our shortcomings deliberately and methodically. We need to make up our minds to become more honest with ourselves.

Let's begin with the three things that make us good at our jobs. Take a personal inventory of how you stand in these categories:

- **Intangibles:** things like integrity, dependability, honesty, gifts, and other good things that can't be taught or easily learned

- **Education:** our constant education and learning through classes, seminars, conferences, degree programs, and so on

- **Experience:** our experience level, which comes only from doing

Try rating yourself in these three categories, or better yet, have someone else rate you. A lack of knowledge or skills is by far the easiest shortcoming on this list to address. That's because there is a host of educational opportunities available to us. You can take a class at a local tech school, buy some books, or even use free online resources (see sidebar). If you need knowledge or skills, you have little excuse for not getting further educated.

Experience doesn't come from taking a class. Instead, you must go out and actually do things in the field to gain experience. In classes you get theories and case studies, but on the job you get practical situations, and these are different things. Gaining experience involves making judgments, and sometimes making mistakes. It is no coincidence that the word *experience* is closely related to the word *experiment*. Mistakes are OK if you learn from them, and in fact, you learn a lot more quickly when you make mistakes. Experience teaches you things you would never learn from a class or a book. You can also learn secondhand through the experiences of others, and you can accelerate that by getting a mentor.

Online Learning Resources

Cybrary–https://www.cybrary.it/

Cybrary is an open-source cybersecurity and IT learning and certification preparation platform. Connect to an ecosystem of people, companies, content, and technologies to create and access an ever-growing catalog of online courses and experiential tools providing cybersecurity learning opportunities to anyone, anywhere, anytime.

Information Assurance Support Environment (IASE)–https://iase.disa.mil/eta/Pages/index.aspx

This is a US government–sponsored training environment offering cybersecurity awareness training, cybersecurity training for IT managers, cybersecurity training for cybersecurity professionals, cybersecurity technical training, NetOps training, cyberlaw awareness, and cybertools training.

Offensive Security Metasploit Unleashed–https://www.offensive-security.com/metasploit-unleashed/

The Metasploit Unleashed (MSFU) course is provided free of charge by Offensive Security in order to raise awareness for underprivileged children in East Africa. If you enjoy this free ethical hacking course, you can make a donation to the Hackers for Charity Food Program, a nonprofit 501(c)(3) organization.

SANS Cyber Aces Online–http://www.cyberaces.org/courses/

SANS Cyber Aces Online makes available, free and online, selected courses from the professional development curriculum offered by the SANS Institute, the global leader in cybersecurity training. SANS's goal in making these courses available as open courseware is to help grow the talent pool and accelerate the rate at which skilled cyberprofessionals can enter the information security industry, filling critical jobs currently going unfilled.

But what if you are short on the intangibles? Take integrity for instance. The word *integrity* has two different meanings.

The first meaning refers to a disposition toward ethical and honest behavior. I'm afraid there isn't much anyone can do for a person who lacks a sense of ethics as an information security professional. Ethics and honesty are intangible dispositions rooted in a person's character; either you have a moral sense or you don't. If you are one of these people (who lacks a sence of ethics), and you don't change, I hope you get found out before you do too much damage for the rest of us to clean up. Unfortunately, as we continue to struggle with finding information security talent in our industry, we will come across more people who lack moral integrity.

The other meaning of *integrity* refers to the formation of an integrated whole, a state of being undivided. Our industry may appear to some to be undivided, and this may be the result of the lipstick we apply. The fact is, we're not unified. We are divided, and in this respect, we absolutely lack integrity. The integrated whole means that our industry needs to get honest with itself and unify as group around a common mission.

There's food for thought. What is our "common mission"? If we had one, we'd probably be more integrated, unified, and cohesive. More integrity is the goal.

The Unicorn That Didn't Grow

We like to do something we call "growing unicorns" here where I work. Most of the time it turns out great. We hire someone for the intangibles—the things we can't teach, like integrity, honesty, natural abilities, and gifts—and then we teach them what they need to know to be great in this line of work. Occasionally, this approach backfires, and it usually backfires because the unicorn that we're growing doesn't have the *patience* to learn from *experience*.

On one occasion, one of our unicorns was very ambitious and highly skilled. He worked his butt off to study and pass certification exams.

He had a very promising career ahead of him. He lacked only one thing: *patience*. In time, he would have gained the *experience* to lead a team of unicorns and progress through the company; however, due to his lack of patience, he forced the issue. Forcing the issue led to resentment among his team members, and eventually he left the organization.

In this story, the unicorn was convinced that he was the man for the job. Despite being told more than once that he just wasn't ready, he wouldn't let it go. His pride got in the way, and his career suffered for it. Too much pride blinds us to the fact that we all have a lot to learn. Had he taken an honest and humble look at himself in the mirror, he would have realized the truth.

We all could use more honesty and humility.

Another Unicorn

Here's the story of another unicorn. This one has a genuine desire to help others and make a positive difference. He does his work, steps up regularly, and does so for the right reasons. He doesn't mind recognition, but he is not motivated by pure ego. He has an impeccable reputation and people love working with him.

The strong desire to help others motivates this unicorn to create solutions, and the time has come for him to step out from the shadows and tout some of the solutions he's created. It's an uncomfortable situation for him, but he knows that it's important to share his ideas with everyone.

Most important is the fact that he has not fallen into the trap of being too proud of himself. This industry could use better performance, leadership, relationships, and cooperation. Our industry could use more humility.

Peer Pressure

The people in our industry need to hold one another accountable. Not in a prideful manner that tears others down, but in a coaching manner that builds others up, and in a collegial manner that reminds us we are all in this together.

When a person on our team has integrity, but lacks other qualities there is a great opportunity for mentorship and coaching. It's my responsibility to my team and my profession—our industry—to take as many junior information security professionals as we can find and give them everything we've got.

The two most important things we can improve upon with our peers are accountability and mentorship.

Truth to Power

Boards of directors and other executive managers must have the truth if we expect them to make wise decisions. There are boards and executives who want the truth, but don't get the truth, and there are boards and executives who say they want the truth, but really don't. We get paid to tell people the truth, not what they want to hear. If we work for a board or executives who don't want the truth, we have options:

1.   **Continue to fight the fight.** Find common ground and under-standing and hope they'll come around.

2.   **Sell your soul.** Just keep feeding the board and other exec-utives what they want to hear. (This shouldn't even be an option, but it is, and some people work this way.)

3.   **Live to fight another day.** You can strategically pick your bat-tles or go find a new job. Our industry has more than three hundred thousand open jobs; surely some of those positions report to a more transparent management team.

Option 2 is difficult when our integrity is involved. If we decide on option 3, the good news for us is that the unemployment rate in our industry is 0 percent, and there are plenty of directors and executives who value the truth. Let's be honest with our employers and consis-tently tell them the truth. Of course, we'll fare much better when we use facts versus opinions. Honest facts and a humble approach when presenting to executives will go a long way.

Our Industry Should Get Honest with Itself

How can our industry get honest with itself when it isn't unified? When it has no integrity in the second sense, when it doesn't form a whole? We're so disparate and segmented. We have so many different approaches to seemingly everything. Everybody's got a solution, but nobody's got a solution we can all agree on. The admission that our industry is broken is a main theme of this book.

Our industry can't get real with itself unless our industry becomes unified. Just as an individual needs the inner harmony and synchronized workings of the heart, the mind, and the gut, so too must we form a unified organization with a common mind, a compassionate heart, and the guts to do the right thing together.

> The information security industry needs a single professional organization to create unity, define our profession, establish a single standard, create common methodologies, and work for the greater good.

Take politics and selfish financial interests and put them aside for a second to entertain the idea of a single way of doing things. If we, as an industry, could align ourselves well and agree on the fundamentals, we would all come out better in the long run, both economically and socially. Until this happens, things will get worse before they get better.

Until we decide to unify, we're left as individuals working with other individuals, each trusting others to do things right. Individually, how do we get real and use lipstick only where we need to? It's up to us as individuals to work this out as a grassroots effort.

This is where things get personal.

PROBLEM #3: TECHNOLOGY IS THE MOST COMMON LIPSTICK

When we use technology as a replacement for something else that we should be doing, then we're using technology as lipstick on our pig.

The single biggest application of lipstick is when technology controls are used to replace administrative controls or physical controls. The reason we do this is rather obvious. Administrative control means you must deal with people, and that is a difficult challenge. It is much easier—though much more expensive and much less effective—to use technology instead.

Our definition of *information security* goes beyond technology, even though technology is an important part of what we do. But it is not everything. Technology and information security are complementary.

Here's an example from an organization that our company recently worked for. It spent hundreds of thousands of dollars on the latest and greatest endpoint protection product, the greatest security information and event management (SIEM) solution, awesome data loss prevention (DLP) technology, and just about everything else. Executive management and the information security staff were very confident in what they'd assembled. On the surface, they looked impenetrable.

This organization wanted us to perform a penetration test to show management how awesome they were. At the planning kickoff meeting there was so much cockiness, you'd think there was no way these guys could get taken down.

How long do you think it took for our team to obtain an account with Domain Admin–level privileges from an external source without detection?

Twelve minutes.

We used a simple phishing attack with some slight variations. It wasn't out of scope, nor should it have been.

The organization's cockiness quickly turned to borderline despair. Executive management's false sense of security was shattered, and this was a good thing.

All their shiny new technology did not stop an employee from getting duped by a fake email. Employee training is an administrative task. Technical controls can complement administrative controls, but they cannot replace them altogether. People like to use technical controls as replacements for the other control types because they're sexier, easier, and less risky (for the security professional). Administrative controls are more boring, harder, and riskier (for the security professional). Administrative controls mean dealing with people. Who likes that?

Another simple example is the practice of vulnerability management. Patching operating systems and applications and catching configuration errors is a difficult challenge for most organizations. They spend millions of dollars on software for this, but the problems aren't technological ones. The fundamental problems are often related to administrative controls, like not having a handle on asset management, access control, and/or change control. The lipstick is the inappropriate tools used to treat deeper problems.

Asset management and change control require solid administrative controls (policies, procedures, training, and whatever else) to work properly. Again, we should complement our administrative control processes and practices with technology, but not replace them. We like technology more and tend to rely too heavily on it. When technology is used as lipstick, it can be a big problem.

SOLUTION #3: WE SHOULD USE TECHNOLOGY ONLY WHEN AND WHERE IT'S NEEDED

Technology is beautiful, and its proper use can literally change lives. There are limitations to what technology can do for us though, and these limitations must be acknowledged with honesty and integrity. Take administrative controls, for instance. Technology can be a compensating control for administrative controls, but not a replacement control. If technology is used beyond its intent or capabilities, it quickly become lipstick.

If we have human beings interacting with information, we'll have to do the hard work of educating them and influencing their behaviors through interaction. We shouldn't overcompensate with technological controls.

We shouldn't be overly impressed with the hundreds of thousands of dollars we've spent on technology when we consider that the normal people continue to exhibit insecure behaviors. And let's not forget that having the technology is one thing; using it appropriately is another.

PROBLEM #4: LAYERING ON LIPSTICK MAKES THINGS WORSE

" Complexity is the worst enemy of security. **"**

–Title of an interview with Bruce Schneier by Chee-Sing Chan, *Computerworld Hong Kong*, 2012

Bruce Schneier is one of the true pioneers of our industry, and it was an eye-opener to learn about his views on the harm caused by needless complexity. Interviewer Chee-Sing Chan asked Schneier, "Are we actually any more secure today than we were five years ago?" (Source: https://www.computerworld.com/article/2493938/cyberwarfare/complexity-the-worst-enemy-of-security.html)

"In short, no," said Schneier. "And the answer is that fundamentally the problem is complexity."

The logic is very clear. Added complexity means greater vulnerability. A process of thirty steps is more difficult to secure than a process of three steps. There are more opportunities for things to go wrong.

"The thing is we absolutely love complexity," continued Schneier. "It's down to using these new apps on our smartphones, it's using Skype on our work device while using the airport WiFi. We all like these things and having access to our data at all times, but this creates more complexity and it makes security harder."

We overcomplicate things. We use complexity unnecessarily in our industry because we don't know any better, we are unable to affect necessary changes within our organization, and/or because we miss the fundamentals. Most of the time, complexity creeps in unintentionally.

Whether it's intentional or not, needless complexity amounts to just slathering on the lipstick. A more complex environment may look impressive, but it's a lot harder to secure.

SOLUTION #4: WE NEED TO SIMPLIFY

It's very common to find organizations with extremely complex systems and processes that struggle with information security. In every area where there is needless complexity, simplicity must reign. A conscious effort must be made to reduce the number of steps in any process.

Process mapping is not necessarily a fun exercise, but it can be very valuable. Map processes to information security risks. Look for ways to simplify everywhere. A good process mapping exercise will include the technological steps too. When we simplify, we identify areas where we can be more efficient and secure. It's a win-win. More efficiency can save money that can be spent on more effective controls. There's also the value of knowing our systems better. The better we know our systems, the better we can secure them.

These are the virtues of simplification:

1. more efficient processes, fewer steps
2. reduction in ineffective or unnecessary controls
3. better security

Most of us don't know how to do process mapping, and admittedly it's not the most fascinating discipline in the world. It's not as sexy as buying a cool tool or blinky light (lipstick), but it's often more valuable. There are hundreds of great (and often free) resources available for process mapping. Check them out.

Simplify everything. Remember, layering on technology after technology adds to complexity, and complexity is bad.

4

Pipe Dreams

" This is your last chance. After this, there is no turning back. You take the blue pill–the story ends, you wake up in your bed and believe whatever you want to believe. You take the red pill–you stay in Wonderland, and I show you how deep the rabbit hole goes. Remember: all I'm offering is the truth. Nothing more. **"**

–Morpheus in *The Matrix* (1999)

The information security industry is broken because reality is a hard pill to swallow. Reality can be a hard pill to swallow, but it is the only pill that works. Blue pill versus red pill is a metaphor between choosing:

- a false sense of security, happiness as a virtue, and the blissful ignorance of illusion (the **blue** pill)

- a true sense of insecurity, knowledge, and the harsh truths of reality (the **red** pill)

The philosophical meaning behind it all is: are we OK with ignorance as long as we are happy, or do we desire the truth even if it's hard to embrace it?

If you were to describe our industry, which of the following word lists would you pick?

- *blissful ignorance, panic* (when something goes wrong), and *fantasy*
- *understanding, calm,* and *reality*

Judging by the behaviors we witness in most of our industry, the answer is obvious. Most people choose the first list of words. The words in the second list are antonyms of the words in the first list. This illustrates the difference between what we see when we look at ourselves in the mirror, and what we wish we would see.

In 2012, General Keith Alexander, then-director of the National Security Agency (NSA) and commander of US Cyber Command, stated that the loss of industrial information and intellectual property through cyber espionage constitutes the "greatest transfer of wealth in history." (Source: https://foreignpolicy.com/2012/07/09/nsa-chief-cybercrime-constitutes-the-greatest-transfer-of-wealth-in-history/) That's a seriously bold statement. He went on to claim that the $1 trillion (or more) that was spent to combat security-related crime in 2011 was "our future disappearing in front of us."

The self-proclaimed "world's leading researcher and Page ONE for the global cyber economy," Cybersecurity Ventures, said, "Cybercrime will cost the world $6 trillion annually by 2021." (Source: https://cybersecurityventures.com/hackerpocalypse-cybercrime-report-2016/) Here, five years after General Alexander's statement, the same claim is made that we're witnessing the greatest transfer of wealth in history.

Hype and fearmongering, or truth? Who would know for sure?

Some of us require the truth and reality: the red pill. Some of us are fine with the status quo and perceived happiness: the blue pill. The red pill wakes us up; the blue pill lulls us back into our deep sleep. It's the difference between reality and a pipe dream.

In our industry there are plenty of pipe dreams, ungrounded fantasies that people accept as real. In this chapter we'll examine the problem of ignorance and try to blow away the smoke that shrouds aspects of our industry in fantasy.

Problems covered in this chapter include:

- Problem #1: Ignorance is no excuse for poor information security.
- Problem #2: Panic and anxiety stem from our lack of understanding.
- Problem #3: Fantasies make for bad decision making.

Some of the potential solutions we'll explore include:

- Solution #1: Understand what we should know and learn it.
- Solution #2: Plan for the worst and hope for the best, a sense of calm.
- Solution #3: Expect reality using logic and facts.

The Problems

The problems in our industry stem from ignorance, panic, and fantasy. Business leaders, and even some of us, are ignorant of the basics, and poor decisions are made because of it. We fear the things we don't know due to our ignorance, and we live in a fantasy world where we tend to think the things that aren't possible are possible.

PROBLEM #1: IGNORANCE IS NO EXCUSE FOR POOR INFORMATION SECURITY

> " Ignorance isn't bliss, it's breach. "
>
> —ME

Broadly speaking, ignorance is a lack of knowledge. But it is more complicated than that. Professor Emeritus James Carse of New York University says there are three kinds of ignorance:

1. **Ordinary ignorance**, which means that somebody doesn't know something.

2. **Willful ignorance**, which occurs when someone knows the truth or has access to knowledge but chooses to ignore it.

3. **Higher ignorance**, which embraces the vast mysteries of the universe.

> (Source: https://www.psychologytoday.com/blog/look-around-and-look-within/201111/willful-ignorance-penn-state-and-dont-ask-dont-tell)

We are all ignorant, so it isn't necessarily a derogatory word. Where ignorance gets us in trouble is when we don't know things that we should know. The most troublesome form is willful ignorance, or deliberately avoiding knowledge for some temporary advantage—as if ignorance were bliss. Some people refer to willful ignorance by another name: tactical stupidity.

Ordinary Ignorance at Work

Examples of ordinary ignorance in our workplace are everywhere. Nobody knows everything, and we can go only so far in combatting this disease. Some examples of ordinary ignorance include the following:

- Your organization is too small or insignificant for attackers.

- You have nothing of consequence to protect.

- You don't have a role to play in information security.

- Information security is an IT issue.

- You have a very good CISO, so you're OK.

The possible examples of ordinary ignorance are endless.

Willful Ignorance at Work

A worm outbreak hit a tech company, and its IT department struggled to contain the outbreak. For hours IT played bop the weasel as the worm kept popping up throughout the system. IT finally called in an outside consultant. The fight continued throughout the night, and eventually things were brought back to normal. The organization was off-line for about twenty-four hours.

During the incident response, the consultant noticed several ways the organization could have done better. The worm spread through the exploitation of a well-known vulnerability for which the manufacturer had provided a patch many months earlier. Patch management was a concern.

The organization also took too long to detect what was happening. A quicker detection would have led to a quicker response, and the worm wouldn't have been nearly as disruptive. It seemed reasonable that the organization would take the lessons learned from this incident and make itself better.

The consultant wrapped up her work and asked the CIO if he would like some advice on how the company could improve its prevention, detection, and response capabilities.

"No," he said. "We don't want to know what we could do better. If we know about something bad, then we must do something about it. We'd rather not know."

Does this sort of logic shock you as much as it does me? I've heard the same sort of willful ignorance many times, but it still gets me every time.

Maybe you've heard one of these:

- "We don't want a risk assessment because then we'd have to fix all the things that we know about."

- "A penetration test will just make more work for us."

- "Just get us compliant. We don't want to know about all the other things."

- "We're not pleased that you found all the things you found. Next time, we want to know only the things that we must know."

This kind of willful ignorance is dangerous, and it's a problem for too many people.

SOLUTION #1: UNDERSTAND WHAT WE SHOULD KNOW AND LEARN IT

The truth is that the better we know something, the better we can secure it. We should embrace the opportunity to dig deep into all parts of our security program, stop defending bad practices, stop making excuses, and get to the root of our issues.

Understanding

The opposite of ignorance is understanding. The more we understand, the better we can operate effectively.

For the most part, ignorance of the law is no excuse. Take something as simple as speeding, for instance:

Police officer: "Do you know how fast you were going?"

Motorist: "No, sir, I'm not sure. Was I speeding?"

Police officer: "Yes, you were going sixty miles per hour."

Motorist: "Oh, really? I'm not sure what the speed limit is here."

Police officer: "The speed limit is thirty miles per hour."

Motorist: "Sheesh. I didn't see a sign anywhere, and I didn't feel like I was speeding."

Is it legal for the police officer to give the motorist the ticket? Of course it is. Additionally, the motorist is unlikely to mount a sufficient defense to fight the ticket and will probably end up accepting whatever penalties are coming his or her way. The law is the law. It probably doesn't matter if it's criminal law, civil law, or administrative law. Ignorance is probably not going to be defensible.

Someone who is unaware of a law cannot escape liability for violations because of simple unawareness. This is a legal principle. I'm no lawyer, but I do understand the logic. In Latin, the words are *ignorantia legis neminem excusat*, which means "ignorance of law excuses no one."

In our industry, at one time ignorance was a defense. Boards of directors and executive management could claim that they didn't know any better. Times have changed. Information security ignorance is no longer defensible. These days the board and top executives are held liable for breaches at their firms.

Ignorance is no excuse.

Battling Ordinary Ignorance

The way to tackle ordinary ignorance is through effective learning and education.

We've known this for years, and it is standard for organizations to require information security training of its employees. However, the workers aren't improving their understanding as quickly as we need them to, and often we're not training them on what they need to know.

Perhaps we need to change the way we approach information security training and awareness to better reflect contemporary corporate cultures. Our normal, dry information security training and awareness programs are boring and less effective than interactive and enjoyable ones. We spend millions of dollars on this training only to be continually disappointed with the results. Traditional information security training and awareness programs don't work.

Here are some characteristics of traditional programs:

- pushing information out
- mandatory training (We all like mandatory, don't we?)
- topic focused
- viewed as dry and boring by many

Why don't we try to make our information security training more fun? Then people will pay more attention and participate. What do people find enjoyable and fun? People like games, competitions, awards, recognition, and free stuff. Here are some characteristics of nontraditional programs:

- employees pulling information
- encouragement to participate
- voluntary opportunities to learn more
- focused on behaviors (not information)
- proactive rewards for good behaviors

These are some of the leaders in our market for information security training and awareness:

- Wombat Security
- Cofense PhishMe
- KnowBe4
- MediaPRO
- Inspired eLearning

The best way to combat ordinary ignorance is by making information security learning fun. More and more organizations are turning to the gamification of their efforts. We are making progress in this area, and we should keep going down this path.

Make sure information security training and awareness exercises are personally relevant and fun.

Training programs also need to be tailored for people in different positions at an organization. The knowledge and skills needed by an accountant are different from those needed in customer service. Board members and executives have their own requirements. We need to map out the needs in these various positions and develop training and materials that are role specific and relevant.

Battling Willful Ignorance

"Tis but a scratch."

–The Black Knight after losing an arm in battle, in *Monty Python and the Holy Grail*

People in our industry deploy willful ignorance in two ways. One way is when people willfully claim they don't know something that they do know. The other way is when people ignore any input that contradicts their core beliefs or their inner model of reality.

At the heart of the second type of willful ignorance is confirmation bias. Classic examples are conspiracy theorists who cling to a plot regardless of the facts refuting it. They simply refuse to acknowledge any established facts, evidence, and/or reasonable opinions that contradict their "reality."

We can combat willful ignorance in two ways:

1.   Carefully and respectfully coach a person out of willful igno-rance by offering a way to transition without having to give up their own pride and sense of reality. You start out with their model of reality, and slowly walk toward objective reality by fitting facts inside the discussions in an agreeable fashion.

2.   Force the issue. When willful ignorance can no longer be tol-erated, the truth and reality must be forced.

Because willful ignorance is such a danger in our industry, we cannot tol-erate it. Our method of combat depends upon our specific circumstance.

PROBLEM #2: PANIC AND ANXIETY STEM FROM OUR LACK OF UNDERSTANDING

A panic broke out in the industry worldwide in mid-2017, when a ran-somware outbreak named WannaCry (aka WannaCrypt, WanaCrypt0r 2.0 and/or Wanna Decryptor) made big news. People were freaking out from the attack. The ransomware, allegedly leveraged from a sto-len NSA exploit, would encrypt a computer's files and then demand a ransom of hundreds of dollars worth of Bitcoin. It seemed like dooms-day was finally upon us. More than one information security expert called it a "bloodbath."

Panic reigned.

Well, turns out that the world didn't end. The "bloodbath" lasted about four days (although we still have some lingering effects today) and resulted in the compromise of approximately three hundred thousand systems. That translates to about .003 percent of all systems worldwide.

As in the story of the little boy who cried wolf, the moral is that if we panic enough times, nobody will listen anymore. There seems to be a panic news story in our industry just about every month, at least—whether it's Meltdown and Spectre, Equifax, or the next scary thing.

Panic is anxiety carried to an extreme. What the two emotional states have in common is that they are irrational and conducive to poor decision making.

According to research conducted by scientists at the University of Pittsburgh, anxiety works to disengage the part of the brain that is critical to good decision making. In a research paper published in the *Journal of Neuroscience*, the scientists explain that anxiety interrupts the brain's capacity to ignore certain distractions by numbing a group of neurons in the prefrontal cortex that are specifically involved in making choices. (Source: http://www.jneurosci.org/content/36/11/3322.abstract)

SOLUTION #2: PLAN FOR THE WORST AND HOPE FOR THE BEST, A SENSE OF CALM

Panic and anxiety in the right dose can awaken a person from apathy. In that sense, these emotions can be good motivators, but they should never be *the* motivators for information security. Too much anxiety causes us to make bad decisions and even leads to health problems.

Dealing with Anxiety

People who work well under pressure in high-anxiety situations don't panic, because they understand what needs to get done and they get to work. They can focus on the task at hand, regardless of the distractions or panic going on around them. We should do what we can to emulate these calm heads. Here are some tips to hold onto your mind while the world is panicking around you.

1. Remind yourself to stay calm.

2. Breathe.

3. Take your time; don't rush.

4. Defer decision making if necessary.

5. Take a step back and put things into perspective. The world doesn't end if we get something wrong.

6. Be careful with the words you use, because words can cause others to panic. Avoid inflammatory words like *bloodbath*, *pandemic*, and *catastrophic*.

7. Keep an eye on the symptoms of anxiety (see sidebar).

As always, with more experience, you can avoid getting caught up in the wave of hysteria. It all begins by stopping yourself and trying to look at the big picture. The more you understand the situation, and the more you've planned for it, the better you will perform when the time requires it.

> We need to do our best to stay calm in every situation. Step back or step away if necessary.

Be very skeptical of others who choose to use panic words and those who jump to conclusions without a basis in fact.

Plan for the Worst

We know that no matter what we do, we live with risk. It doesn't matter how many controls we put in place or how effectively they operate: bad things will still happen. What will you do when the inevitable happens?

There's no excuse for not planning for what we know to be inevitable. Likewise, there is no excuse (or shouldn't be one) for not having a defined, robust incident management process that is tested regularly. You, and the organization you work for, should always be well prepared for an incident, or breach. Entire books have been written about incident-response planning, and there are mountains of freely available resources.

I'd argue that the failure to plan for an incident is indefensible.

PROBLEM #3: FANTASIES MAKE FOR BAD DECISION MAKING

Why do we get so upset with organizations that suffer a breach and lose our information? Did we think it was possible for them to prevent all breaches, at all times, and in all situations?

It's predictable for victimized consumers to respond with visceral anger when they learn their private information has been stolen in an information security breach (see sidebar).

Anxiety can get out of hand for some people, and there are real signs that there may be a need for help. Here are some signs of generalized anxiety disorder (GAD):

- Excessive, ongoing worry and tension
- An unrealistic view of problems
- Restlessness or a feeling of being "edgy"
- Irritability
- Muscle tension
- Headaches
- Sweating
- Difficulty concentrating
- Nausea
- The need to go to the bathroom frequently
- Tiredness
- Trouble falling or staying asleep
- Trembling
- Being easily startled

(Source: https://www.webmd.com/anxiety-panic/guide/generalized-anxiety-disorder#3-8)

Although the exact cause of GAD is not fully known, there are treatment techniques available to anyone who is suffering. A good source for more information and help is the Anxiety and Depression Association of America (ADAA).

Healthy anxiety is a natural defense mechanism; unhealthy (or prolonged) anxiety must be treated. Don't let pride get in the way of getting help if and when you need it.

I get it. Anger is an emotion that can stem from all sorts of places, but especially when your expectations suddenly crash and it affects you personally. But why the high expectations? You are asking for a big letdown if your expectation is rooted in a fantasy. That's unhealthy. We know it's not possible to prevent all bad things from happening, right? It's not possible to prevent all breaches in all circumstances either.

Headlines after Recent Breaches

- "Angry about Equifax? Here's Why You Should Be Outraged" (Source: http://www.sandiegouniontribune.com/opinion/editorials/sd-equifax-hack-143-million-20170922-story.html)

- "Literally Everyone Should Be Thinking about Suing Equifax" (Source: http://www.businessinsider.com/equifax-security-breach-everyone-should-be-thinking-about-suing-2017-9)

- "T-Mobile CEO: 'Incredibly Angry' about Experian Data Breach" (Source: http://www.channelfutures.com/mobile-computing/t-mobile-ceo-incredibly-angry-about-experian-data-breach)

- "Target Customers Angered over Response to Credit-Card Data Breach" (Source: https://www.dailynews.com/2013/12/20/target-customers-angered-over-response-to-credit-card-data-breach/)

- "Feds Anger Grows over Data Breach, amid Fears That the Number Affected Could Rise" (Source: https://www.washingtonpost.com/news/federal-eye/wp/2015/06/28/feds-anger-grows-over-data-breach-amid-predictions-that-the-number-affected-could-rise/?utm_term=.43252f3c9f26)

- "K Box Members Feeling Angry and Insecure after Hackers Leak Personal Data" (Source: http://www.straitstimes.com/singapore/k-box-members-feeling-angry-and-insecure-after-hackers-leak-personal-data)

Risk Elimination

A widespread area of misunderstanding—and hence fantasy—is the nature of risk. Many believe the goal of information security is to eliminate risk. Risk elimination means zero risk, and it's impossible. On the other end of the scale, infinite risk is also impossible. We live with risk, and we will always live with risk.

> Risk elimination and the expectation of it may be the single most prevalent and elusive pipe dream in existence.

Our sense of higher ignorance tells us there are way too many things we don't know. Something unforeseen can always happen. Therefore, risk elimination is a pipe dream.

100 Percent Prevention

Along the same lines as risk elimination is another fantasy that afflicts too many people. The fantasy is the belief that 100 percent prevention is possible. It's simply not. Unpredictable events can and will always happen, which is why our prevention efforts must be complemented with detection and response strategies. These are required for all organizations, regardless of size, location, shape, or industry.

One example of a client who was a happy resident of Fantasyland was a local bank president (BP). I was telling him about the importance of having an incident-response plan, but he didn't see the value in it.

"BP, you really should consider formalizing your information security incident-response plan."

"Why? We feel very confident in our security measures here at the bank."

"I agree that you have good preventative security measures in place, BP, but bad things can still happen and will happen. You should be better prepared."

"Bad things, like what?"

"There are thousands of things that could happen. Let's say one of your employees falls for a phishing attack, discloses his or her credentials, and it goes unnoticed for some amount of time. An attacker could do some damage before you ever notice anything amiss."

"Well, that's just not going to happen. We conduct awareness exercises regularly, and we've implemented very strong technical controls, such as email filtering and web filtering. This has never happened to us, and I don't think it's likely to happen anytime soon."

"OK, take something else, like a physical theft of a computer."

"That's not going to happen either, and if for some reason it did, we employ full disk encryption on all workstations and laptops."

I realized at this point that it didn't matter what scenario I gave him; he was going to have a rebuttal for it and miss the point I was trying to make.

"BP, I get it. You have invested heavily in prevention, and your controls really are impressive. If you can guarantee that one of your systems will never be compromised, if you can guarantee that you will never experience a breach, and if you can guarantee that an employee won't make some unforeseen mistake that results in a bad thing happening, then I guess you don't have any need for an information security incident-response plan."

BP thought for a few moments.

"Well, I can't guarantee that."

"Exactly the point."

We cannot guarantee to anyone that we can prevent breaches. In our industry, we spend too much time on prevention at the expense of detection and response, as if 100 percent prevention were the goal.

Expectations

"My expectations were reduced to zero when I was twenty-one. Everything since then has been a bonus."

–Stephen Hawking

An expectation is a belief that someone will or should achieve something. Another definition of the word *expectation* is the strong belief that something will happen in the future.

What does executive management expect from information security? What does the board of directors expect? If we'd taken the time to ask and listen, we'd probably be surprised by the answer. One problem is that we don't ask. Try it sometime. Ask and see what the answer is. See how close it matches with reality.

I've asked this question of business executives, and here are the most common answers:

- I expect that information security will keep us safe.

- I expect it will protect the information belonging to our company and our customers.

- I expect it to keep us out of the headlines.

- I don't know what to expect of information security, to be honest.

- I expect that information security will make us compliant.

Each of these answers requires clarification. What do the words *safe* and *protect* mean? Keeping us out of the headlines makes sense, but is it realistic? Becoming compliant is an easy one, assuming compliance means doing what the last auditor or examiner told us to do. You can see how establishing expectations can be harder than it seems.

For many of us, expectations aren't communicated at all. If they are, they're not clear enough to manage.

Expectations run the gamut from the unknown to the unrealistic and everything in between. The bar is set between disappointment and satisfaction. Exceed expectations, and people are satisfied. Fail to meet expectations, and people are disappointed and angry. That is why it is essential to have this conversation about expectations with others. Otherwise you risk accidentally communicating the wrong expectations. Who knows what kind of fantasy world they may live in?

We've affirmed some basic realities in this chapter:

- We cannot possibly eliminate all risk.

- We know that we are never secure if *secure* means 100 percent prevention.

If we know that these things are true, then why do we feel so angry and disappointed when a breach becomes known? Why do we lose our jobs?

SOLUTION #3: EXPECT REALITY USING LOGIC AND FACTS

Reality is found deeply rooted in fact. When we go into a board meeting, we should feel confident when we're armed with facts and a little less confident going in with opinions. Facts and opinions can both be challenged; however, facts stand on their own.

What are the facts, and where can we find them?

A fact is a piece of information presented as having objective reality. The key word in the definition of *fact* is *objective*. Objective (or objectivity) is *expressing or dealing with facts or conditions as perceived **without distortion by personal feelings, prejudices, or interpretations***.

Finding fact in today's world seems harder than ever. Everyone seems to have an agenda behind what they report as fact. Dig enough, and we'll find "facts" everywhere. Observations without interpretations are facts. We don't have a formal risk-management function. If this is true, then it's a fact. The impact of not having a risk-management function requires an interpretation, and this becomes opinion (assuming we don't have factual data to support our assertion).

> We must become masters at discerning facts from opinions.

Opinions aren't necessarily bad, they just aren't as good as facts. Opinions, masked as fact, can have bad consequences. We need to adopt the stance that we get paid to tell people the truth, and we don't get paid to tell people what they want to hear.

Risk Management

During a recent talk that I gave, one of the people in the audience asked a good question. He asked, "Is it possible to put the genie back in the bottle?" I assumed he was talking about going back to a day when we didn't have rampant breaches, as we do today. My answer was simple: "The genie was never in the bottle. The challenge is getting comfortable living with the genie." The point here is that risk elimination (putting the genie back in the bottle) is not possible and can't be the goal. The goal is to understand the genie, manage the genie, and live with the genie.

> The goal is risk management, not risk elimination.

Risk elimination isn't and can never be the goal. The real goal is risk management. Managing risk is the key to managing information security.

We can learn a lot about the nature of risk in our daily activities, where we confront risk to some degree in practically everything we do. Taking a shower is risky because you could slip on the soap and hit your head. Walking down the stairs is risky because you could trip and break your back. Driving a car is risky because you could crash. Speeding through a yellow light is risky because a car could slam into you or the police could give you a ticket. Playing on a stony cliff in the rain is risky because you could fall to your death on the rocks below.

Obviously, these risks don't stop us from living our lives. That's because experience has given us a sense of likelihood and impact (pun intended). Likelihood and impact are the essence of risk. We use our common sense to assess daily risks, and many of them we choose to accept. We just learn to be careful when taking a shower or driving a car.

The same thing must be true in information security. Risk is risk. To manage risk, we must assess where the risks are and how important it is for us to do something about them. Risk management must start with an assessment, and the assessment must be followed by decision making, and the decision making must be followed with action. It's that simple in concept. The difficulty comes in applying the same logic across hundreds and thousands of different scenarios related to an information security program.

This difficulty is compounded by the fact that we have no universal approach to risk assessment in our industry. There are hundreds, maybe thousands, of different methodologies being used, and many of them are incompatible with one another. Information security risk assessments are usually expensive endeavors—a good share of the $90 billion a year spent on information security—yet we can't guarantee the assessments are effective. Too many risk assessments in our industry are a waste of time and money. Some assessments aren't even risk assessments at all!

To hark back to the theme of this book: the way we assess information security risk today in our industry is broken. We are faced with a dilemma. Poor information security risk assessments are a problem; however, risks must still be assessed. After all, how can we know where to invest our next information security dollar without some assessment of the most significant risks? How can we manage risk if we don't know where our risks are?

Here are some of the things that make for a bad information security risk assessment (the opposites would make for good ones):

1. **Subjectivity:** Opinions are great, but they are not good enough for an information security risk assessment. Opinions are based on an individual's ethics, education, and experiences, and these things aren't shared by others universally. Opinions create a gray area that is often debated.

2. **No reflection of risk:** We've defined *risk* numerous times in this book already. A bad information security risk assessment doesn't use the same (or a similar) definition. Risk assessments that measure only maturity or vulnerability are maturity assessments and vulnerability assessments, not risk assessments.

3. **No data support:** Data doesn't lie, assuming we've collected the correct data and our interpretations are correct. Data supports the objectivity of an assessment, lending itself to a more credible outcome.

4. **Cookie-cutter recommendations:** Recommendations that are not actionable will not lead to measured improvement.

5. **Metric manipulation:** A risk in using metrics is manipulating the measurements to reflect what we want them to reflect versus reality. Metrics must remain constant.

6. **Narrow focus:** The scope of any information security risk assessment must be clearly defined and communicated. Remember our definition of *information security*; it's not purely technical.

7. **One use only:** There are numerous internal and external audiences for an information security risk assessment. Doing a separate information security risk assessment for each audience is wasteful.

Organizations must quantify information security risk as much as is possible. A good information security risk-management approach enables the organization to demonstrate due care and diligence to stakeholders, comply with current and future laws and regulations, and spend its information security dollars most wisely.

Understanding through Quantification

At a recent client board meeting, I presented the results of a FISASCORE we completed for the organization. It scored exceptionally well, in the 700s on a scale of 300 (very poor) to 850 (excellent). This is an organization that takes information security very seriously, and one of the directors asked what it would take to get a score of 850. I explained to him that it wasn't possible. It is theoretically possible, but not practically possible. He asked me what I meant. I explained to him that an 850 means that there is no risk, and no matter what we do, we will not be able to prevent a breach with 100 percent certainty. He looked shocked, but he understood what I was saying. Up until that point, this director had never thought about security this way. He had never thought that a breach was inevitable and unpreventable. No more fantasy.

We know that risk elimination isn't possible, but this doesn't stop us from trying. When trying means that we think risk elimination is possible, then we're living a fantasy.

Detection and Response versus 100 Percent Prevention

So, 100 percent prevention is not possible. What to do? Detect and respond. What we cannot prevent, we must be able to detect and respond to.

The good news is that our industry appears to be waking up to this fact. According to Gartner, organizations were transforming their security spending strategy in 2017, moving away from prevention-only approaches to focus more on detection and response. Let's hope that this continues to be a priority for organizations moving forward.

Infragard is a nonprofit organization serving as a public-private partnership between US businesses and the Federal Bureau of Investigation. At a recent talk at an Infragard meeting on the subject of prevention, I asked the one hundred or so information security pros in the audience to estimate the percentage of their day that was focused on prevention versus detection and response. They figured they spent less than 5 percent of their time on detection and response. Whatever amount of time or money that we're spending on detection and response, let's see if we can double it. This would move us more in the right direction.

It's refreshing to read that Gartner expects spending on improving our detection and response capabilities will be a key priority for us, at least through the year 2020. (Source: https://www.gartner.com/newsroom/id/3638017)

Spending money on detection and response is one thing; spending time on formalizing our processes is another. In 2017, less than 10 percent of all organizations who called us for incident-response help had any formal or viable incident-response plan or procedure.

> Every organization must have an incident-response plan and supporting process.

Establishing Expectations

Getting input from people is a nice start to establishing expectations. We should ask the stakeholders in our information security programs what they expect from information security. Start with the board of directors, and then ask executive leadership, and then ask the users. The answers are going to vary from person to person. We may be able to identify some semblance of a consensus, but we won't likely get a unanimous direction from our stakeholders.

We'll also need to tell people what they can expect from us, for their expectations may not be realistic or achievable. Keep in mind that we're communicating with normal people who don't speak our language. Regardless of this difficulty, it will be our job to manage their expectations.

What Should Stakeholders Expect from Us?

Obviously, our stakeholders can expect that we will support the mission of the organization. The mission is why the organization exists in the first place, and our information security efforts must be in alignment. Our stakeholders can expect that we will uphold and live out the core values of the organization. This should go without saying as well, yet it means more when we're explicit about it.

Can we commit to not being a barrier to business? Let's hope so. If we become a barrier to the business we serve, we'll either need to change our ways or look elsewhere for a job.

Can we commit to reducing risk? Maybe, but this could be troublesome in a literal sense if we are already operating with an acceptable level of risk. This is also difficult because we don't control the risk decisions. The *business makes the risk decisions*, so our hands would be tied if we're the ones charged with reducing risk.

There are two expectations that our organization should have for us (*only two*—keep it simple):

1. We will provide consistent and high-quality information that enables the CEO and the board of directors (if one exists) to make effective information security risk decisions.

2. We will see to it that risk decisions are implemented in a manner consistent with the organization's mission and core values.

This, of course, requires the CEO and board of directors to participate in the risk decision-making process. Pipe dream or reasonable expectation? Now we have an expectation in reverse. We have an expectation of the CEO and board of directors: that they will participate in risk decision making, which seems reasonable. Business leaders don't need to be involved in all the details, but they do need to make the risk decisions that affect the business for which they are responsible.

Stakeholders can expect the following from us:

1. We will provide consistent and high-quality information that enables the CEO and the board of directors (if one exists) to make effective information security risk decisions.

2. We will see to it that risk decisions are implemented in a manner consistent with the organization's mission and core values.

More than ever before, CEOs are being held accountable for information security:

- Former CEO of Yahoo, Marissa Mayer, forfeited her multi-million dollar cash bonus.

- Target CEO Gregg Steinhafel resigned in the fallout of Target's 2013 breach.

- Equifax CEO and chairman Richard Smith stepped down after the massive 2017 breach.

- The former CEO of Austrian aerospace company FACC, Walter Stephan, was fired shortly after FACC's spear-phishing breach in 2016.

- Sony Pictures chief Amy Pascal was fired in the wake of the 2014 Sony breach.

- Former Altegrity CEO Sharon Rowlands was sued (personally) by Altegrity's Chapter 11 plan administrator following the company's bankruptcy after the US Investigation Services (USIS) breach. Personally. Let that sink in. (Source: https://cases.primeclerk.com/Altegrity/Home-DownloadPDF?id1=Nzc0OTYy&id2=0)

Today, boardrooms are blaming CEOs, and we've seen how these things continue to bubble up to the top. It seems that it's only a matter of time before some of the postbreach derivative actions will start to hit home successfully with the board of directors.

Tim Erlin, vice president at Tripwire, says, "Accountability starts with the CEO, but information security is a shared responsibility across every function and level of an organization. Data breaches are a problem that the board-level executives need to be responsible for addressing, which means that the CISO must be involved in those board-level discussions. The board can't take meaningful, productive risk-management action without that expertise in the room." (Source: http://www.information-age.com/ cyber-security-professionals-blame-ceos-data-breaches-123467499/)

Regulators are also expecting board-level involvement. Boards of directors and/or CEOs must be making the information security risk decisions on behalf of the organization.

What Can We Expect from Leadership?

Let's assume that the board of directors and CEO will not commit to active participation in risk decision making. Perhaps they will delegate this authority to someone or some group with more time to spend on these matters. In these cases, the board and CEO still need to be informed regularly using truth and facts (where available).

Stakeholders and information security should be able to expect the following from the CEO and board:

1. Active participation in risk decision making.

2. Empowerment to enact the decisions that have been made.

We've touched on this earlier in the book, but it's worth repeating here. Assume that we get five minutes with the board and/or CEO. What would we tell them to make the most valuable use of their time?

Here are five suggestions.

1. **Tell them the current state** of our information security program. This is best represented by a number, score, or graph:

   ▪ from a risk assessment

- relative, between two numbers, an upper bound and lower bound

- objective and based in fact, as much as possible

- entire security program in scope

- accounting for risks in administrative, physical, and technical controls

There are numerous different scoring mechanisms available to choose from. A scoring mechanism that fits the criteria in the list above is best.

2.   **Tell them the goal state** for our information security program. This is the acceptable, or suggested acceptable, status for our information security program. This is what we're shooting for, based upon risk decision making.

The scoring mechanism used previously is used to measure the delta. This is the planned progress. The acceptable level of risk is a business decision, and it must be set by the board of directors and/or CEO.

1.   **Tell them how long** it will take to reach our goal. This will require project planning and resource allocation.

2.   **Tell them how much it will cost** our organization to reach our goals. This becomes budget.

3.   Tell them one or more of our **most significant risks** and what we're doing about them.

If we can agree to advise our board members and CEOs consistently with this information, it will go a long way toward helping us define realistic expectations.

If we know that we cannot possibly prevent breaches, it would be safe to expect one or two. If we develop and share expectations that are more founded in fact, there will be fewer surprises and more educated decisions.

5

The Blame Game

Somebody's got to pay . . . unless that somebody is me.

The information security industry is broken because people don't want to own it. It's human nature. When things go right, we take the credit for it. When things go wrong, we blame somebody. It's the blame game, and in our industry, it happens to be a very popular pastime. All too often it's a matter of shifting the blame and placing it where it doesn't necessarily belong. This is another indication our industry is broken.

It's not accidental that we blame people. Science writer Susan Krauss Whitbourne, PhD, came up with five reasons why we want to blame someone. (Source: https://www.psychologytoday.com/blog/fulfillment-any-age/201509/5-reasons-we-play-the-blame-game) The five reasons are:

1. "Blame is an excellent defense mechanism."

2. "Blame is a tool we use when we're in attack mode."

3. "We're not very good at figuring out the causes of other people's behavior, or even our own."

4. "It's easier to blame someone else than to accept responsibility."

5. "People lie."

Here are some headlines from recent notorious breaches:

- "Senators Want 'Massive' Fines for Data Breaches at Equifax and Other Credit Reporting Firms" (Source: http://www.latimes.com/business/la-fi-equifax-data-breach-fines-20180110-story.html)

- "It Was Uber's Big Year for Blundering" (Source: http://www.autonews.com/article/20171230/MOBILITY/180109998/2017-blunders-uber-tesla)

- "Florida Oncology Company to Pay $2.3 Million after Data Breach" (Source: https://www.hcanews.com/news/florida-oncology-company-to-pay-23-million-after-data-breach)

- "Class Members Rip Proposed $115M Anthem Data Breach Deal" (Source: https://cei.org/content/class-members-rip-proposed-115m-anthem-data-breach-deal)

- "Who's to Blame for the Anthem Hack?" (Source: https://www.cnn.com/2015/02/06/opinion/sutter-anthem-hack/index.html)

- "Department of Homeland Security Suffers Data Breach" (Source: https://www.bleepingcomputer.com/news/security/department-of-homeland-security-suffers-data-breach/)

- "Former Yahoo CEO Apologizes for Data Breaches, Blames Russians" (Source: https://www.reuters.com/article/us-usa-databreaches/former-yahoo-ceo-apologizes-for-data-breaches-blames-russians-idUSKBN1D825V)

You can probably think of instances when people have used one or more of these reasons to place blame on others. If we're honest, we've all done it. We can think of times when I've done it myself for one or all these reasons.

Problems covered in this chapter include:

- Problem #1: There's no shortage of people or things to blame for our shortcomings.

- Problem #2: We all live in glass houses.
- Problem #3: We fear blame and reprimand.
- Problem #4: We're not good at or ready for attribution.
- Problem #5: There's no recourse for faulty products and services.

Some of the potential solutions we'll explore include:

- Solution #1: Define roles and responsibilities.
- Solution #2: Accept that we all have our problems.
- Solution #3: Cultivate transparency and incentives.
- Solution #4: Plan for attribution.
- Solution #5: Hold people accountable.

The term *blame game* refers to a situation in which people try to blame one another for something bad that has happened. You see it every time anything goes wrong. Every time there's a breach, people start throwing blame everywhere. They're like sharks in a feeding frenzy.

PROBLEM #1: THERE'S NO SHORTAGE OF PEOPLE OR THINGS TO BLAME FOR OUR SHORTCOMINGS

In the broadest sense, to blame someone is to assign responsibility to a single individual as being the cause for something bad happening. But we know the world is a complicated place, and there are likely many contributing factors for anything that happens. It seems arbitrary to select one cause among many upon which to pin the blame.

Let's say our company suffered a breach due to a compromised vendor who was provided remote access to our organization's network.

Think of everyone we could blame:

- **The vendor**—for failing to periodically test its employees' resilience to phishing attacks

- **The vendor**—for using weak authentication

- **The vendor**—for permitting users to authenticate with their workstations as "administrator"

- **Our organization or ourselves**—because of our failure in, or absence of, vendor risk-management practice

- **Ourselves**—for the failure to isolate the vendor's network traffic or for using weak remote access authentication

- **Our organization's executive management**—for failing to fund our information security efforts adequately

- **The attacker**—for targeting the vendor and attacking us

- **Our security operations team**—for failing to identify the attack earlier

- **Our incident-response team**—for failing to test our incident-response capabilities more often

> " One of the most destructive human pastimes is playing the blame game. It has been responsible for mass casualties of war, regrettable acts of road rage, and on a broad interpersonal level (social, familial and work-related), a considerable amount of human frustration and unhappiness. "
>
> –Elliot D. Cohen, PhD (Source: https://www.psychology today.com/us/blog/what-would-aristotle-do/201207/ stop-playing-the-blame-game)

Blame can be destructive, and it can seriously hurt other people. Often, blame hurts us personally, and we're not even aware of its effects.

The blame game is a group sport too. In any major breach, consumers are going to want to blame someone, and the pundits will certainly join in on the fun. That's what happened with the Equifax breach. The giant credit rating company was compromised through an unpatched Apache Struts vulnerability, which was months old when it was finally discovered. Reports surfaced that Equifax had a patching policy that should have ensured a patch would be applied to the vulnerable server within forty-eight hours. Obviously, Equifax had a failure where they didn't follow their policy and rules for identifying and applying patches in a consistent manner. The vulnerability was not identified on the compromised system, and the patch was not applied.

The company policy outlined a two-stage process: a manual process to apply the patch, and an automated process to scan the system to ensure that all known vulnerabilities had been accounted for. Neither of the processes called for in the policy had been enforced. The system was eventually discovered by one or more attackers, and the rest is history.

But the powers that be chose to focus in on an individual, the CISO. She was raked over the coals by the media because she happened to have a master's degree in music composition, and her CEO Richard Smith singled her out when he testified before Congress. Thankfully, there were many people in our industry who came to her defense; however, it wasn't before she was seemingly forced into hiding.

One reporter in his trashy article claimed that her "identity is being scrubbed from the internet," implying that it was because she "studied music composition." (Source: https://www.marketwatch.com/story/equifax-ceo-hired-a-music-major-as-the-companys-chief-security-officer-2017-09-15)

What did this blame get us? Did it make anything better? The answer is no. The system is still broken, and we're still using social security numbers in a manner that is fundamentally wrong.

The mature approach would be to ascertain what went wrong and make sure it doesn't happen again. The ego-driven response is to quickly blame someone to avoid being blamed yourself. This is no way to learn from our mistakes.

SOLUTION #1: DEFINE ROLES AND RESPONSIBILITIES

The opposite of scurrying to blame someone (anyone) is the willingness to accept responsibility and be accountable for one's actions. *Accountability* is a positive and reinforcing word. *Blame* has a negative connotation and is a more punitive word. Focusing on accountability is one way to quit playing the blame game.

The question becomes: who is accountable for what?

Board of Directors

The ultimate responsibility in any organization lies at the top of the hierarchy, with the CEO and/or the board of directors (if there is one). The buck stops there.

Since the board is supremely responsible for the entire corporation, it is consequently accountable for information security. The board's specific information security responsibilities must be documented, communicated, and carried out in practice. The board doesn't need to be composed of expert technologists, but it must be informed appropriately so that it is empowered to make sound decisions.

Given the importance of information security in today's business environment, and in every facet of our lives, the failure to document the board's responsibilities is fast becoming inexcusable (if it's not already inexcusable).

> Document the specific information security responsibilities of the board of directors and ensure that they are followed. This ends up helping them significantly in the long run, because it shows due care.

Chief Executive Officer (CEO)

The CEO is the highest-ranking executive in a company, and in some cases is the ultimate decision maker. It behooves us to ensure the CEO has the best information possible on which to base his or her decisions. Specific information security responsibilities for the CEO must be defined and documented. If they are documented, and the CEO can demonstrate having fulfilled those responsibilities, then there's some defensibility in his or her position when the inevitable breach occurs.

Like those of the board of directors, the CEO's specific information security responsibilities must be defined and documented.

Here's a general statement of the top three CEO responsibilities in information security: (Source: https://pdfs.semanticscholar.org/94e0/7446a534e1cba8e831b94489bdbcbe3f24ae.pdf)

1. Support the information security department's initiatives as they relate to the mission of the business.

2. Ensure responsible funding is provided for ongoing security operations.

3. Hold the components of the business accountable for achieving their objectives in a secure manner.

Chief Information Security Officer (CISO)

The CISO, whenever possible, should be a role that reports directly to the CEO. As the role becomes separated from the CEO by more layers, it becomes less likely that the CEO has the best information possible.

The two primary responsibilities for the CISO were covered in the previous chapter. There may be a large list of additional responsibilities for the CISO, but most (if not all) should be tied to these two primary ones.

The CISO must:

1. Provide consistent and high-quality information that enables the CEO and board of directors (if one exists) to make effective information security risk decisions.

2. See to it that risk decisions are implemented in a manner consistent with the organization's mission and core values.

Managers

Because managers are closer to the action, they have insights the rest of us don't have. They know how our information security requirements and controls are working and they know how they're not. Managers know how users are circumventing our controls, and they know if users are pleased or frustrated with our efforts. Managers can be our greatest allies, or they can be our most feared foes. They make or break our efforts, so we need to treat them well.

Information security responsibilities need to be defined for all managers. Still, we need to be careful of the load we put on them. We need to respect their time, but more importantly, we need to respect their feedback.

Manager information security responsibilities should encourage the following:

- strong relationships (with information security)
- feedback
- cooperation

Build rapport with managers first, before asking for more specific responsibilities. Regardless, manager responsibilities for information security must be defined, documented, and managed.

We need to work on rapport with managers because we'll want to use them to help with noncompliance issues. If we already have the rapport, then we can document the responsibilities to assist with noncompliance in their workforce. If we don't have the rapport established, then we shouldn't rush it. Establish rapport first; ask for stuff later. Eventually, their cooperation with noncompliance, education, and communication will all need to be added to their responsibilities; however, these things often take time.

Human Resources

The human resources (HR) department plays a critical role in numerous information security–related processes, including (but not limited to) the following:

- conducting background checks and other potentially necessary employee vetting

- onboarding, employment change, and termination processes

- training and employee culture programs

- employee disciplinary processes

- employee benefit and incentive programs

HR functions as they relate to information security must be defined, documented, and managed.

Users

We will have issues if there is a disconnect between what we expect from our users and what are they capable of and willing to do. We solve this problem by communicating with them and their managers to come up with creative solutions to accomplish our goals. We won't be able to define user responsibilities in the comfort of our offices or cubicles.

> User responsibilities must be defined, documented, communicated, and managed through collaboration.

If there's a failure in the fulfillment of responsibilities among the users, it's more likely to be because of poor collaboration and communication than for any other reason.

Get real, though: we'll always have our challenges with users. They're human. Expect mistakes here and there, and plan for them.

Conceptual (but Real) Responsibilities

Conceptual responsibilities are tied to roles that aren't defined by job title or job descriptions. Conceptual roles are important because they divvy up information security responsibilities among the people who are most intimate with our information resources, including information, systems, and applications. These are also the people who rely upon the systems the most to do their jobs.

The two primary conceptual roles are owner and custodian.

For example, let's say your organization uses Salesforce as its customer relationship management platform. The person responsible for the platform may be conceptually defined as the Salesforce system owner. The person responsible for its security functions—such as creating new users, assigning permissions, and removing old accounts—may be conceptually defined as the Salesforce system custodian.

These conceptual roles and responsibilities bring together the foundational components of asset management and access control.

Information/System/Application/Data Owner

Every asset requires an owner, whether it's a physical asset, a software asset, or an information (data) asset. There are system owners who are responsible for the operations of the system (hardware and operating system); there are application owners who are usually responsible for the operations of the application (that runs on the system); and there are data owners who are usually responsible for the usability, quality, and security of the data. Sometimes these roles can be shared.

Most organizations are terrible at assigning and managing conceptual roles and responsibilities, and a big reason is because they're also bad at asset management in general. If we don't have a solid asset inventory and asset-management program, then we're going to struggle significantly in assigning conceptual roles and responsibilities.

Typical owner responsibilities are:

- the design and implementation of business processes associated with an information asset

- attaining and maintaining knowledge about how the information is acquired, transmitted, stored, deleted, and otherwise processed

- determining the appropriate value and classification of information associated with the asset

- communicating the information classification when the information is released of the department and/or organization

- controlling access to the information and consultation when access is extended or modified

- communicating the information classification to the information custodian so that the information custodian may provide the appropriate levels of protection

Information/System/Application/Data Custodian

The responsibilities for this conceptual role are a little easier to define and implement. The custodian is a role delegated by the owner. Custodians are most often responsible for the maintenance of the information resource or asset at the direction (implied or explicit) of the owner.

Avoid Blame

Once all responsibilities have been defined and documented, they must be assigned and communicated. Only then can we begin holding people accountable. There are many creative ways to do that without using blame. If we must use blame, then at least we should use it when it can be justified, after responsibilities have been clearly doled out.

PROBLEM #2: WE ALL LIVE IN GLASS HOUSES

Those who live in glass houses should not throw stones is a is a wise proverb because everybody has faults of one kind or another, so it is hypocritical to obsessively criticize others.

Whenever a breach makes headlines, there's no shortage of finger wagging. It's alarming how much condemnation comes from people who aren't doing any better with information security than the one who suffered the breach. Most of the stone throwing comes in the form of commentary, online or in person.

There are four irrational beliefs that drive the blame game, according to Elliot D. Cohen, PhD: (Source: https://www.psychologytoday.com/blog/what-would-aristotle-do/201207/stop-playing-the-blame-game)

1. "If something has gone wrong (or is not the way it should be), then someone other than myself must be identified and blamed for causing the situation."

2. "This person/s' malfeasance diminishes the respect he/she deserves as a person."

3. "So, it is permissible (and only fitting) to treat this person/s in ways he/she deserves to be treated such as ignoring, name-calling, and in extreme cases, physical assault."

4. "I must not accept any significant degree of responsibility for the situation since to do so would be to admit that I am myself also diminished as a person, and therefore deserving of the same disapprobation and negative treatment."

Hypocrites are the best blamers.

SOLUTION #2: ACCEPT THAT WE ALL HAVE OUR PROBLEMS

" Embrace this imperfect universe and the fallible beings in it, yourself and others–and stop blaming people for it. "

–Elliot D. Cohen, PhD (Source: https://www.psychology today.com/us/blog/what-would-aristotle-do/201207/ stop-playing-the-blame-game)

Why do we insist that for every incident, someone always has to be blamed and made to pay? Everyday life isn't a court of law, and you aren't the judge and jury. Accept yourself and others unconditionally. This doesn't mean you can't rate your own actions or those of others negatively; but it does mean that you shouldn't berate yourself or others.

Recast responsibility as a way to learn from your mistakes as well as those of others. Accept your fallibility as a route toward self-improvement. Try to make things better, but rest content that you live in an imperfect world.

Psychology writer Andrea Blundell says, "The more self-worth you have, the more you will able to manage being responsible for yourself. And the more you can accept your own humanness and capacity for error, the more you are likely to accept and understand it in others, too." (Source: https://www.harleytherapy.co.uk/counselling/why-we-put-the-blame-on-others.htm)

PROBLEM #3: WE FEAR BLAME AND REPRIMAND

The habit of blaming others carries consequences. A culture of blame is extremely dangerous to our organizations and makes our jobs as information security professionals difficult. Where I work, we do hundreds of projects a year, and occasionally one goes off the rails. It's a fact of life, because we're human beings. When a project doesn't meet our expectations, we do an investigation into the facts and look for opportunities to do better the next time. The purpose of the investigation is to look for opportunities to improve, not to place blame. We're consistently clear about the purpose. Despite our best efforts not to look for or place blame, our employees still feel the need to defend themselves.

Those responsible get defensive. Why? I think that there are two reasons. One can be healthy, and the other is not.

1. They take a lot of pride in their work and set high expectations for themselves. This is usually a healthy characteristic but can become unhealthy when our expectations are unrealistic (like 100 percent customer satisfaction). Consistently unrealistic expectations lead to stress and burnout.

2. They fear reprimand and feel threatened when they've fallen short. In the blame game, you can get blamed, shamed, and fired for mistakes, even if the mistakes are not your own,

for instance: an unhappy client is unhappy simply because they're a difficult client, not because of anything you did.

Users

How about our users? They are our most significant risk. More than 90 percent of all successful data breaches involved phishing attacks, according to the 2017 Verizon Data Breach Investigations Report (DBIR).

It is easy to get emotional and angry at them. Those damn users! Why are they so stupid? I've seen disrespectful behavior toward them, including ignoring, shaming, name-calling, and, in extreme cases, physical assault.

These emotional reactions lead to actions and reactions that are not productive in improving our information security program. Blaming and shaming our users isolates them from us and us from them. They don't want to share their thoughts and feelings with us. For fear of blame and reprimand, they don't want to tell us that they accidentally clicked on a link in an email or that they may have made some other mistake.

We shoot ourselves in the foot when we angrily blame users. They are arguably our best incident detection tool, and if they fear reporting things to us, we've lost a significant input into our incident-response processes, not to mention their cooperation in prevention.

CEOs

CEOs are responsible for some of this mess, but not all of it. It starts with accountability, which is not quite the same as blame. Accountability is an obligation or willingness to accept responsibility or to account for one's actions. Blame is to find fault with or to hold responsible. So the ideas are close, but not the same.

CEOs need to be held accountable first; reserve blame for now. I'll explain more later in this chapter. Besides, blaming the CEO won't make your security better.

SOLUTION #3: CULTIVATE TRANSPARENCY AND INCENTIVES

A culture of transparency and positive reinforcement leads to better information security. For years, we've been the people who've said no to things, and the only time normal people really heard from us was when they did something wrong. The old-school method of cracking down on people for noncompliance doesn't work. It doesn't foster collaboration, because users don't like dealing with us.

> Leverage transparency and positive reinforcement (or encouragement) consistently. Use sanctions and punishment only as a last resort.

Sanctions and blame-based information security programs do not work. In some cases, they backfire and get us canned.

A better approach is a transparent approach that rewards people for good behaviors, such as reporting unusual events to us. We should give them something they'll value to show our appreciation. When people invite us to project kickoff meetings or conference calls, that's a good thing. Give them a reward. Positive reinforcement will lead to better collaboration, better cooperation, and better information security. These little gestures will encourage individuals to improve their security practices.

It is true that people are the greatest risk, but it doesn't mean that they're totally to blame when they click on a link or fall for a phishing attack. If the email arrived in their work mailbox, wasn't it us that delivered the malicious email to them in the first place? We control the infrastructure. There are many technical controls that we could implement to reduce the number of these emails that land in users' inboxes, and there are additional controls that we could implement to reduce the impact associated with user mistakes.

> Always look for ways to reward desirable information security behaviors.

Where there's still a gap (or risk) between technical controls and administrative controls, I would much rather a user report having made a mistake than find out later through some other means.

PROBLEM #4: WE'RE NOT GOOD AT OR READY FOR ATTRIBUTION

A logical place to put the blame is on the attackers who exploit our weaknesses every day. The big problem is that in most cases we don't know who these perpetrators are. They use a variety of tools and techniques to cover their tracks. If by chance, luck, or skill we can identify the computer that was used, we still have extreme difficulty identifying the person who was at the keyboard.

When a breach is first detected, there's a knee-jerk impulse to identify the source of the attack and catch the bad guys, but as a practical matter, we don't even try to identify the attacker, because our focus is on determining the extent of the intrusion (or breach), removing the threat, and resuming normal business operations. In a clear majority of cases, attribution isn't even possible because of the lack of evidence that's available. By the time we get called, evidence has already been destroyed, if it ever existed in the first place.

We still want someone to blame, though, don't we?

Maybe we can blame the Russians, the Chinese, or the North Koreans. It must have been a state-sponsored attack of some sort, right? This is a convenient false narrative, and it might get people off our backs. False attribution is not much different than no attribution, except that we spread a lot of misinformation. Either way, it's a problem.

SOLUTION #4: PLAN FOR ATTRIBUTION

In the world of information security, attribution refers to the whole process of tracking and identifying the culprit in order to lay blame. This effort usually turns out to be a waste of valuable resources. Most of us don't possess the necessary experience, skills, time, money, or tools to track down the source of an attack. Furthermore, most of us haven't prepared our environments sufficiently to protect the necessary evidence needed for the investigation.

Even if we did find the attacker, what would we do with this information anyway? File charges? Sue them? If you've tried to report a common incident to the FBI or local law enforcement, you know how these things usually turn out. Holding the perpetrator accountable is like trying to catch the wind.

On rare occasions, some incidents warrant a search for the perpetrator. These cases are sufficiently large in scope and impact, and usually require experts to conduct the investigation. That's why it's a good idea to identify some experts and add their contact information to your incident-response plan.

> Define *attribution* in your organization before attempting to perform attribution, and then prepare.

Part of the process of conducting an attribution search is to obtain general intelligence to address the who and the why of nefarious activity. This is absolutely necessary to enable us to make good decisions on how to better prevent, detect, and respond to future incidents. This sort of attribution process takes planning, however. We need to implement the necessary processes and configurations to support the preservation of evidence, and our detection processes must be able to detect the incident early enough to use the evidence. Finally, our incident-response processes must be sufficient to investigate the incident.

PROBLEM #5: THERE'S NO RECOURSE FOR FAULTY PRODUCTS AND SERVICES

In what other industry can one create and sell a product or service with known flaws, where the exploitation of these flaws can cause damages—including lost revenue, damaged reputations, financial hardship, lost privacy, and potential physical harm—and not have any substantial recourse? These possibilities are true for the information security industry, for the software development industry, and, I suppose, for IoT manufacturers.

In most industries, when something bad happens, manufacturers, such as car manufacturers or medical device makers are held liable. Of course, flaws in cars or in medical devices can result in physical damage or death. Sadly, it might take the direct loss of human life before software development shops are held liable for the creation of the buggy, insecure software behind IoT, medical devices, cars, and the like.

So why are software developers not held accountable for the security of the products and services they provide?

Race to Market

Innovation and information security seem to be at odds with each other.

Both developers and consumers are anxious for new products to reach the market as soon as possible. Companies spend millions in the effort, which gives them a great incentive to release hardware and software as soon as possible to recoup costs and turn a profit. Consumers get excited because the new hardware and software products may allow them to do something really cool.

This frenzy over the latest innovation burst upon the scene at the dawn of the internet age, and with it the attitude of "release it now, fix it later." It would take time and add costs to try to fix every defect, and it's a pipe dream to ever expect zero defects. Consequently, sometimes the new hardware and software are released with vulnerabilities or suboptimal information security features—some of which may even be known to the company.

The explosion of IoT devices is also leading to new security headaches, and these will only get worse. Imagine if we developed airplanes or cars in the same way that we develop IoT gadgets and software. We're already starting to combine transportation with technology in such a way that airplanes and cars can now be hacked. Allegedly, experts at the Department of Homeland Security were able to compromise a commercial plane's avionics system while it was parked at an airport. (Source: https://www.thedailybeast.com/could-terrorists-hack-an-airplane-the-government-just-did) Cars have also been the target of numerous attacks over the past few years.

At what point do we hold someone accountable or liable for releasing hardware and/or software with security flaws? The answer is soon, but our industry isn't ready for it just yet. (Sources: http://foreignpolicy.com/2017/07/28/bad-code-is-already-a-problem-soon-companies-will-be-liable/ and https://techbeacon.com/software-security-liability-coming-are-your-engineers-ready) Be prepared, though: increased security will mean increased costs and probably slower innovation.

This problem doesn't affect only companies that develop products for commercial sale. It also applies to organizations that develop their own internal software and IT projects. In many companies, information security protections are not formally considered early in the project, if at all. This same problem is compounded for organizations where innovation is a key differentiator.

SOLUTION #5: HOLD PEOPLE ACCOUNTABLE

How do you hold someone accountable for something that they don't feel like doing and for which they don't perceive any direct benefit to themselves? The thought (conscious or unconscious) is that security is a hassle. Security is inconvenient. It slows us down, and for what benefit? Sure, someone suffers if I take security shortcuts, but as long as it's not me . . . This mentality plays out in our industry every day.

Information security isn't about information or security. Information security is about people. People suffer when we don't do our jobs well. If people weren't affected by our lack of skill or motivation, then nobody would care.

Product and Service Providers

When we purchase a product—software or hardware—what assurance should we have that security is considered in the product's design and implementation? We assume that the product is developed in a manner that ensures security and quality; however, there is no way to be certain of such things. At what point do we, as an industry, define what's acceptable and what's not, specifically, for software and hardware products? New products are hitting the streets faster than we can secure them—if securing them is even possible.

We must define our requirements for software development and product suppliers. The status quo isn't working, and we can't just keep patching and hope for the best. We need to define things like acceptable bug density for software development products and security standards for IoT devices. We need to define things like what types of testing must be implemented at what stages of the software development life cycle and what types of results are satisfactory. This needs to be universal.

As an industry, we need to demand better. It is not acceptable for companies develop and release software to the public with known vulnerabilities that will cause harm.

Beyond Blame

We need to get out of the blame game and get better at making productive changes.

Playing the blame game stunts our personal growth, diminishes our power, steals our empathy for others, erodes our ability to maintain healthy relationships, and instills negativity where we need more positive attitudes.

We need to shake off our habit of pointing accusing fingers, and instead calmly ascertain areas of accountability and responsibility to improve our overall security.

We need to get out of the blame game and into the information security game.

6

The Herd Mentality

"If everyone is thinking alike, then somebody isn't thinking."

–George S. Patton Jr.

The information security industry is broken because people focus on others instead of themselves. We Americans like to think we are total individuals who think and act in unique ways. While this is a pleasant sentiment, social scientists will tell us that nothing is further from the truth. In fact, they say people tend to unconsciously mimic the crowd; they fall into a herd mentality and behavioral conformity. This is true for people around the world, and for many animals as well.

People of a similar sort tend to flock together, like birds, and through peer pressure they reinforce one another's beliefs into an uncritical uniformity, like sheep. Advertisers influence us by telling us that a new movie or restaurant is wildly popular. Everyone is going there, and so should you. When we have trouble making a decision in our crazy, complicated world, we guide our choices by doing what everyone else is doing. When we go to a new place and are not sure how to behave, we copy what other people are doing and deem it proper etiquette.

It feels safe in the herd, but living in the herd can be dangerous. The herd mentality has also been referred to as the mob mentality or the gang mentality. A lynch mob, for example, takes on a life of its own, with most of the crowd unthinkingly following the lead of the radical few.

But wait a minute: businesspeople—business leaders—don't like to be compared to sheep. Leaders are built to lead.

A recent study of crowd behavior was conducted in England. Researchers at Leeds University asked a group of volunteers to walk silently around a large room in no specific pattern. The volunteers walked randomly without speaking to one another. The researchers then picked a few of the volunteers out of the pack and instructed them to walk and act as though they knew where they were going, remaining silent and not urging any of the others to follow in any way. Before long, the rest of the volunteers began to follow the very small group of volunteers who no longer walked in random patterns.

The findings show that as the size of a crowd increases, the number of informed individuals decreases. In large crowds of two hundred or more, 5 percent of the group is enough to influence the direction of the whole group. (Source: http://www.leeds.ac.uk/news/article/397/ sheep_in_human_clothing__scientists_reveal_our_flock_mentality)

A mere 5 percent can greatly influence the decisions of the other 95 percent without anyone even realizing it. The herd mentality is obviously real, and it's obviously very powerful! We need to become aware of how the herd mentality functions in our industry so that we can figure out when to go along with herd mentality and when to think outside the box.

The herd mentality is compounded by other factors in our industry, like the lack of common sense and knowledge about what information security is. The herd mentality leads people to buy products they don't need or can't use. The herd mentality leads us to advise clients to do things that don't make sense. The herd mentality, if left unchecked, can be a very destructive force to anyone in our industry.

Problems covered in this chapter include:

- Problem #1: There's a false sense of safety in the herd.
- Problem #2: Herd mentality leads to poor choices.
- Problem #3: Even if the herd is right, it still won't fit us.

Some of the potential solutions we'll explore include:

- Solution #1: Use the herd to your advantage.
- Solution #2: Take the time to research.
- Solution #3: Focus on you and what you can control.

PROBLEM #1: THERE'S A FALSE SENSE OF SAFETY IN THE HERD

It feels safe in the herd; therefore, it must be safe.

Safety

It's true that there is (some) safety in the herd. We call it "safety in numbers." It feels more comfortable and safe to be surrounded by your peers and to not stand out. The safety is real, but it comes at a significant cost.

The herd mentality isn't all bad. It comes from our core human tendency to mimic and emulate others, and science confirms that the fastest, most effective way to develop and grow as leaders is by watching others. (Source: https://generalleadership.com/trading-tulips-the-fallacy-of-the-herd-mentality/) The herd mentality also grants its members collective power and safety from others outside the herd who may want cause harm, as perceived by members of the herd.

Collective power is hard to quantify, but it exists in the form of driving others to cater to the needs of the herd. Take Microsoft Windows, for instance. Let's say that you have to choose between Microsoft Windows or Linux as your company's server operating system. Regardless of the individual benefits of Windows versus Linux, you are granted a certain collective power by choosing Windows. If you choose Windows, you'll benefit from the collective power on things such as a broader choice of widely supported applications to run, a more abundant and cheaper talent pool to support the platform, more peripheral hardware options, and so forth. The fact of the matter may be that Linux is the best fit for you, but choosing Linux over Windows will make you a member of a smaller and potentially less powerful herd.

Safety within the herd means that members of the herd can realize some protection from perceived harm. The perceived harm comes from sources outside the herd, and it is "perceived" because to members of the herd, it is harmful. The sources of harm can be lawyers (opposing counsel in litigation), regulators, examiners, auditors, and the like. The harm is lost revenue or less money—either money paid outright in the form of fines, levies, or settlements or revenue lost because of lost customers, reputation, or consumer confidence.

The herd, in terms or protection from perceived harm, represents "reasonableness." *Reasonable* and *prudent* are two very important words when people are determining fault or liability when something goes wrong (such as a breach). We live in a litigious society, and when a breach occurs, there is usually no shortage of lawsuits filed against the party who is perceived to be at fault. When the lawsuits come, it appears there is one primary or prominent argument.

Was due care practiced by the organization?

"Due care refers to the effort made by an ordinarily prudent or reasonable party to avoid harm to another, taking the circumstances into account. . . . The precise definition is usually made on a case-by-case basis, judged upon the law and circumstances in each case." (Source: https://definitions.uslegal.com/d/due-care/)

In the simplest sense, if an organization didn't practice due care in securing the information that was exposed or compromised in a breach, then the organization is more likely to be found at fault and liable. If you don't know what due care is with information security, what better way to demonstrate due care than to do what everyone else in your herd is doing? Besides, how can so many people (the herd) be wrong?

So, as you can see, the herd mentality isn't all bad.

Psychologists say that the two most common reasons for us to become, or want to become, part of the herd are *social pressure* (also known as peer pressure) and a *belief* that so many people couldn't possibly be wrong. There's little doubt that these two reasons exist in our industry.

Two additional reasons for the herd mentality are *fear* and *ignorance*. These are bad things about the herd mentality. Relying upon the herd mentality too much has consequences. In our industry we rely on the herd mentality too much because of fear—or worse, because we don't know any better.

> **"** Creating an environment of thinking small, being insignificant and choosing a world of mediocrity has become acceptable. Even more than that, it has become the norm. People play a safe game. When did mediocrity become OK?**"**
>
> –Angela Kambouris, leadership coach
> (Source: https://leadersinheels.com/career/
> leaders-can-break-free-mediocrity/)

Mediocrity

Unfortunately, the herd mentality fosters *the state or quality of being mediocre*. Many of us settle for mediocrity.

Comfort lives inside the herd, and if we're comfortable, we're settling. Comfort is the enemy of progress and innovation.

How many times have we heard that it's good enough? Our security is good enough. If we're not as bad as the other guy, we're in good shape. Hogwash.

Would you agree that most organizations have inadequate information security programs?

Would you also agree that most people are inadequately protected from harm?

151

Figure: Here is an illustration of the herd-mentality bell curve

If the answer to these questions is yes, which it most likely is, then why would we settle for being part of the herd?

Let's imagine a bell curve that maps out the one thousand or so organizations I've dealt with in my career, graphed according to the quality of their information security programs. The clear majority of them have inferior programs, so they'd be the bell part of the graph. The outliers would be those that have no program at all, or those that we could judge to have good or adequate programs. Would you really want to be in the herd on this graph? People who follow the herd settle for mediocrity, which in this case is inadequate. Yet they have the comfort of their peers, who convince one another that they're all OK. But good enough is not OK if it simply means good enough for the herd. In our industry, we can't afford this.

There are extremely talented people in our industry—the outliers—who do not settle for mediocrity. There are thousands among us who work our tails off to stand out from the herd. This is not the norm in our industry, which means there is plenty of room for improvement.

Information security is a skill that requires critical thinking and constant striving for excellence. We settle for mediocrity. We settle for good enough. We need more information security leadership, more critical thinking, and less settling for good enough. When we're not careful, our overreliance on the herd for safety robs us of our ability to do our best.

> **"** Our desire to fit in leads us to all too easily trade creativity for conformity. **"**

–General John Michel, USAF
(Source: https://general leadership.com/trading-
tulips-the-fallacy- of-the-herd-mentality/)

Triteness

One antonym for *creativity* is *triteness*. The word *trite* means worn out and boring from too much use. Something that's trite is neither original nor fresh. The herd mentality steals our creativity and makes us trite from reusing the same old ideas.

The trite aspect of our industry is that we're still facing many of the same risks that we faced ten, fifteen, twenty years ago. Sure, we have areas of creativity where we are seeing advances—artificial intelligence, blockchain, quantum computing, endpoint protection, and others. But overall, creativity isn't commonplace in practice. If we were so creative, then why are we still running into the same problems over and over?

Why haven't we solved more of our fundamental problems? Why are we still getting in the way of business too often? Why do we still deliver training and awareness in ways that don't work? Why aren't we reporting to CEOs more frequently? Why aren't we advising boards of directors more often? Why do we still have too many shoddy information security programs? Most us lack the creativity to solve difficult challenges, and we must attribute some of this lethargy to our herd mentality.

At a recent conference where I spoke about the importance of asset management, one attendee came up and said he disagreed with me.

"Asset management is too difficult for my company," he said. "We've decided to just do enough to get by."

"What do you mean by 'get by'?" I asked.

"We just want to cover the basics," he said.

"And what do you mean by 'the basics'?"

"As long as we're doing as well or better than everybody else," he said, "then we're fine with that."

I get it. This is a decision that the company is consciously making. I just disagree with it on two fronts. When he says asset management is too difficult, what I hear is that he lacks creativity and/or he's lazy. A creative and driven person would devise and implement methods to ensure that asset management is effective and that it doesn't unnecessarily interfere with the organization's mission. Many of us get paid well in this industry, and we should do better than this guy.

He equated the basics to what the herd was doing. The problem is that the herd sucks at the basics! Only a small percentage of organizations seem to get the basics correct. The herd mentality stole this guy's creativity.

SOLUTION #1: USE THE HERD TO YOUR ADVANTAGE

Businesses are in business to make money, and every organization exists to serve a mission or purpose. Rather than mimicing other members of the herd and basing strategic decisions on what our peers are doing, we should escape from that habit of thought and develop strategies founded on what best serves our company's purpose.

We should be finding ways to use our information security dollars more wisely. Can we can use information security as a differentiator and drive more business? Information security is a cost center in most herds, but we should strive for a different mindset.

Capitalize on Security Investments

We shouldn't spend a dime on information security investments that don't help us make more money and/or serve our organization's mission. Let that sink in. Why would we invest in anything else? We should spend our next information security dollar in the place where we'll get the most bang for our buck, as opposed to spending it on the hottest new thing the herd is buying.

Spending decisions should be based on two factors: our risk assessment and an analysis of the impact that our risk decisions may have. Can we devise a risk-mitigation control or strategy that would actually make our organization more efficient and more profitable? If so, this is a no-brainer. It makes information security more of a business driver and less of a business drain. Solving these difficult challenges moves us out of the herd and helps make our organization a leader.

Take Risks

Standing out from the herd can be risky, but it can serve us quite well.

We have a saying at our company: *Failure isn't optional; it's mandatory.* The point is that if we're not taking calculated risks from time to time—making decisions in which failure is a possibility—then we're not pushing ourselves enough. We're not being creative, we're not tackling difficult challenges, we're not innovating. Failure to take calculated risks is failure in and of itself. We shouldn't hold back from doing the right things because they're risky. We just need to make sure we're fighting for the right things.

Let's say we want to redesign how we handle identity and access management because the existing processes are overengineered and complicated. We are convinced that it's the right thing to do, but other executives are lukewarm to the idea. We could stick with the status quo and succumb to the group thinking, or we could take a risk and continue our efforts.

We could give up, or we could do additional research, build a better case, ensure that we've accounted for the best- and worst-case scenarios, and push forward. The more we venture into this territory, the riskier it will get. We know it's the right thing to do, and to date, all our research into the issue supports this assertion. Still risky.

Eventually, the other executives may warm up to the idea due to our persistence, and we get the buy-in we've been looking for. We thought it was risky before; now it gets crazy risky. Although the other executives eventually buy in, some of them are still very skeptical. With the first hiccup, things could get hot.

We need to take more calculated risks. Nobody likes failure, but it's a by-product of some risks. This is the way it works. The alternative is to go with the herd and continue the status quo. The status quo doesn't work; it's broken.

Think Outside the Box

Although this phrase has become a cliché, the practice of creatively thinking beyond traditional ideas will never get old. The traditional ideas inside the box are the realm of the herd mentality. There is resistance to changing the traditional approaches to information security, even if they don't work. It's very encouraging to see places in our industry where outside-the-box thinking prevails, and there are tons of new ideas floating around.

Here's an example of our flawed, inside-the-box approach. You'd better have information security policies. The common wisdom sayis that if it's not written down, it doesn't exist—or if it's not documented, you're not actually doing it. The absence of a critical policy is a big problem for compliance and audit.

Many of us make people sign off that they've read, with understanding, our policies, even though we know they haven't. Think about that for a second. We could threaten them with physical violence, knowing they still won't read the policies, yet we make them sign something saying they have. They sign, they lie. We tell them to lie. This is no way to start a new employee-business relationship.

This approach is flawed.

Policies fit within a type of control that we call administrative controls. The purpose behind administrative controls is to influence and drive human behaviors. The purpose of a policy is not to have a policy; the purpose of a policy is to influence and drive human behavior.

It's our less-than-creative attempt to influence human behavior that's the problem.

Policies are important, but they're just not as important as some people think they are. Think of policies as being the rules for a board game. In this case, the name of our game is information security. When you sit down to play your new board game, does everyone read the rules? It's unlikely. Usually one person takes the lead, reads the rules, and disseminates them to the other players. When there are questions about the game play, someone refers to the rules for additional guidance.

This is how policies are supposed to be used. One person masters the rules and disseminates them to the other players (employees). The rules are made available as a reference document when there are questions. Policies, therefore, are (1) the rules for our game and (2) reference documents.

Think outside the box. Take risks by creating new solutions and approaches to problems that could work better than our traditional methods do.

One of the best ways to think outside the box is to listen to others. Listen to other people who aren't part of our herd. Listen to others who don't think the same way we do. In an organization, we need to sit down and spend more time with normal people. Normal people come up with some of our best outside-the-box solutions to our problems.

PROBLEM #2: HERD MENTALITY LEADS TO POOR CHOICES

> " Herd mentality, mob mentality and pack mentality, also lesser known as gang mentality, describe how people can be influenced by their peers to adopt certain behaviors on a largely emotional, rather than rational, basis. "

> –Wikipedia

History is full of examples in which the herd mentality led people to make bad choices. Extreme examples of mob mentality include

157

the French Revolution's Reign of Terror, the Salem witch hunts, the Holocaust, the Red Scare, the anti–civil rights race riots, the Sand Creek Massacre, and so on (too many to list).

These are extreme examples, so what does this have to do with information security? I'm getting there.

There were times in my childhood when I made dumb choices, and times when I contemplated making a decision that would end poorly. At one point or another during your childhood, you must have heard the phrase, "If your friends jumped off a bridge, would you do it too?" I certainly heard this from my mother more than once.

Of course, we wouldn't jump off a bridge! We weren't stupid or crazy, but we were children, and we belonged to a herd populated by our friends.

I wonder if members of the Oxford University Dangerous Sports Club heard the same motherly advice I heard before they decided to take the plunge off the 250-foot Clifton Suspension Bridge in Bristol, England. The date was April 1, 1979: bungee jumping was born. Ten years later bungee jumping became a commercial enterprise, and since then, millions of people have jumped off a bridge.

Take that, Mom!

But that brings us back to a question: If I had gone bungee jumping with my friends, would I have done it because they did it? Or would I have made a rational decision of my own to go jump off a bridge?

Research has consistently shown that human nature drives us to want to be part of the "in crowd," an innate desire that is so strong that it can cloud our judgment and lead us to make bad decisions. In some cases, the herd mentality and cognitive bias are so strong that we unconsciously follow along without making any conscious decision at all.

I've run into companies that have spent thousands of dollars on technologies like SIEM, DLP, or Network Access Control (NAC). When we've asked them why they decided to make the purchase of one particular product versus another, many times we'll find that they bought the product because someone else they know (a peer) had bought the product. Was it the best product for them? Maybe. Did they have more significant risks to attend to? Maybe. Did they just waste their money? Maybe.

And if their friends had jumped off a bridge, would they have done it too? Maybe.

The findings from one study suggest that these purchases were not just a fluke. Researchers found that when people did not have a strong opinion about which products to buy, they would mimic the purchasing choices of the people around them. The study "Social Defaults: Observed Choices Become Choice Defaults" was published in the *Journal of Consumer Research*. Rather than asking questions of the product vendors or spending time learning about the products, people just deferred to the "social default," even when it was a clearly inferior product. (Source: http://careymorewedge.com/papers/SocialDefaults.pdf)

All people—even business leaders—and their decisions are strongly influenced by the herd mentality. The most common question we receive from business executives when discussing information security is "What are other companies doing?" They want to know where the herd is at. There's some logic to this, because we may think that somewhere within the herd is the "reasonableness"—the difference between negligence and due care.

Too often, the reason business executives ask this question is because they lack the information necessary to make good decisions on their own. It's our job to find and deliver this information so that we can make good decisions and shed the herd.

The Latest News

Another bandwagon effect that mobilizes the herd is the news, regardless of whether it is true or false. Nothing drives interest in an information security technology or service more than prominent news reports. After the Target breach, everyone became aware (if they hadn't been before) of the need for payment card security, network segmentation, and vendor risk management. These were very hot topics and easy sales opportunities. Were payment card security, network segmentation, or vendor risk the most significant risks or highest priority security tasks? Yes, if you were driven by the herd mentality. Maybe they weren't, if you were focused on your own information security risks.

After the Equifax breach, the hot topics were application vulnerabilities patching, web applications patching, web servers patching, and web application vulnerability scanning.

The Heartland Payment Systems breach in 2008 spurred a hot market for checking web applications for input validation and conducting SQL injection scans/testing.

Wireless network security was huge after the TJX Companies breach in 2006.

The herd is always tuned into the latest news, and it has a significant impact on herd members' purchasing decisions. It doesn't matter if it's wireless networking, mobile-device security, encryption, patching, or the scary Intel chip vulnerabilities. The herd tends to be overly influenced by the top stories of the day, which is no way to define or manage an information security strategy.

Following Trends

Another annoying herdlike habit is basing information security strategies according to what's trending.

Trends aren't bad per se, but they ought not be the sole basis for rational decision making. They are merely insight into what the rest of the herd is doing.

Look at these hot trends according to a recent magazine article: (Source: http://www.information-age.com/10-cyber-security-trends-look-2018-123463680/)

- cybersecurity regulations improvement
- data theft turning into data manipulation

- demand continuing to rise for security skills

- cybersecurity and IoT

- attackers continuing to target consumer devices

- attackers becoming bolder, more commercial, less traceable

- attackers getting smarter

- breaches becoming more complicated and harder to beat

- cyber-risk insurance growing more common

- new job titles appearing, such as chief cybercrime officer (CCO)

We can agree or disagree with the items on the list, and this is all interesting information. We should consider these things, but not change our strategy significantly to account for them. A CCO does sound sort of cool, though.

Running off the Cliff

Once you're headed for the buffalo jump, it is too late.

Native Americans and bison have a long shared history. The people used every part of the bison to supply their needs. *Tatanka* ("bison") was at the core of the Lakota culture of North America. The Native Americans were masters at hunting American bison. One method of hunting, used by the Blackfoot Indians, was the buffalo jump. This was a V-shaped pathway that ended at a sheer cliff. The people would chase the herd over the cliff. This type of hunting was very successful for the people; however, as you can imagine, it was a very violent way for a member of the buffalo herd to die.

Let's apply the concept of a buffalo jump to our industry.

A danger that comes with the herd mentality is that you go where the herd goes. Sometimes you go where the herd goes unwittingly or blindly; sometimes you go willingly, like an excited puppy following its master. If the herd is headed for a virtual buffalo jump, you too are headed for that buffalo jump.

One of the most recent buffalo jumps was related to the Meltdown and Spectre exploitation of critical vulnerabilities in most of the modern processors used in computers today. (Source: https://meltdownattack.com/)

Another buffalo jump was buying a security information and event management (SIEM) solution because everyone else seemed to be buying one. You buy it because the herd buys it, not because you're sure that you need it or know how to use it. This seems like a minor buffalo jump, but the lack of critical thinking can result in potenial poor spending where there are limited funds available and a potential false sense of security.

Other possible buffalo jumps include the misuse of standards such as ISO 27001 and NIST SP 800-53, doing the minimum number of things necessary to keep up with the herd (checklists are common here), and buying technology and other solutions without going through the proper reasoning or justification.

If you're wondering what proper justification is, then that might be an indication you're following the herd. Proper justification should be any unacceptable risk that you or your organization has chosen to mitigate.

SOLUTION #2: TAKE THE TIME TO RESEARCH

There are two things that are most effective in combatting the herd mentality: critical thinking and time.

Research shows that we make poorer decisions and are more reliant on the herd mentality when we're rushed and don't take time to think. Taking time to think may seem impossible to us because we are so busy. We are working at capacity and then some, and every salesperson under the sun wants just five minutes of our time. We're going one hundred miles per hour just to try to handle everything.

We're all in a time crunch.

Regardless of our specific situation, something must give. There are only so many hours that we can commit to any working day. Understand that when we don't take the time to slow down and think, we're more prone to poor decision making. If we need more resources, then we need to get more resources. If we can't get more resources, despite our most sincere and creative efforts to do so, then we're forced to live with the consequences, which may include living with a poorly designed information security program or leaving to find a job with an organization that will properly staff and fund our efforts.

I would be lying to you if I said that I haven't been guilty of demonstrating improper work-life balance. The results can be devastating. We burn out, our health can suffer, we pile poor decisions on top of poor decisions. We need to slow down, take our time, think things through, and make good, rational decisions for ourselves, and not because the herd made them for us.

Here are some potential solutions to help you find more time:

- Find more time through using your time better; by mastering time management in these and other ways:

  - Hold fewer or more effective meetings.

  - Waste less time on politics.

  - Automate everything that can be automated.

- Make and win the case for more information security talent.

- Go to work at a place where you are empowered to do your job through buy-in, trust, funding, human capital, and so on.

Slowing down requires mastering time management. You'll need to set appropriate expectations for your time with yourself and with others. Begin by sorting out things that require short bursts of time and things that require a dedicated thinking session.

Your goal is to carve out a stretch of at least ninety minutes each week that is not followed by any important meetings. Forget about all your other concerns and let your mind go blank. Let the speedometer rest at zero.

When you feel relaxed, start thinking about your problem from every direction—the big picture, your experience, how other people may see things, and so forth. It may help to write down your thoughts. It is OK to let your mind wander, because some of the best ideas come out of nowhere. Clarify in your mind the decision you need to make and write it down as a question. You might find that the way you frame the question determines certain possible solutions. Try restating the question. That alone may open up a new array of possible answers. Some critical decisions require research, and research takes time. That's OK. Give it time.

You are now officially out of the herd and have taken steps toward thinking as an individual.

PROBLEM #3: EVEN IF THE HERD IS RIGHT, ITS STILL WON'T FIT US

When we're immersed in the herd mentality, we focus heavily on what others are doing. We mistakenly believe that if we just do what others are doing, then it will work the same way for us. If they use a certain solution, and we believe that they're secure, then if we do the same thing they do, we will be secure too.

It's one thing to learn from others; it's another thing to emulate them. The first is always healthy; the second may not be.

The one-size-fits-all type of thinking can be dangerous, because there's a big difference between *feeling* secure and *being* secure. That's part of the comfortable delusion of herd mentality.

Wouldn't it be nice if you could just do what everyone else was doing and all your problems would be solved? The brutal fact of the matter is that copycat solutions won't work, because information security is not a one-size-fits-all discipline.

The only universal element in our industry is the guiding principle embodied in our definition of *information security*: information security is managing risks to the confidentiality, integrity, and availability of information using administrative, physical, and technical controls.

It would be great if everyone used this same definition. It would be healthy. What would be unhealthy is if everyone applied the definition in the same exact manner in all organizations and situations. When we apply the definition in practice, each part of it needs to be customized to fit the unique characteristics of each individual organization.

How many times have we seen organizations copy information security policies from another organization, or use templates, and expect them to work the same way? Maybe they're just checking a box (a different problem). The point is that policies, processes, training, technologies, and other controls used in one organization will not work the same way in another.

The problem in considering a universal application of the information security definition is that we don't employ all the same people, we don't all operate in the same physical location, and we don't all use the same technologies in the same way. If we have these fundamental differences, then how would we expect the same controls to be effective in the same manner that they're effective in another organization? The logic doesn't work.

The risks in one organization are different than the risks in every other organization. A fallacy and a danger related to the herd mentality is that we may mistakenly think that one organization's controls will work the same way in our organization.

> " Winners focus on winning. Losers focus on winners. "
>
> –Anonymous, but quoted by many "winners."

SOLUTION #3: FOCUS ON YOU AND WHAT YOU CAN CONTROL

Nobody knows my information security program like I know my information security program. Nobody knows what's best for me like I know what's best for me. It's not that we don't rely on peers and family members we trust to keep us in check. It's that honest introspection is a very valuable tool. In fact, it is an invaluable tool in fighting the herd mentality. If I'm honest with myself, then I know the things I need and the things I don't need. The same is true with you.

As the above quote suggests, if we want to have a winning strategy, we should be spending a lot more time on achieving our goals (winning) and a lot less time focusing on what other people are doing. It's not that we don't notice the others. It's that we don't focus on them. It's not that we don't notice admirable qualities in our competition. It's that we just don't let them distract us from what we're doing to win.

What's Winning?

Define it for yourself. For me, winning is simple. It means the following:

1. being the best information security resource that I am capable of

2. building the best information security program that I am capable of building

I know I've won when I put specific goals, objectives, and measurements around what winning means to us. I may even tie them to some of our organizational communications, like achieving our future state for information security on time and under budget. You may remember from previous chapters that these things are in alignment with what I may have told executives and the board:

1. our current state
2. our future state—winning
3. when we'll get there—winning
4. how much it's going to cost—winning

Do I always win? Absolutely not! However, defining what winning looks like in the organization and striving for the prize is noble and defensible (should it ever come to that).

Did you notice all the "I" statements in this section?

When I'm working on an information security program, I take it personally. I view the program as my program, even though it may belong to a client. I want to build the best information security program that I am capable of.

I don't want to build the best security program that should be used by everyone in the herd. That would be impossible. Information security is not a one-size-fits-all discipline. It's a discipline that is customized for each organization. The principles are universal. The language is universal. But the applications of the language and principles cannot be universal.

Take information security personally yourself. For us to build the best information security programs possible, we must focus on ourselves first. Take notice of the herd, learn from the herd, but don't focus on or obsess over the herd.

Break from the Herd

The herd isn't responsible for my information security program, and they're not responsible for yours either. The herd doesn't suffer any real and direct consequences from a single poor security program, and if anything, the herd will laugh at it and keep moving on. The solution for escaping herd mentality is grounded in individuality, knowledge, and experience.

You be you.

From Amy Morin, psychotherapist and author of *Thirteen Things Mentally Strong People Don't Do*, are these tips for breaking out the herd mentality: (Source: https://www.forbes.com/sites/amymorin/2014/07/25/study-shows-the-power-of-social-influence-5-ways-to-avoid-the-herd-mentality/2/#278a97bc430d)

1. Don't work on autopilot.

2. Consciously form your own opinion.

3. Take your time making decisions.

4. Be aware of how stress affects your decision making.

5. Be willing to be different.

Weaving Amy's advice into our work would go a long way toward making us better information security practitioners.

7

Because I Said So

The information security industry is broken because people don't want to do the right thing. Let's get something straight, right off the bat: compliance and information security are completely different things.

There are four primary motivators, or reasons, why organizations establish information security programs:

1. **Compliance:** They are forced to do so to comply with mandates thrust upon them by governments, the industry at large, and other companies they want to do business with.

2. **Incident:** An incident has occurred, and they are defending against what has become a new set of attackers (customers, lawyers, regulators, and the like).

3. **Right thing:** Leadership and the organization see information security as the right thing to do for one or more reasons, including civic duty, responsibility, profitability, or market differentiation.

4. **Other:** There are times when an organization doesn't even know why it's spending money on information security.

Which do you think predominates in the industry?

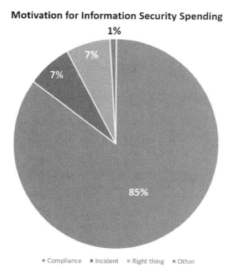

Motivation for Information Security Spending

Figure: This illustrates motivations for information security spending

In the past ten years, since we started FRSecure, we've done a few thousand projects with more than one thousand clients. Of the thousands of projects we've done, we estimate that 85 percent of them would not have happened had it not been for compliance, directly or indirectly. The primary motivation for 85 percent of our projects was compliance; 7 percent were motivated because of an incident, 7 percent were motivated because they want to do the right thing, and 1 percent aren't sure why they're doing one or more security projects.

" There are two levers for moving men—interest and fear. **"**

–Napoleon Bonaparte

Compliance is by far the number one motivation for information security investments of time and money. The driving motivation, as Napoleon points out, is fear—fear of the consequences if they fail to comply. They fear being sanctioned and paying fines, they fear losing customers, and they fear that someone might find out that they're not compliant.

It is another symptom of a broken industry that most of our information security programs—if they deserve to be called that—are the product of reactions to demands from others who have motives other than the best interests of our organization.

Governments, whether they be federal, state, or the European Union (EU), make security demands on behalf of the citizens in their jurisdictions. They want us to serve them. The ways in which this plays out are fraught with all kinds of problems, vagaries, and weaknesses. These makeshift security programs are not built upon strong foundations; they're built piecemeal and are subject to change depending on the next new government policy.

Contrast that to the solid information security program that I advocate in this book, programs guided by the foundational principles embedded in our oft-repeated definition: information security is managing risks to the confidentiality, integrity, and availability of information using administrative, physical, and technical controls.

Information security programs built upon this foundation are intended to be comprehensive, vigorous, and dedicated to the mission, best interests, and profitability of the organization.

In this chapter we dwell on the difference between compliance-based security efforts (and their attendant flaws) and proper information security programs.

Governmental compliance stems from dozens of state and federal laws, and increasingly, mandates from the EU. The best example for compliance in our own industry is the Payment Card Industry Data Security Standard (PCI DSS). The third source for compliance is between organizations and comes in the form of vendor risk management or vendor security management.

To its credit, compliance has prompted a greater security infrastructure than we might otherwise have. However, we wouldn't need others to tell us what to do if we knew what to do and we did it. The best way to be secure is to start with wanting to be secure.

Problems covered in this chapter include:

- Problem #1: We have so many laws, but so little direction.
- Problem #2: We have no choice but to comply.
- Problem #3: Compliance makes a crappy foundation.

Some of the potential solutions we'll explore include:

- Solution #1: The intent of the law is key.
- Solution #2: How we comply is where we find our choices.
- Solution #3: Focus on the foundation.

Imagine how much more secure an organization would be if it actually wanted to be secure.

PROBLEM #1: WE HAVE SO MANY LAWS, BUT SO LITTLE DIRECTION

Compliance isn't working, or at the very least, it isn't working well enough for information security. This will become clear as we examine some of the primary federal mandates, especially in health care and the financial sector.

Let's pick on HIPAA. It's an easy one to pick on.

HIPAA was signed into law by President Bill Clinton in 1996. The law caused quite a stir when it was signed, and it still does today. It contains five sections, known as titles. When it comes to information security, the most applicable section is Title II: Preventing Health Care Fraud and Abuse. It contains the Privacy Rule and the Security Rule, both of which became effective in 2003. The industry rushed to become compliant with the Privacy Rule; however, compliance with the Security Rule was a different story.

The Security Rule contains the Security Standards for the Protection of Electronic Protected Health Information, which can best be seen as a simple checklist of things you must do (what it does not explain is how you should do these things and why):

- Implement policies and procedures to prevent, detect, contain, and correct security violations—check.

- Conduct an accurate and thorough assessment of the potential risks and vulnerabilities to the confidentiality, integrity, and availability of electronic protected health information held by the covered entity—check.

- Apply appropriate sanctions against workforce members who fail to comply with the security policies and procedures of the covered entity—check.

- Implement procedures to regularly review records of information system activity, such as audit logs, access reports, and security incident tracking reports—check.

These are good statements with good intentions. However, they are also vague. Language like *apply appropriate sanctions* and *conduct an accurate and thorough assessment* is open to various interpretations. Unfortunately, this is how compliance must work. The statements cannot be too exact, because they apply to a wide range of different organizations that employ different people in different places following different processes and using different technologies. Remember, information security is not one-size-fits-all. Programs must be customized to each unique organization.

In 2009, Congress passed the Health Information Technology for Economic and Clinical Health Act (HITECH) as part of the American Recovery and Reinvestment Act (ARRA). ARRA contained incentives designed to accelerate the adoption of electronic health record (EHR) systems, but one of the key provisions for reimbursement was to conduct an information security risk analysis. HITECH also clarified the intent of the Security Rule and implemented the Breach Notification Rule. HITECH added more teeth and clarification to the HIPAA Security Rule, and organizations rushed to become compliant. It may have taken money as an incentive, either in the form of increased fines or the EHR incentives, but the intent of the law was becoming clearer for some. The result was better information security—not great, but better.

HIPAA has been around for more than twenty years. The Security Rule—the one we're most concerned about here—was finalized more than fifteen years ago. HIPAA underwent additional revisions and has been amended with additional clarifications multiple times since then. How's it going? You'd think that with all this time and these revisions, security in the health-care industry might be rock-solid by now. It's not. Information security in health care may actually be worse.

According to a recent news article, using data from a survey conducted by the Ponemon Institute, health care organizations experienced an average of sixteen cyberattacks each in 2017, up from eleven the year before. The majority of respondents said patient data had been breached or lost in the last year.

From a risk perspective, this is troubling information. Furthermore, health care organizations are under increased attack because (1) they have very valuable data and (2) they are still an easy target. The data is more valuable than ever to attackers because of the significant rise in health-care costs, including health insurance. Attackers can sell the data for more, and the data has a longer shelf life. People are receiving treatments under other people's health insurance. This is a dangerous situation for the victims. The second point exposes the fact that HIPAA compliance isn't working, or at the very least it isn't working fast or well enough.

HIPAA isn't very prescriptive, for it can't be. HIPAA applies to thousands of diverse organizations, and to make the regulation too prescriptive would cost more than anyone is willing to pay. I get the sense that most health-care organizations want to do the right thing and play by the rules. Yet most of them need more direction.

The Office for Civil Rights (OCR) is the agency for the US Department of Health and Human Services in charge of enforcing HIPAA's Privacy, Security, and Breach Notification Rules. The OCR embarked on a mission to further define requirements and provide more prescriptive guidance. The result was the HIPAA Audit Protocol and the HIPAA Audit Program. The Audit Protocol is a checklist of things that must be in place to comply with the law. There's more prescriptive guidance, but it's still not producing adequate results.

Not long after the Audit Protocol was established, the Office of the National Coordinator for Health Information Technology (ONC) produced the Security Risk Assessment Tool (SRA Tool) to guide health care organizations with performing their information security risk assessments, a common problem area for many health care organizations. According to the ONC, the tool is not required by the HIPAA Security Rule but is meant to assist providers and professionals as they perform a risk assessment. Furthermore, the SRA Tool is not intended to be an exhaustive or definitive source on safeguarding health information from privacy and security risks.

Seem confusing yet? HIPAA compliance may not be confusing if you're an expert working with it, but it is as confusing as hell for normal people.

Maybe this is just health care. Clearly the financial industry must be better. It is, but not as good as it could be. The pinnacle of regulations in banking and finance is the Gramm Leach Bliley Act (GLBA). According to the Federal Trade Commission (FTC), GLBA requires financial institutions—companies that offer consumers financial products or services like loans, financial or investment advice, or insurance—to explain their information-sharing practices to their customers and to safeguard sensitive data.

There are numerous government agencies involved with the further definition of the law and its enforcement. Their intent is to be helpful, but the interpretation and enforcement of GLBA compliance is confusing enough, without having guidance from each one. Compliance really comes down to doing what the last regulator or examiner told you to do.

Information security compliance in the financial services world is further ahead than in health care. That's because financial services organizations provide access to the one thing that everyone wants: money.

The information security pushed through GLBA compliance is still checkbox security and doesn't adequately fit our definition of information security in most organizations.

Indirect Compliance

Indirect compliance works the same way as direct compliance, but it comes under the guise of vendor (or third-party) risk management. Instead of a direct HIPAA, GLBA, or other regulatory driver, the same sort of requirements are pushed through from a customer with these specific requirements. The requirements for the vendor may take the form of a SOC 2 report, ISO certification, a specific risk assessment, or some other means.

All the principles related to direct compliance also apply to indirect requirements, just in a different form.

SOLUTION #1: THE INTENT OF THE LAW IS KEY

The letter of the law is easy. It is basically a checklist of things that we've been told to do. The letter of the law doesn't mean much, however, until it's been interpreted. This can be a conundrum because it's the intent of the law that will be enforced. Every time there's a new law or regulation, people scramble to determine the intent of the new law or its impact. This commotion distracts us from the things we're currently working on, as if we don't have enough to work on already. It takes valuable resources and can result in all sorts of off-budget expenses.

The latest compliance mandate is for the EU's General Data Protection Regulation (GDPR). GDPR is meant to "strengthen and unify data protection for all individuals within the European Union." (Source: https://www.infogovbasics.com/what-is-gdpr/) The letter of the law is extensive, but it's the anticipation of the interpretation or intent of the law that has people scrambling. Some claim to know how GDPR will be interpreted, but nobody really knows until it actually gets interpreted. Unfortunately, the only way to learn its interpretation will be through enforcement. If you happen to be on the wrong end of the enforcement, meaning you're one of the first organizations that gets audited or acted upon, it could hurt. GDPR fines could get as high as €20 million (approximately $23.4 million) or up to 4 percent of an organization's annual worldwide revenue.

A primary challenge for GDPR compliance is to determine why, where, and how private information is used within the organization. We must figure this out before we can apply any specific requirements. If our asset-management practices already account for information assets, even if they don't account for this specific type of asset with granularity, we've already got a significant leg up in compliance.

How about HIPAA? The same principle applies. The letter of the law is one thing. The intent of the law is to manage information security risk well, especially as it relates to electronic protected health information (ePHI).

Our definition of *information security* starts with "managing risks." So if we were already running a well-designed information security program, based on our definitions and using our solid foundation, then we would already be compliant with HIPAA. Any changes to the interpretation of the regulation would already be accounted for within our information security program, or, in worst cases, would be with slight modifications.

Let's look at the letter of the law for HIPAA, specifically one of the first Administrative Safeguards statements. 45 CFR 164.308(a)(1)(i) states: "Implement policies and procedures to prevent, detect, contain, and correct security violations." In a checklist mentality, or compliance-first mentality, we could comply with this statement in about an hour. The intent of the law, however, is to create a set of policies and procedures that (1) are formally approved by executive management, (2) reflect executive management's intentions and expectations for the protection of sensitive information (to be defined also), and (3) cover all aspects of our security program, including but not limited to roles and responsibilities, asset management, and access control. The intent is to use the policies to govern a good, foundational information security program.

You get the point. The letter of the law is easy, but ineffective. The intent of the law is harder, but very effective. We can offset the difficulty in attainment of the intent of the law by having a good information security program in the first place. The more effective and viable approach, especially in the long term, is to start with a solid information security program. The less effective and less viable approach is to start with a compliance program based on the letter of the law.

I used GDPR and HIPAA in this example, but the same is true of most every other information security–related regulation that I can think of, including GLBA, Federal Information Security Management Act (FISMA), FINRA, and Cybersecurity Information Sharing Act (CISA).

Understand the true intent behind administrative controls (policies, standards, guidelines, procedures, training, and so forth). The intent of administrative controls is not to have administrative controls. The intent of administrative controls is to influence human behaviors.

Having documentation for the sake of having documentation is not the purpose of the documentation. Manage risk well, and compliance is much, much more advantageous. Managing compliance without managing risk well is a crapshoot.

PROBLEM #2: WE HAVE NO CHOICE, BUT TO COMPLY

Which of these seems more attractive to you?

1. building a security program because you want to, and you see how you will benefit from it

2. building a security program because you've been told you must, and that you must build it in the way you're told, regardless of whether you benefit

The first option produces results and a pursuit of excellence. The second option produces an attitude of doing the fewest number of things possible to get a box checked, regardless of risk.

 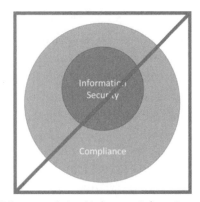

Figure: This example illustrations the best and the worst relationship between information security and compliance.

A few years ago, we helped a large health-care system conduct a security risk analysis to comply with a federal security mandate. As I presented my results at an executive meeting, the CFO posed a simple question: "Has anyone figured out if there is an ROI for this?" Typical CFO. The reply was equally simple: "Regardless of any ROI, it's the law, and we don't have a choice."

It's true that we have no choice but to comply with the law. You do, however, have a choice in how you comply with the law. In our industry, the number one driver for information security focus and spending is compliance. In most cases, it's because we don't know any better. We don't want to do security, so we approach it like we must.

If we know that the letter of the law does not necessarily match with the intent of the law, due to interpretation issues and our inherent tendency to take shortcuts, then why would we design a security program according to the letter of the law?

A security program built inside a compliance program will require changes, and sometimes significant and fundamental changes, with each new interpretation. With each new interpretation by a regulatory agency of an auditor comes a new wave of changes. Every time an examiner or auditor comes to review your program, he or she will reach conclusions based upon his or her own interpretation of the law at the time of the review.

It's like a ship getting tossed upon the waves of interpretation. Each new interpretation is a new wave that tosses the ship from side to side. Sometimes the interpretations change so much from year to year that they almost capsize or sink the ship.

Too many of us build compliance programs with security added on, when we should be building security programs with compliance added on. We have no choice but to comply, but we have choices regarding how we comply.

SOLUTION #2: HOW WE COMPLY IS WHERE WE FIND OUR CHOICES

We don't have a choice in whether to comply, but we do have a choice in how we comply and in what attitude we have when we comply.

Do we feel like we're forced to comply, or do we feel like we get to comply? Do we want to comply because we want to comply, or do we comply because we must? The changes in the wording are slight; however, the difference in attitude is actually very telling. One approach is reluctant and leads to doing the least amount possible—checklist security, shortcuts, and getting by. The other approach has a proactive attitude leading to doing things right, managing risk, and thriving.

Take two competitive organizations. One complies because it must and the other complies because it wants to. The first organization takes a shortsighted approach, and every time there's a new regulation, or a change to an existing regulation, there's a significant disruption in operations. The disruption comes in the form of putting other projects on hold while staff attend to compliance initiatives and an increased budget to account for controls that may or may not fit into the strategic direction of the organization.

The second organization takes a strategic approach to information security. It welcomes new regulations because it already has a solid foundation in place. It welcomes the new regulations because they won't be overly disruptive to the operations, and staff know that it will result in a competitive advantage. The second company can easily accommodate any additional controls into its strategy if these haven't already been accounted for.

Our choice can lead to significant competitive advantage.

The answer to how we choose to comply is by fitting compliance into our security program versus the other way around. Compliance-driven information security programs are less effective than risk-driven information security programs. Risk-driven information security programs are simply information security programs, according to our definition.

Best Interests

Most of us can agree that nobody has our best interests in mind more than we do. Nobody cares about the well-being of our organization more than those who have a stake in the success of our organization. It's sad that too many of us take direction on information security from people who don't have our best interests at heart. I'm not saying that regulators, examiners, and auditors don't care about us. I'm saying that they don't care about us nearly as much as we care about ourselves.

This is yet another case for an information security program focused on our needs, with compliance built in.

PROBLEM #3: COMPLIANCE MAKES A CRAPPY FOUNDATION

As you may recall from chapter 2, the foundation of an information security program includes (at a minimum) asset management, access control, and change control. What is the foundation of our information security program if compliance is the primary or only driver?

I Get Compliance

Compliance reminds me of growing up. I am an only child, and my mother and father were in the Marine Corps. It's where they met. So—two Marines as parents, and me being the sole focus of their parental attention. I seriously get compliance!

When either of my parents told me what to do, I complied. Compliance was ingrained into my being from an early age. There was a set of tasks that I was required to complete each Saturday, and noncompliance was not an option. Otherwise I faced some serious sanctions.

Cleaning the bathroom was one of the tasks on my checklist. If, after cleaning the bathroom, I noticed that the dishes were piled up in the sink, do you think I would touch the dishes, even though I clearly knew that they needed to be taken care of? The answer is no. It wasn't on my list. This is how one is conditioned to think when working on somebody else's checklist.

My parents were much smarter than I was, so they changed the rules. My father said, "If you see something that needs to be done around the house, and I have to tell you to do it, then it's too late. Don't make me add chores to your list when you know it's a chore that's not on your list." In non-Marine terms, what he meant was: Don't stick to the checklist. Do tasks as they arise.

Who would have thought that my father's wisdom given to me at a young age would have such a significant impact on my work? I despised the instruction at the time, but I have grown to value it as a core life lesson. Thanks, Dad!

The same mentality that applied to me as a child applies to our adult lives and our work lives. If we must be told what to do, it's too late. When we rely on being told what to do, we'll do what we're told and not much else. This is a terrible foundation for information security. In fact, it's not even a foundation at all.

Mediocrity and Triteness

There they are again. Mediocrity and triteness.

Not unlike the herd mentality from the previous chapter, compliance can, and often does, steal our desire for greatness, excellence, innovation, and creativity. When we rely on compliance, our information security initiatives are defined by regulators, examiners, and auditors.

We find ourselves settling for mediocrity. Compliance initiatives, if not handled properly, can easily become checklist exercises in which our only goal is to check every box off the list as quickly as possible with the least amount of work. Mediocrity is good enough. Excellence is not on the checklist.

Our motivation must be to strive for excellence in information security. Until we change our motivation, we'll certainly continue to face significant problems: confusion, poor security programs, increased frequency and impact of breaches, and lackluster innovation.

SOLUTION #3: FOCUS ON THE FOUNDATION

The road to excellence is through mastering the foundational concepts of information security. It isn't easy, and the work isn't sexy, but it is essential. Nail these concepts now, and compliance will be much easier going forward. We need to make things easier on ourselves in the long run anyway. Focus on the foundation now, and we'll save ourselves a boatload of grief down the road.

A solid base for an information security program was covered in chapter 2. The foundation consists of planning, strategy, buy-in, asset management, access control, and change control.

8

Empty Promises

We don't say what we mean or mean what we say, and we can't prove any of it.

The information security industry is broken because we don't commit and keep our word. We all make promises and commitments to others. Sometimes we make commitments that we have no intention of fulfilling; we lie. More commonly, we make commitments that we have every intention to fulfill; however, events occur that keep us from doing the things that we set out to do. (In other words, sh*t happens.) There are even times when we make commitments without even realizing that we did, through a communications or expectations mixup. For us, and for this chapter, an empty promise is any commitment that we fail to live up to, whatever the reason.

Every empty promise we make leads to an erosion of trust and credibility. Trust and credibility are two extremely important concepts for us. They're woven into everything we do in our industry.

Problems covered in this chapter include:

- Problem #1: Troubles with commitments

- Problem #2: Money as a demonstration of commitment
- Problem #3: Thinking obscurity makes us secure

Some of the potential solutions we'll explore include:

- Solution #1: Making commitments carefully
- Solution #2: Putting our money where our mouth is
- Solution #3: Taking our head out of the sand

A promise is a commitment. It's an obligation we've made to someone: a stakeholder, a peer, an employee, a customer. Promises are made in our personal lives to our wives, husbands, friends, children, and others. Something as simple and as seemingly insignificant as promising a spouse that we'll do something around the house, coupled with a failure to deliver, can lead to an erosion of trust or a belief that we can't be taken at our word.

In organizations, and in our industry, empty promises aren't always so cut and dry. Executives often make promises that they intend to fulfill but then realize that the commitment is more than they bargained for. Some organizational leaders desperately want to show their commitment to information security, but don't know how.

The organizational leaders who make promises without any intent to deliver on them are poor leaders who give us nothing more than lip service. These are the worst of all.

PROBLEM #1: TROUBLES WITH COMMITMENTS

Organizations today make a lot of promises. There are promises about customer experience, new product innovation and strategy, career advancement opportunities for employees, and social responsibility (including information security). Each of these promises is a commitment to the audience for which it was intended. As organizations struggle to keep their commitments, many of them experience a reality called "commitment drift." According to Elizabeth Doty, a former lab fellow of Harvard University's Edmond J. Safra Center for Ethics, "Commitment drift is dangerous, because it leads people to neglect the investments needed to maintain key capabilities, sustain customer relationships, retain employees, execute strategies, and pursue innovations. It also introduces the risk of breakdowns in safety, privacy, and ethics, and erodes the trust of employees, customers, shareholders, and the public." (Source: https://www.strategy-business.com/article/00267?gko=c4691)

We experience more than our share of commitment drift within organizations when it comes to information security. Information security

Here are some of the reasons why we make commitments, often without a full understanding of what it takes to fulfill our promises:

- **Fear of disapproval**: This is arguably the most common reason people make empty promises. Imagine an executive stating that he or she doesn't take information security seriously.

- **Need to please**: We strive to make others happy, even at our own expense.

- **Difficulty saying no**: This is a common cause of overcommitment.

- **Desire to be (seen as) trustworthy**: A fulfilled promise leads to trustworthiness, which is the goal. Unfortunately, we shoot ourselves in the foot when we can't deliver.

- **Speaking without evaluating**: This is when we speak too soon. I do this too often when I commit to something without checking my calendar first.

- **Intentions to persuade**: We make a promise as a form of manipulation. If you do this for me, then I'll do this for you. Parents like to use this one.

- **Bridging awkwardness**: This empty promise is innocent, and we all do it. We run into an acquaintance at the coffee shop, and we say something like, "Hey, we should get together soon," but we have no intention of following up.

takes a commitment, and any good organizational leader would say that they take it seriously. Their words—their commitments—don't always translate to action, and their commitments become empty promises all too often.

Some of our problems stem from the fact that our leaders don't know what they're committing to in the first place. They don't have all the necessary information to make good decisions, and they suffer from short-termism, complexity, reactivity, and conflicting operational issues.

We may commit to security, but we don't know what security is, we don't put our money where our mouth is, and lastly, we misunderstand what the commitment is because we don't think we're really at risk in the first place.

We all say that we take information security seriously, but do our decisions and actions support what we say? Empty promises with information security result in saying one thing but doing something completely counter to the thing that was just said.

Commitments in Information Security

There have been hundreds, maybe thousands of articles and books written about the importance of executive management commitment to information security. The top-down approach to information security is critical to program success. Nobody doubts the importance of senior executive commitment, and most of the articles say the same things: information security is everyone's responsibility, executive management buy-in is critical to the success of information security, information security must be a priority for senior executives, and so forth.

It's not as if we don't already know that executive management and director commitment is critical to information security. Where we miss the mark is in how we demonstrate the commitment and how we measure the commitment. What executive manager would ever admit to not taking information security seriously? Would the CEO of a company publicly state, "I don't believe in the importance of information security"? This is highly unlikely. Instead, a CEO would say, "I am absolutely committed to information security." Significant problems exist, however, if the CEO:

1. doesn't understand what the commitment actually is

2. doesn't know how to demonstrate the commitment

3. doesn't know how to measure the commitment in a meaningful way

How can we help CEOs define solutions to these problems? It's our job to help them define what the commitment is, or should be, and then to communicate the commitment in a manner that they will fully understand. We are the principal advisor to other executive leaders, especially in areas where we are the experts and they are not. It's our job to define for and advise CEOs on ways that they can demonstrate their commitment, and it's our job to find ways that they can know if they are fulfilling their commitment well (measurement).

We can all agree that the CEO and board of directors are ultimately responsible for information security in the organization. We can all agree that the CEO and board of directors must make a commitment to information security. It's not always their job to define what the commitment should be, but it's definitely their job to agree with the commitment. It's not necessarily their job to define how they can demonstrate their commitment, but it's definitely their job to agree with methods of demonstrating commitment. It's not their job to measure their commitment, it's our job to measure their commitment and help them adjust where necessary.

We should never expect a CEO or a board member to be the expert on information security. We are the experts, and we empower them to make good decisions about these matters.

Board Commitment

Commitment #1 for executives: get involved.

The first commitment for executives and boards of directors is to get involved in information security, and more and more are doing just that. In a research study, Accenture asked two thousand security executives across twelve industries and fifteen countries whether "cybersecurity is a board-level concern supported by our highest-level executives," and 70 percent said yes. (Source: https://www.accenture.com/t20170406T041440Z__w__/ us-en/_acnmedia/PDF-48/Accenture-The-Acn-Security-Index-new.pdf) Now that we've got their attention, we better make it count.

Another study found that despite increased "cybersecurity" investment, the frequency of board briefings on information security appears less than optimal. About 36 percent were briefed only once a year, 34 percent reported quarterly (or more often), 21 percent reported twice per year, and 9 percent were not briefed at all. (Source: https://www.bdo. com/insights/assurance/corporate-governance/2017-bdo-board-sur- vey/2017-bdo-cyber-governance-survey)

A 2018 study by PwC found that "only 44 percent of respondents say their corporate boards actively participate in their companies' overall security strat- egy." (Source: https://www.pwc.com/us/en/cybersecurity/information-secu- rity-survey/strengthening-digital-society-against-cyber-shocks.html).

The truth is that most boards are not adequately involved in information security, and it must become more of a demonstrated commitment by them.

Executive Commitment

Just like directors, most C-level executives will tell you, "Of course we take information security seriously." Yet in most companies today, information security still reports through the CIO, or a person with a similar role within the organization. Surely CIOs take information security seriously. They do, but heading into 2017 only 10 percent of CIOs listed information security as a top business priority (Source: https://www.pcmag.com/article/350665/

only-one-in-10-cios-view-security-as-a-top-business-priority), and according to more recent research from Deloitte, "only 49 percent of CIOs identified security and privacy as a strategic investment." (Source: https://www2. deloitte.com/uk/en/pages/technology/articles/cio-survey.html)

Another study says that 87 percent of CIOs believe their security controls are failing to protect their business. (Source: https://www.venafi. com/assets/pdf/wp/Venafi_2016CIO_SurveyReport.pdf) So, 87 percent of CIOs know that their controls are failing, yet still only 10 percent list it as a top priority? I know—these are separate studies using different methodologies. However, there must be some correlation between the facts and CIO commitment.

It's probably safe to assume that most CEOs have delegated information security responsibilities to the CIO, and the CIO has other top business priorities, in addition to the responsibility for protecting the organization's information.

Let's consider organizations that have made a strong enough commitment to information security at the top and have hired a dedicated chief information security officer (CISO) who reports directly to the CEO. The number one contributing factor to CISO turnover is lack of a serious information security culture (31 percent), followed closely by not actively interacting with other executives (30 percent). Higher compensation elsewhere was the third most common reason cited for CISO turnover, at 27 percent. (Source: https://www.techrepublic.com/article/the-real-reason-companies-dont-take-security-seriously-their-money-isnt-on-the-line/)

The fact that we still tolerate information security reporting through the CIO is frustrating for at least three reasons:

1. Information security is *not* an IT issue; it's a business issue.

2. Information technology and information security objectives are sometimes at odds with each other. It's the nature of the work that each function performs. Information security and IT are peer functions, not one subordinate to the other.

3. Information security is enough of an issue for most organizations that it requires direct communication to the CEO and board.

If we continue to treat information security as if it's an IT issue, we'll continue to hamper our ability to communicate risk and execute effectively on risk decisions.

Demonstration of Commitment

Most CEOs and directors care about keeping their word, yet there is a disconnect between their stated commitment to information security and what really happens.

How should a board of directors and CEO demonstrate their commitment to information security? The most common methods are through oversight of an information security program, including allocation of resources (money, people, and time), regular reporting, and public announcements of support. CEOs (or a delegate) will approve information security policies to ensure that everybody plays by the same rules. The fact that nobody reads policies, few employees can find them, and they aren't uniformly enforced are all issues that are often tolerated in the name of business. These things eat away at the commitments that were made and make the rules ineffective.

Dell's End-User Security Survey in 2017 showed that most users will ignore information sharing policies; 80 percent of them expressed frustration that security policies hurt productivity. (Source: https://datasecurity.dell.com/wp-content/uploads/2017/09/Dell-End-User-Security-Survey-2017.pdf)

Some CEOs do make strong commitments to information security, but these commitments get clouded over by short-term goals like quarterly earnings, product deadlines, and competing urgent issues. This creates a downward spiral of disengagement that leads to what some call "institutional corruption." Good people with the best intentions divert the organization from its stated information security purpose.

Bottom Up

I have had the opportunity to work with several boards of directors and CEOs—both before and after breaches. On far too many occasions, the executives and directors have not been armed with accurate information. Even when given the chance to communicate with executives, we've fallen short in giving them the most pertinent and accurate information available to enable good decision making.

It's far too common for these leaders to be blindsided by things that they should have been told about ahead of time. This includes everything from common incidents to very high-profile breaches.

According to a 2014 survey conducted at Black Hat, most organizations are not spending their time, budget, and staffing resources on the problems that most security experts consider to be the greatest threats. Whose problem is this? If you said that it's ours, then I agree. It's our job to enable executive management to fulfill its obligations. Rather than complaining at a security conference, maybe we should spend more time solving our own problems.

Small Businesses

The commitment to information security by small businesses is shrouded in ignorance and the false belief that obscurity provides security. A survey conducted by CNBC and Survey Monkey showed that only 2 percent of small-business owners viewed the threat of a cyberattack as the most critical issue they face. However, the fact is that half of the 28 million small businesses in the United States have been hacked, according to the 2016 State of SMB Cybersecurity Report. This clearly shows more must be done to protect data across all sizes of business.

SOLUTION #1: MAKING COMMITMENTS CAREFULLY

We should commend our organizational leaders who want to commit to information security and want to demonstrate their commitment beyond mere words. Most leaders are people of integrity who want to keep the promises that they've made. In rare cases, there are leaders who say one thing but have no intention of following through. The leaders in the latter category are poor leaders. Our focus is on the former category, the leaders who care.

Organizational leaders have thousands of issues and interests that compete for their time, energy, and money. It can be a real struggle even to remember what we've promised and to whom, let alone to ensure that we're backing up our promises with action. If we make information security as automatic as possible, if we make it a part of how we do business, then this will go a long way toward ensuring that we're not making empty promises.

An organization's board of directors has the responsibility to govern the organization. Board directors have a critical and strategic role in ensuring that proper oversight is given to information security risks; however, it has been a constant struggle and ongoing debate as to what their specific responsibilities are. Recognizing the struggle that boards have with information security responsibility, the National Association of Corporate Directors (NACD) released an updated edition of its *Cyber-Risk Oversight* director's handbook in January 2017.

It's refreshing to see that more companies are prioritizing information security at the board level. A quick look at a handful of public company annual reports will show that their boards of directors appear to take information security seriously. For instance, Walmart talks extensively about information security in their 2018 Annual Report (http://s2.q4cdn.com/056532643/files/doc_financials/2018/annual/WMT-2018_Annual-Report.pdf). So do Berkshire Hathaway, Apple, and many of the Fortune 500 companies.

Two concerns. One, it's easy to talk the talk, but it's a lot harder to walk the walk. Living up to commitments that are made is walking the walk. There still aren't enough companies who live up to their commitment, and there are plenty of companies who don't even know how to. The second concern is that there aren't enough companies who make the same commitments that these Fortune 500 companies appear to. Commitments to information security shouldn't be reserved for large, highly visible companies. Commitments to information security should be made by all companies, no matter their size or shape. We need to make this the norm in our industry.

Careful Commitments

I opened this chapter, in part, with advice from Elizabeth Doty, a former lab fellow of Harvard University's Edmond J. Safra Center for Ethics. In her article titled "Does Your Company Keep Its Promises?" she presents seven strategies to help organizations stave off commitment drift.

These are great strategies to implement for the commitments we make for information security. Commitments are best driven from the top down and are best implemented in a manner that operationalizes them, thus ensuring that they become a matter of normal business. Our commitments start with the first strategy listed in the sidebar, and then become operationalized in strategies two through seven. Let's look at each one in more detail. Most of us don't sit on boards of directors, so our ability to affect commitments made at the top is limited.

> **Elizabeth Doty's Seven Strategies to Stave Off Commitment Drift**
>
> 1. Make fewer, better commitments.
>
> 2. Track your key commitments.
>
> 3. Ask for commitment from others.
>
> 4. Connect the dots between groups.
>
> 5. Focus on processes, not heroics.
>
> 6. Know what commitments you are inheriting in a new role.
>
> 7. Continually check for contradictions.
>
> (Source: https://www.strategy-business.com/article/00267?gko=c4691)

Commitment Drift Strategy #1: Make Fewer, Better Commitments

What are the few and better (or best) commitments that should be made from the top? Whatever we decide, we should document them.

Documenting commitments is a good way to ensure that the multiple people who agreed to them in the first place are reminded of what they committed to.

Commitment #1: Involve the board and management.

The first commitment of the board of directors and executive management should be to be involved. The level of involvement varies from organization to organization, but the commitment to be involved should be nonnegotiable.

Commitment #2: Ensure that information security and risk are defined.

The second commitment should be to ensure that information security and risk are defined in a manner that is understood by all members of the organization.

Commitment #3: Provide training that is specifically designed for directors and executive management on an annual basis.

A third commitment would be to provide on an annual basis information security training that is customized for the specific needs of directors and executive management.

Commitment #4: Implement and oversee an enterprise-wide information security risk management program.

A fourth commitment is to implement and oversee an enterprise-wide information security risk-management program that provides credible information about the organization's current risk state, including the organization's most significant risks and sufficient information for decision making.

Commitment #5: Keep board and management informed of the current information security state, represented as risk.

A fifth commitment might be to receive regular updates as to the status of the organization's information security program. The status should be represented in a manner that is quickly grasped and understood by the board and executive management, and it should be supported by objective and credible information, using facts whenever possible. The basis for the status is risk.

Commitment #6: Approve the organization's risk-treatment strategy or information security strategy.

A sixth commitment is to approve a risk-treatment strategy that enables the information security program's future state or strategy.

Commitment #7: Ensure that the organization's risk-treatment or information security strategy is adequately funded.

A seventh commitment is ensuring that the implementation of the organization's information security strategy is adequately funded with a dedicated information security budget.

Commitment #8: Hold the organization accountable for the execution of the risk-treatment or information security strategy.

An eighth commitment is to hold the organization accountable for the execution of the information security strategy and all related projects and tasks.

These commitments should be made in writing, should be attainable, and should be measurable. None of these is overly disruptive, and all could easily become part of normal business operations.

Five-Minute Rule

In five minutes or less, be able to objectively explain the following:

1. our current state

2. our planned future state

3. when we'll get there

4. how much it will cost

5. **BONUS:** our top significant risk and what we're doing about it

Policy

Most importantly, make every effort to not commit to things that cannot or will not likely be attained. For instance, anything and everything that is written in policy, assuming it has been approved by executive management (which it obviously should be), must be enforced. No policy can be enforced, however, in all instances on all occasions. For these unusual circumstances, a policy waiver or exemption process should be employed.

Commitment Drift Strategy #2: Track Key Commitments

Commitments that are documented and objective are easier to track. Take the sample commitments outlined in the previous section, for example. At a minimum, these key commitments can be easily tracked in meeting minutes and in meeting notes. Most boards and executive managers should receive updates on information security commitments, status, and objectives quarterly, if not more often. If we can keep ourselves to the five-minute rule, we'll fare much better.

Commitment Drift Strategy #3: Ask for Commitment from Others

The commitments that the board of directors and executive management decide to make are ultimately their decisions to make. Good, reasonable, and attainable commitments from the highest levels of the organization go a long way toward empowering others to make good decisions and to make supporting commitments.

Commitment from others can come in the form of an information security road map or strategy that has been approved by the board or executive management. For instance, some of the risks that are cited in the risk assessment will require help from others within the organization. Their commitments should be built into the operational process.

Commitment Drift Strategy #4: Connect the Dots between Groups

An enterprise-wide information security risk-assessment and risk-treatment strategy requires cooperation and collaboration across business units. If the risk-treatment or information security strategy doesn't call specifically for connecting the dots, it may require our intentional effort to communicate with members of different departments.

Commitment Drift Strategy #5: Focus on Processes, Not Heroics

I used the word *operationalize*. *Operationalize* means simply to put into operation, to start working. My intent behind the use of the word is to support the commitments made to information security into operation through devising and implementing the necessary supporting processes. Commitments that are unreasonable are those that require extraordinary effort.

Commitment Drift Strategy #6: Know What Commitments You Are Inheriting in a New Role

Commitments that are documented in road maps and strategies are commitments that are assigned to specific roles. Changing roles should not significantly change any single commitment.

Commitment Drift Strategy #7: Continually Check for Contradictions

This is the purpose behind continual reporting and tracking against the committed road map and/or strategy. Larger or more complex organizations will organize and implement an internal audit function that may review internal compliance. This is a complement to the commitment, not necessarily a commitment in and of itself.

Our Commitment to the Board and Executive Management

We are the most trusted advisors to the board of directors and executive management with respect to information security. If this isn't true, then we have some work to do.

PROBLEM #2: MONEY AS A DEMONSTRATION OF COMMITMENT

The amount of money allocated to information security is the most common measure for an organization's commitment—or lack of commitment, I suppose. Three questions come to mind when discussing spending on information security:

1. Do we have an information security budget?

2. Is our information security budget sufficient to support our commitments?

3. Is the money allocated to information security spent well?

Businesses are in business to make money, and organizations are in business to further a mission. Information security is an afterthought for most; even so, these seem like legitimate questions that should be answered. Unfortunately, too many of us don't have good answers for these questions—and this is another problem.

Budget

Many organizations do not have an information security budget, they don't know how much it is, or they don't know how much it should be. This means that they're spending money on information security, but don't truly know how much it is or where it's being spent. According to Gartner, "In most instances, the chief information security officer (CISO) does not have insight into security spending throughout the enterprise." (Source: https://www.gartner.com/newsroom/id/3539117)

Is it too far-fetched to say, "No budget, no commitment?" Probably, but there is a correlation between an organization's commitment to something and how much it's willing to pay. If information security priorities are set in a budget, it at least shows that the information security is top of mind.

How much should we spend on information security? The answer is always "it depends." We found that most companies don't have a dedicated information security budget. Others spend a given percentage of their information technology (IT) budget on information security. There is no consensus on what the appropriate percentage should be, however.

If you have a dedicated information security budget, then congratulations! You know that you are the exception, right?

Regardless of budget, we know that organizations are spending more money than ever on information security. Some experts predict that worldwide information security spending will increase by 12 to 15 percent year over year through 2021. (Source: https://www.csoonline.com/article/3083798/security/cybersecurity-spending-outlook-1-trillion-from-2017-to-2021.html). Gartner predicts $93 billion will be spent in 2018 (Source: https://www.gartner.com/newsroom/id/3784965), and worldwide information security spending is expected to exceed $124 billion in 2019. (Source: https://www.gartner.com/en/newsroom/press-releases/2018-08-15-gartner-forecasts-worldwide-information-security-spending-to-exceed-124-billion-in-2019) We have increased our spending on information security, which begs two additional questions:

1. Is it enough?

2. Is it well spent?

Enough Money

One study says organizations spend an average of 5.6 percent of their overall IT budget on information security. That ranged from 1 percent on the low end and 13 percent on the high end. (Source: https://www.gartner.com/newsroom/id/3539117)

Another study found the overall median budget for information security was projected to be between 7 percent and 9 percent in fiscal year 2016. (Source: https://www.sans.org/reading-room/whitepapers/analyst/security-spending-trends-36697) Smaller companies appear to spend slightly less (6 to 7 percent) than larger companies do (7 to 9 percent).

Information security spending is increasing everywhere in our industry. For example, 81 percent of US health-care organizations and 76 percent of global health-care organizations were estimated to increase information security spending in 2017. (Source: https://www.thalesesecurity.com/about-us/newsroom/news-releases/2017-thales-healthcare-data-threat-report-organizations-spending) And 86 percent of financial services firms were expected to increase their information security spending in 2017. (Source: https://www.esecurityplanet.com/network-security/86-percent-of-financial-services-firms-to-increase-cyber-security-spend-in-2017.html) Globally, the market couldn't be much hotter for increased spending, with some estimates of 10 to 15 percent annually, year over year.

Is your information security budget sufficient? The answer for most organizations is that they don't know. If you're one of the few with a dedicated information security budget and a solid logical answer to this question, you're better off than the rest of us!

Assuming we've answered whether we're spending enough money on information security, the next logical question is are we spending it well?

Money Well Spent

Where we spend our information security dollar does not always (or often) align with where we *should* spend our next information security dollar.

A recent example comes from working with a multibillion-dollar, multinational organization. We were discussing its information security program, and just talking shop one day. The topic of vendor risk management came up, and we started to discuss some of the news articles we'd both read that claimed that more that 60 percent of all data breaches are caused by third parties, directly or indirectly. Naturally the conversation turned to what this company was doing with vendor risk management. Turns out that it employs roughly three thousand vendors and does its best to do risk assessments with two full-time staff members. I was amazed.

"You are able to assess all three thousand vendors using two full-time employees?" I asked.

"No, we probably get to assessing about eighty of them each year."

"You'll never make it through all of them at this pace. Something doesn't seem right."

"We have only a $185,000 budget for vendor risk management, so it's the best we can do."

OK. It's obvious that vendor information security risk management is a glaring hole in this company's information security program, yet it has budgeted only $185,000 for it? Its information security budget overall was about $10 million.

Does this seem right to you?

We like to spend money on information security gadgets and easy buttons, regardless of what our most significant risk may be.

SOLUTION #2: PUTTING OUR MONEY WHERE OUR MOUTH IS

A dedicated information security budget goes beyond just spending money and can go a long way toward backing up our commitment, because it shows that information security is important enough in the highest levels of the organization to warrant dedicated financial consideration.

A dedicated information security budget is also evidence that the organization is properly tracking its commitment.

> Create, approve, and manage information security expenditures according to a dedicated information security budget.

Many organizations simply do not know their security budget, partly because few cost accounting systems break out security as a separate line item, and many security-relevant processes are carried out by staff who are not devoted full-time to security, making it impossible to account accurately for security personnel. In most instances, the chief information security officer (CISO) does not have insight into security spending throughout the enterprise. (Source: https://www.gartner.com/newsroom/id/3539117)

It's true that many things in information security cost money, but there are many things that don't. Of the things that do cost money, make sure that you're spending your money wisely (we'll cover this more in the next chapter). For now, establish an information security budget and spend your information security dollars where they help the most. They help the most where they address the unacceptable risks the most. Don't know where that is? Go back to the basic information security risk-assessment and treatment plan that we've covered several times in this book.

PROBLEM #3: THINKING OBSCURITY MAKES US SECURE

Here's the truth: security through obscurity isn't security at all.

Using obscurity as an excuse is false logic. If you've been around long enough, you've heard excuses like these:

- We're too small for anyone to notice or care.

- We don't have any information that anyone would care about.

- Who would want to hack us anyway?

This sort of logic would lead us to believe that nobody would ever care about an HVAC vendor located in Sharpsburg, Pennsylvania. There's nothing interesting about a full-service mechanical contracting company specializing in the design, engineering, installation, and service of supermarket and convenience store refrigeration and HVAC systems. What's so interesting about this company that would attract the attention of an attacker? They don't process large amounts of sensitive information like health records or private data.

We've inherently known for quite some time that security through obscurity is no security at all, even before this company, Fazio Mechanical, became famous when it was found to be the early weak link in the Target breach. The Target breach is one of the most publicized breaches of all time, and after such instant fame, you'd think that obscurity logic would have been thrown out the window. Unfortunately, it wasn't. This false logic is still alive and well today. Here are some examples from just a few weeks in my small corner of the world.

- An entire county in Minnesota was taken off-line from a series of malware infections.

- A food services company was infected by ransomware—not once, but three times.

- A distribution company lost over $800,000 in payment fraud.

We're all connected, and everything has value to somebody. Organizations that use obscurity as a reason to pooh-pooh information security make themselves easy targets for financial fraud, ransomware, pivot attacks, and more.

In the United Kingdom, two-thirds of small businesses don't think that they're vulnerable to cybercrime. (Source: https://www.gov.uk/government/news/cyber-security-myths-putting-a-third-of-sme-revenue-at-risk) The sad fact is that these businesses are more targeted today than large businesses, because the return on an attacker's investment is higher; it's easy money. There are more troubling statistics related to small- to medium-sized business, including:

- 60 percent of small businesses that suffer a breach are likely to go out of business within six months.

- In 2016, more than 14 million companies in the United States suffered a breach.

- Counter to the logic in the first two statistics, more than half of small- and medium-sized business leaders are convinced that their business is *not* a target.

Source: https://cdn2.hubspot.net/hubfs/1747499/ Content%20Downloads/Switchfast_SMB_ Cybersecurity_Report.pdf

You may think that the obscurity (false) logic is reserved for small companies, but it's not. While doing work for a very large bank, I had the opportunity to sit in on the CISO's information security team meeting. The meeting was held in a large auditorium, because his team was so large. He made one comment that really stood out to me. He said, "We only need to be more secure than the next guy, the other banks. We don't need to do anything more than that. If we don't unnecessarily draw attention to ourselves and make ourselves a target, we'll be fine."

What?! Did he just say that?

Not only did he say it, but he meant it too. He must have forgotten that a bank has the one thing that everyone wants: money. Secondly, he falsely implied that we need to protect only from the opportunists that happen to stumble upon us. Just fly under the radar and they'll go after the other guys instead.

SOLUTION #3: TAKING OUR HEAD OUT OF THE SAND

Every single organization is a target, no matter how big, no matter how small, no matter where, and no matter what industry. This is the reality.

Granted, no two information security programs look the same. Yet every organization must have an information security program based upon our common definition of *information security* and *risk management*.

> Every organization requires an information security program based upon the definitions of *information security* and *risk management*.

Ignorance of the information security challenges facing an organization is not a defensible position for board members and/or executive leadership. Some of the companies that have had their head in the sand are learning this lesson the hard way, maybe not as much in terms of legal liability, but certainly in terms of lost customers and lost dollars.

Ignorance, either normal or willful, is quickly becoming unethical and contrary to the strategic, legal, and fiduciary responsibilities to shareholders, customers, and employees that board members assume.

9

The Money Grab

" A business that makes nothing but money is a poor business."

–Henry Ford

The information security industry is broken because money is more important than your security. The information security market has never been hotter or more exciting. New companies, innovative products, and massive investments are entering the market every day. Not only is worldwide spending on information security products and services expected to exceed $124 billion in 2019, but mergers and acquisitions (M&A) activity is at a frenzy too, with dozens of significant transactions every month. Check this out: Cybersecurity Ventures predicts that $1 trillion will be spent globally on information security between 2017 and 2021. That's $1,000,000,000,000!

In general, this bodes well for the industry, as executives recognize the value of information security and raise budgets accordingly. A lot of good can come from this.

At the same time, such a huge transfer of wealth brings out the money-grubbers. These people are in it only for the money, and they will cross ethical lines to get a piece of the pie. Some of the things they'll do are downright

205

fraudulent. They are not interested in what is best for the information security industry or the businesses they purport to protect. The money-grubbers are focused only on the almighty dollar, and the dollars they want are yours.

> Have a computer and a website? It's all you need to become an information security "expert" overnight.

These days, anyone and everyone can enter the game with a few bucks, a website, and a computer. Experience and skills are optional. Besides, who's going to know anyway? Not the customers.

People in our market don't need experience or skill to make a ton of money. The result is a market flooded with unscrupulous salespeople and products and services that won't work as promised or are vastly overpriced. Some of these products and services will be financially successful, making millions and millions of dollars—which is not an indication that they actually work.

Knowing that not all the new products and services entering the market are truly innovative or brilliant brings confusion and uncertainty to the buyers. Too many of us will be sucked into the hype and fooled into buying a product or service that does more harm than good. We'll invest in things that don't fit with our most significant risks, leading to a waste of our hard-earned information security dollars. It can be intimidating to sort through the offerings to find the products and services that actually help us and are fairly priced.

Problems covered in this chapter include:
- Problem #1: There's plenty of snake oil for sale.
- Problem #2: Fear and sex sell lots of stuff.
- Problem #3: Money spent poorly is bad money.

Some of the potential solutions we'll explore include:
- Solution #1: Do your homework.
- Solution #2: Fight FUD and be a little less sexy.
- Solution #3: Buy what you need.

It seems there are never enough information security dollars to do all the things we want (or need) to do. Information security dollars are precious, so we must spend them wisely.

PROBLEM #1: THERE'S PLENTY OF SNAKE OIL FOR SALE

Take this, and it'll cure what ails you. Buy this, and it'll make you more secure.

Clark Stanley developed and sold his Snake Oil Liniment in the late nineteenth and early twentieth centuries. He claimed that his amazing concoction provided immediate relief for a vast array of maladies, from rheumatism to insect bites. People believed his incredible claims, and Stanley made a lot of money. His rattlesnakes and Snake Oil Liniment were hit attractions at the 1893 World's Fair, the Columbian Exposition in Chicago.

Finally, Stanley was taken to court, and in 1917 experts examined his oil. They found that Snake Oil Liniment didn't cure anything, and it didn't even contain any snake oil. It turned out to be mineral oil spiced up with various additives, including red pepper and turpentine. From then on, the term *snake oil* referred to any idea, product, or service that made big promises but was actually worthless.

Inevitably, a portion of the $96 billion dollars spent this year on information security will go to snake oil. Along with a new ransomware strain, or zero-day attack, our biggest fear should be our vendors selling us stuff that we don't need.

Sometimes the product or service itself is suspect, but more commonly it's the marketing used to sell us the product or service that leaves us misinformed, confused, and less secure.

Commercialization Everywhere

Not enough of us are in it to win it anymore; we're in it to make a ton of money. Money ain't all that bad, but it is bad if we've sold out.

Do you remember when information security conferences were more about information security than they were about selling things to us? Some security conferences have sold out to the money gods. Vendors flock to them because this is where the buyers are.

RSA and Black Hat USA are arguably the most attended and followed information security conferences in the world. RSA has been running for more than twenty-five years and attracts tens of thousands of attendees. Black Hat has been around for more than twenty years and attracts thousands of attendees too. The first Black Hat conference that I attended was an amazing experience where attendees had

---

Snake oil in our industry takes on different forms:

- **Products and services that claim to do something, but don't:** "We can predict your next breach with 90 percent certainty," "Our product is guaranteed to prevent ransomware," and "Our product provides your company with absolute security" are all claims that are either snake oil or need serious validation. Most likely they're snake oil.

- **Products and services full of buzzwords and features that are hard, if not impossible, to validate:** "Our NextGen firewall does a synchronous deep dive inspection of your data flow, then leverages our proprietary hivemind architecture built on big data analytics and artificial intelligence to identify threats in real time."

- **Products that are sold to address a need you don't have, or one you didn't know you had:** There's a fine line between an objective recommendation for a product or service and being sold something you don't need.

- **Products and services that are sold under the premise that they're easy to use but are far from it:** Part of the problem is buying into the sales hype, part of the problem is overestimating our capabilities, and part of the problem is underestimating our constraints (time, people, and/or money).

Figure: This figure shows many of the corporate sponsors of a Black Hat conference.

the opportunity to learn from one another. The conference really was about security, and a few sponsors were necessary to offset some of the costs associated with putting on a high-quality event.

Sadly, when we attend RSA or Black Hat now, we're inundated with marketing hype and pressure to buy things. The conferences have become less about learning and more about making money. The first Black Hat conference was in 1997, and only a handful of sponsors were present. The cost was . . . I don't know . . . was there a cost to attend? The roster of speakers was amazing, and we learned from some of the industry's pioneers.

Black Hat was acquired by CMP Media in 2005, and today's conference is quite a spectacle. There were more than 330 sponsors of the 2017 conference. Sponsorship packages include Diamond, Platinum Plus, Platinum, Gold Plus, Gold, Silver Plus, Silver, and a variety of "startup" packages for things like Innovation City, Career Zone, Lounges, and signage. In addition to all the sponsorship stuff, conference-goers are charged up to $2,795 to attend.

Our conferences are owned by the peddlers selling their wares and convincing too many people that their snake oil is the cure.

High-Tech Snake Oil

A CIO of a retail operation was intrigued by a vendor who mentioned a new product that used artificial intelligence (AI) to detect malicious traffic on a network. Such traffic is typically a prelude to a breach. The CIO asked some questions about AI, and the salesperson responded that using proprietary algorithms, the AI "engine" employs machine learning to gain an intimate understanding of the network. It "learns" the range of normal traffic, and anything different causes an alarm.

The salesperson used at least two hot terms in his pitch: "artificial intelligence" and "machine learning." Throughout the rest of the conversation, the salesperson continued to use buzzwords and spoke with confidence about the product. The CIO agreed to a demo and asked for a proposal. The demo was scheduled, and the proposal investment was $140,000. Once the CIO saw the price tag, she thought that it might make sense to get a second opinion.

She reached out to her information security consultant to vet the sales pitch, the product, and the company. The consultant agreed, and a conference call was scheduled. During the conference call, the conversation quickly went into the technical details and the product's capabilities.

After hearing the pitch from the salesperson, the consultant asked what makes this "new" technology different than an anomaly-based intrusion prevention system, which had been around for ten years. The salesperson insisted that this new technology was not the same as an anomaly-based intrusion prevention system; it was an AI system that autonomously detects and responds to "cyberthreats."

It turns out the product was in fact an anomaly-based intrusion prevention system. A good one, but a spade is a spade. The company didn't want to use that in the description of their product. Instead it chose a cool name and used cool buzzwords like *AI* and *machine learning* to get attention. The CIO was wiser for the exercise, but too many other CIOs buy into the hype without understanding what they're really getting for their money.

The Utility Company

A utility company wanted to have a better view of the events occurring on its network and within the systems on its network. It asked around, and it discovered a seemingly perfect solution to its problem: security information and event management, or SIEM. SIEM is a popular solution, with the market expected to grow to nearly $6 billion by 2021. (Source: https://solutionsreview.com/security-information-event-management/ siem-market-growth-technavio/)

There are more than thirty vendors in the SIEM market, and the utility company was having difficulty determining which solution would be the best fit. It reached out to its information security consulting company, which also happened to sell SIEM products. It may seem like a conflict of interest to provide seemingly "objective" opinions to clients and sell them products that conveniently fit with that advice. Nevertheless, the utility company ended up paying more than $50,000 to the consultant for the SIEM product, with some additional cost for limited support.

Less than a week into the implementation, the utility company realized the implementation wasn't as straightforward as the demo made it appear. Configuration and tuning were time-consuming efforts, and the company was having trouble understanding how to interpret the reports. It paid the consultant an additional fee for these extra services, and it seemed like it was going to be OK. However, once the company's professional services contract had run out, it was apparent that it was going to need a full-time person to manage the solution.

The utility company struggled with the SIEM solution for a few more months before it determined the situation wasn't worth hiring a full-time employee. It began to look for something different to solve the problem of visibility, deciphering incidents from events, and incident response.

The company decided to consider a managed detection and response (MDR) solution, a way to monitor threats that have bypassed other controls. The company was reluctant to use the same consultant that got it to buy the SIEM solution, so it reached out to another consulting company. This one did not sell any products, so there would be no conflict of interest.

The consultant asked the obvious question: "Why are you interested in an MDR solution?" The company replied, "We tried SIEM and found that it wasn't satisfying our needs, so now we're looking for an MDR solution." The consultant then inquired, "What needs did your SIEM not satisfy?" It soon became apparent that this well-run utility company was likely to repeat the mistake with MDR that it had made with SIEM. All told, the company spent almost $75,000 on its significantly underutilized SIEM solution, and now it was thinking about ditching SIEM for MDR. If it didn't make a wise MDR purchasing decision, it could very well waste even more money.

There's a good ending to this one, though. The company did its research and selected a great solution.

Snake Oil Doesn't Solve Information Security Problems

The trouble with snake oil is that it is deceptive. While you think it will fix problems, it ends up causing other problems:

1. Snake oil lulls you into a false sense of security.

2. Snake oil can bring additional complexity that compounds other problems. Remember, complexity is the enemy of security.

3. Snake oil siphons funds away from more productive information security investments.

We're all susceptible to snake oil hype; that's why it's so popular and effective at selling things. Some of the things we need, and some we don't. Buyer beware!

SOLUTION #1: DO YOUR HOMEWORK

Snake oil doesn't cure anything. Before you buy a cure, figure out if you're even sick. If you are sick, figure out the ailment first. Buy cures for the ailments (risks) and make sure that they'll actually work.

Risk is the most common, and arguably the most important, justification for information security expenditures or purchases. We purchase products and services to reduce risk, and we use our risk-treatment plan (or road map) to justify our budget. This approach, while not as popular as it should be, is the correct approach, and it takes some of the pressure off. If the risk decisions (accept, mitigate, transfer, avoid) are made by the business (nonsecurity executives, CEO, board, and so on), then our information security budget decisions are shared.

If we have a budget, we simply spend according to our budget. We'll cover some ideas about what to do if we don't have a budget a little later.

Budgeted Expenses

Our budget may tell us what type of control we need to purchase, but it may not tell us what specific product or service to purchase. The specifics require research and homework. If we've already done our research and homework for the budget, then it's easy: just execute on the budget plan. Research and homework keep us from buying snake oil. Unfortunately, conducting proper research and doing homework takes time and effort.

Doing research by just going out to the market and making calls to various companies isn't enough. This opens the door to the marketing hype, which could easily cloud our judgement and lead us to make poor purchasing decisions.

Companies like Gartner and Forrester will do *some* of the research for us. And while these are good resources for general research, they don't provide enough specific detail to fit our specific situation. We're still going to have to put in our own work.

Let's say that our budget calls for an MDR solution. The purchase of an MDR solution has been justified, but we don't know which one of the thirty or so possible solutions would be best for us. There are thousands of ways to conduct the proper research. Here's one that I've worked through numerous times before.

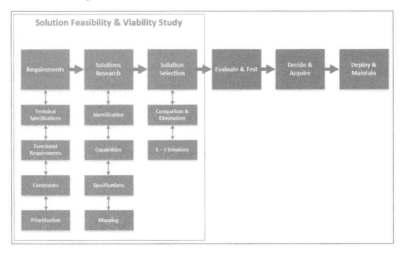

The process starts with defining our own specific requirements for the solution. Before we look to what products can do, we start with what we need the products to do. We determine what the technical and functional requirements are for the MDR solution, what our constraints are (current and planned business processes, time, money, people, and so forth), and prioritize our needs based on the organization's objectives. We can also include features in our evaluation, including things that would be nice to have but aren't necessarily showstoppers. Implementing some sort of scoring mechanism into the process helps make things more objective along the way.

Sometimes it makes sense for a single person to work through the process, and sometimes it makes sense to use a team of interested persons. Questionnaires with ranked characteristics work well for prioritizing requirements and preferences in teams. If we rank the requirements according to criteria such as "must have," "nice to have," and "not important," then we can score them more easily.

The second part of the process is where we do market research, looking for potentially viable solutions, determining various solution features and capabilities, and mapping the capabilities to our requirements. We may need to reach out to the vendor or solution providers to get the answers we need; using a request for information (RFI) form can work well. An RFI works well because it forces all the vendors to answer specific questions in the same manner. This will help us evaluate the vendors and solution providers on a level playing field. Multiple rounds of RFIs may be necessary to complete our research. We can do what we want with vendors and service providers who don't reply to our RFIs. My preference is to eliminate them from contention, because a non-response may be a sign of how interactive they will be during or after our purchasing decision.

Good vendors who make good products will be transparent about their products' capabilities and shortcomings. They will share openly what resources will be required for us to operate their product in our environments, and they'll be happy to teach us how to get the most out of our investment. A common mistake is to not account for all costs, both hard costs (dollars out the door) and soft costs (the overhead related to installing and maintaining the solution). We need to know if a solution will require additional staffing and to account for this in our purchasing decision.

Some people put a big emphasis on customer references. It's a good idea for us to include them in our research; however, we should realize that customer references are often handpicked by the vendor or solution provider. The feedback we get from a handpicked customer reference is more likely to be biased.

Through all this, we've ideally reduced the number of potential vendors from thirty to three or fewer. This is when it makes the most sense to engage on a more personal level through phone calls, in-person meetings, and/or demos.

This is only an example process, but it is one in which we can protect ourselves from buying products and services that won't fit, and it gives us the ability to defend our purchasing decisions when the bean counters come asking.

Here's a simplified version of the process:

1. Establish specific needs and wants.
2. Conduct research.
3. Choose one to three contenders.
4. Engage vendors.
5. Purchase a product or service.

Customers should flesh out what problem they're trying to fix with as much specificity as possible instead of simply wandering into the security market without a goal. Reaching out to potential vendors first, which is the most common approach, is less likely to result in a good purchasing decision.

Off-Budget Expenses

Throughout the year, we are all bombarded with sales calls from organizations who sell some neat things. We also come across seemingly cool products and services that look like they might fit a need that we know we have, or a need that we didn't even know we had. To ignore these influences may lead us to believe that we're missing out on something. Off-budget expenses happen from time to time, but they obviously shouldn't be the norm.

Entertaining the ideas of new products and services is generally good when it's kept in check. We can learn a lot from some sales presentations and demonstrations of new things. Despite the coolness of new things, we must remember our original motivation, which I hope is to manage risk.

Before making any decisions, we should ask ourselves two questions:

1. **Does this product or service address risks that we already know about and that are already accounted for in our risk-management process?**
   If so, what were the risk decisions and what are their assigned priorities? If the risk decisions were anything other

than remediate/mitigate, then we might have a problem that needs to be reconciled first. Another alternative could be that we adjust our road map to account for new information we've learned and proceed this way.

2. **Does this product or service address risks that we didn't know about and aren't accounted for in our risk-management process?** If so, and the risks are legitimate (in our sole or collective opinion), then this could be good information to incorporate into our next risk assessment, or we could conduct a spot risk assessment now. The decision to proceed should then be deferred until a risk assessment is completed.

Obviously, off-budget expenses should receive additional scrutiny and should be avoided when possible.

The point is to use more logic and less emotion in our information security purchasing decisions. We can't eliminate the emotional component altogether, but we can keep its influence in check.

PROBLEM #2: FEAR AND SEX SELL LOTS OF STUFF

> **"** If you're told that cybersecurity attacks are purported by winged ninja cyber monkeys who sit in a foreign country, who can compromise your machine just by thinking about it, you're going to have a fear response. And that's where we are today. The security companies are incentivized to make it sound as scary as possible because they want you to buy their magic amulets. **"**
>
> –Dr. Ian Levy, Technical Director at the National Cyber Security Center (NCSC)

Companies sell billions of dollars' worth of products, and all too often they play on your fear, uncertainty, and doubt (FUD). A typical FUD strategy is to pick scary-sounding headlines to evoke the desired fear-related emotions. Even fake headlines work, like the *Washington Post* article in December 2016 that read "Russian hackers penetrated US electricity grid through a utility in Vermont, US officials say." This was a fake news article that was cited by salespeople immediately after it was published. (Source: https://www.forbes.com/sites/kalevlee-taru/2017/01/01/fake-news-and-how-the-washington-post-rewrote-its-story-on-russian-hacking-of-the-power-grid/#25bfb6ed7ad5).

There's a big difference between raising awareness by disseminating news and instilling fear. A reporter isn't trying to scare you by writing a scary news article—unless it is for a tabloid magazine—but a sales-person who uses the article is most definitely trying to appeal to your sense of fear.

Take the 2017 news of the DoublePulsar exploitation targeting unpatched Windows systems. This was a hyped-up event that was a great opportunity for vendors to use FUD.

Interesting!
new scan suggests ~25% of all vulnerable smb machines publicy exposed are currently infected.

expect more bloodbath. pic.twitter.com/2rR4Yyhxtc

— April 24, 2017

Figure: An April 2017 tweet re: use of the leaked NSA tool DoublePulsar to infect internet-exposed Windows systems

I'm using this Twitter post about the leaked NSA tool as an example. The intent of the person's tweet may well have been to raise urgent aware-ness of a legitimate threat. But then he used a key fearmongering phrase: "expect more bloodbath." Bloodbath is a gory word that doesn't often pop up in everyday conversation. It's a metaphor for a mass slaughter that results in a thick gush of blood. It is a very alarming word, and it's an extreme exaggeration to use it to describe the DoublePulsar threat.

The tweet said, "~25% of all vulnerable smb machines publicly exposed" to the threat.

I have three comments about this:

1. Is it news that if you have SMB open to the internet, your system is prone to attack? Server Message Block is a file-sharing protocol intended for use only on internal networks. You're asking for it from the get go if it is open to the internet— regardless of DoublePulsar. *Don't* allow SMB from the internet!

2. The word *vulnerable* is a pretty important word. Running SMB on the internet without the latest patches is a certain compromise, regardless of DoublePulsar.

3. How many systems are we talking about with "~25% of all vulnerable systems"? If it's a "bloodbath," it must be millions, right? No, the number of systems is much, much fewer than that. According to one researcher, there were an estimated 183,107 systems infected as of the day of the post. According to some conservative estimates, there are about seven billion devices connected to the internet. So, we're basically saying that the infection of 0.0026 percent of the systems connected to the internet is a bloodbath. In context, this isn't a bloobath at all.

I get that DoublePulsar was/is a big deal, and I get that MS17-010 is a very important Microsoft bulletin/patch, but when we put it into perspective, it's not as bad as it seems. Patch your systems, ensure that your vendors are patching their systems, close SMB to/from the internet, and relax. A sure sign of a FUD-related sell is the exaggeration of the problem (vulnerability, threat, risk, and so on) without proper context. The events created by the DoublePulsar news was a goldmine for security companies who were selling you stuff.

FUD sells. Unfortunately, too many of us are buying.

Sex

Advertisers have known for more than a hundred years that sex sells, but how does this apply to the information security industry? Can you imagine a billboard with Justin Bieber, dressed in nothing but his briefs, holding a firewall? I can't. That's because we have a slightly different interpretation of the word *sexy* in our industry. Sexy might be a sleek-looking appliance or a slick program. Sexy might be some of the more mysterious or seemingly glamorous things we do like hacking, penetration testing, or social engineering.

Normal people outside our industry have their own views about what they consider to be sexy in the field of information security. I once spoke to a group of graduate students at a local university about the outlook for the information security industry and meeting the challenges related to our skills shortage. Nobody in the discussion wanted to talk about how we need a basic set of skills to start with; everybody wanted to talk about hacking and the latest sensational headline.

Here are some sexy things in the information security industry:

- cool new gadgets

- sleek-looking appliances

- new features that do cool things

- neat buzzwords like AI, *hivemind*, and *machine learning*

- thrilling and seemingly mysterious things like research, threat hunting, forensics, the dark web, zero-day exploits, social engineering, and penetration testing

When I do interviews with local television hosts, they always ask for advice for the people at home. But when my answers aren't sexy enough, they push for more. For instance, they ask, "What can people do to protect themselves from the Target breach?" I reply, "They should review their financial accounts on a consistent basis and prepare for events like this in the future. They should have multiple credit cards but save one or two for an event where your primary card is compromised." They ask incredulously, "That's it?!" They really wanted something a little more sensational.

When I tell normal people that I work in information security, most of them immediately assume that I have some sort of superpower. They say something like "Oh, wow! You must be busy nowadays with everything that's going on. So, do you like, hack the hackers or something?" I am often tempted to say, "Yes, I hack the hackers, tirelessly, day and night. I fight for the good citizens of this city! I use my superpowers to fight for good, defeat the evil cybervillains, and save the world. I also use my superpowers to change clocks in vehicles, program DVRs, and fix microwave ovens!"

The nonsexy things in our industry are viewed by many to be mundane and boring: policies, procedures, asset-management processes, change control, and the like. The fact, though, is that these boring things are essential to information security, and they help form our foundation. Yet we're constantly tempted by sexy purchases of products and services to make us feel cool and with it, which can give the false impression that we've got information security under control. If we're relying too heavily on sexy things, especially at the expense of utility, then we don't have information security under control.

Stop being impressed with sexy things and get to work on the necessary things.

SOLUTION #2: FIGHT FUD AND BE A LITTLE LESS SEXY

There are two different sets of motivations and emotions behind FUD and sexy stuff. FUD uses our fear or uncertainty of the unknown to motivate and influence us to do certain things. Sex (or sexiness) as a motivator in our industry is more closely related to the things we previously covered in chapter 3, "Lipstick on a Pig."

What fear and sex have in common is that they are both emotional approaches to information security. If we are to use our brains instead of our feelings, the most important justification for information security expenditures is risk. We quite rightly purchase products and services to reduce risk, and we use our risk-treatment plan to justify our budget. This approach, while not as popular as it should be, is the correct approach.

Fight FUD

If there's one thing that FUD takes advantage of, it's ignorance. Ignorance is simply the lack of knowledge or information. FUD is great for selling things to the uneducated masses. The keys to fighting FUD are to educate yourself, gain experience, and exercise discernment.

Educate

Education comes in various forms: online forums, published articles, training (paid and free), seminars, degree programs, and several other options. There is no shortage of education opportunities in this industry, if you just look for them and spend time using them.

If you don't want to become more educated, at least find someone who does and who doesn't have an ulterior motive.

Experience

Experience can't be rushed. It comes with time. Recognize your own experiential limitations. (Be honest.) If you lack experience, find someone who has it, but again be careful with ulterior motives.

Discernment

If you apply education and experience correctly, you can increase your ability to discern FUD selling. My favorite tool for discernment is logic, but I've learned that logic isn't necessarily a universal gift.

(BONUS) Trusted Advisors

Trusted advisors can be hard to find, because it seems that so many of us have a motive of some sort. Trusted advisors must have a solid (and, we hope, long) track record of good, honest, and helpful advice.

Fight fear, uncertainty, and doubt, or FUD. FUD is great for selling things, but not so great for buying things. Combat FUD in all purchasing decisions by using facts.

PROBLEM #3: MONEY SPENT POORLY IS BAD MONEY

"The outgoing Obama administration has proposed increasing federal cyber-security spending by $5bn, or around a third, in the hope of reaching $19bn in 2017." (Source: https://www.theregister.co.uk/2016/02/09/us_gov_security_spending_hike/)

"J. P. Morgan is going to spend a half-billion dollars on security this year." (Source: https://www.forbes.com/sites/stevemorgan/2016/01/30/why-j-p-morgan-chase-co-is-spending-a-half-billion-dollars-on-cybersecurity/#5fffbf9e2599)

"The UK government has announced a £1.9bn increase in spending on cyber-security." (Source: http://www.computerweekly.com/news/450402098/UK-government-re-announces-19bn-cyber-security-spend)

Organizations enjoy touting how much they spend on information security and how much they plan to increase it. It is a good thing for governments and other organizations to demonstrate such strong financial commitments to information security, but there should be accountability surrounding how the money is spent. It is a pipe dream to simply take the amount of money spent and equate it directly to results. They are two different things. Commitment does not equal results—without direction and an understanding of what we're doing.

Three examples come to mind:

1. Target
2. midsize company
3. personal

Target

The 2013 breach was not the first breach that Target had encountered. The retail giant had spent plenty of money on information security before the breach, acquiring some of the best technology available at the time. But these investments did not adequately take into account the problem of vendor risk, or the problems related to process and

223

communication deficiencies. They did not adequately account for weak authentication for vendor access, network segmentation/isolation, or password management either. Of course, hindsight is 20/20. Who could have known that an HVAC vendor would be Target's Achilles' heel?

Soon after the breach, Target started sending questionnaires to many of its vendors to address vendor risk. It had not been much of an issue until the breach. Target definitely took information security seriously, but we can question whether information security dollars were well spent.

Midsize Company

A few years ago, the folks at a midsize company in Los Angeles wanted to discuss what to do about their information security program, now that their CISO had left the company. They were quite proud of their current information security program, telling me that they spent more than $2 million the previous year on "state-of-the-art" information security protections.

"That's great!" I said. "How much did you reduce your risk?"

The room filled with awkward silence. The smiles on the faces of the CFO and CIO were gone in an instant. They didn't have an answer.

Personal

Have you ever heard of shelfware? It's the hardware and software you buy with the greatest of intentions but end up not using, or not using correctly. I'm not proud to admit that I've bought my share of shelfware over the years.

I'm still haunted by my experience at MGI Pharma, one of my favorite jobs. I worked with great people, and loved the company's mission: to discover, develop, and commercialize pharmaceutical products for oncology and acute care applications.

My role was to build and maintain a best-in-class information security program that protected and enabled the company's mission. I had a perfect recipe for success: plenty of trust, executive management endorsement, and funding. Although money wasn't really a constraint for me, I strove to get the most out of every dollar that I spent, because I knew that one wasted dollar on information security meant one less dollar spent on helping someone struggling with cancer.

One year, I bought into the hype surrounding network access control (NAC). It was a newer technology at the time, with impressive potential. I was sold, and it cost only $120,000 (tongue in cheek). We plugged in the appliance and performed the initial configuration. Our team then got pulled into some other projects. We weren't done with the NAC. We needed to configure it more. Then we need to configure it some more. Then we needed to tweak it. Then we needed to watch it. Then we needed to configure it some more. Then we left it alone. Then we gave up and went to work on higher-priority things. What we ended up with was shelfware. Nice blinky lights, but nothing more.

Every misspent dollar on information security is a dollar the organization could have spent on furthering its mission. It might sound extreme, but it felt as if we'd robbed $120,000 from the company's mission.

Effort

Purchasing products and services can make our lives easier. This is good. The purchase of products and services can also hide laziness, and this is a bad thing. Tools, products, and services should complement our efforts, and should never replace them. There's a fine line between using products to make ourselves better information security professionals and using them to mask the fact that we're lax information security professionals.

Low Price

The lowest-price option might not be our best option.

So, an organization needs a penetration test. It doesn't necessarily want to do the test, but its regulator says it needs to. The organization is

EVAN FRANCEN

new to this and not entirely sure what a penetration test is or how to get one, so a staff member decides to consult Google. It's where most of us go in these situations. The staffer Googles *penetration test*, and the search engine returns more than ten million results. That's about 9,999,990 more results than hoped for.

The staffer figures that any security consulting company would know what a penetration test is, searches for *information security consultant*, and gets more than nine million results. So he goes to plan B, checking with his professional network.

He starts asking professional friends who they're using and what their experiences have been. One friend recommends a particular national company. The staffer reaches out to this referral and tells the company that his organization needs a penetration test. After some discussions, he feels more educated about penetration testing, and the company submits a proposal for $15,000. This is much more than he expected, and he's disappointed. The organization doesn't have this money budgeted.

There's got to be a cheaper option. The staffer continues talking to people in his professional network. He receives another referral to another information security consulting company. He reaches out to the new referral and gets a proposal for $2,500. Great! Although this investment isn't budgeted either, this price is more palatable. He goes ahead and signs the proposal, and the work begins. He doesn't see much happening, and there really isn't much communication during the testing. A few weeks later, the consulting company sends him an email containing an attachment labelled "Penetration Test Report." He opens the attachment, and it contains loads of technical stuff he's never seen before. No matter—the organization now has its penetration test report to show the regulator next year.

This scenario plays out thousands of times each year, maybe even thousands of times each month. Is there anything wrong in this scenario? Well, one thing it shows is that the least expensive answer isn't often the best answer.

Another problem is the motivation for the test. The organization's purpose for seeking a penetration test was to appease the regulator, not to improve its information security program or reduce risk. (See chapter 7, "Because I Said So.") One of two things is likely to happen: either the regulator will be pleased and will accept the penetration test report as evidence that the organization did a test, or the regulator will not be pleased and will reject the penetration test report. Let's assume the latter scenario first.

The regulator arrives for the organization's next examination. She reviews all the information security documentation and her notes from last year's exam. She notices from her notes that she had asked the organization to perform a penetration test, so she asks about it. The staffer hands over the report, and she begins her review. Within five minutes, she stops her review, looks up at him, and states that the report isn't evidence of a penetration test. She says it's a vulnerability scan, not a penetration test. The organization's staff member is shocked and confused attempts to explain the company's position. The examiner goes on to explain more specifically what she was looking for, and the staffer soon realizes that he doesn't have a foot to stand on. This seems like a bad scenario, but I think the next one is worse.

The regulator asks for evidence of the penetration test, and the staff member hands over the "Penetration Test Report." The regulator takes a few moments to review the report, then moves on to the next thing on her list to review. Not another word is mentioned about penetration testing. The organization's employee is happy, because he believes he just received validation that the penetration test was a penetration test. He doesn't stop to think about it again, and it doesn't dawn on him that there must be a reason why one vendor quoted him five times the price of the other vendor.

The fact of the matter is: the lower-priced vendor may or may not have done a real penetration test. The decision wasn't based on this; it was based on price alone.

This kind of logic is far too common in our industry.

Low Price Illogic

Several years ago, we were one of seven companies to respond to a Colorado county request for proposal (RFP) for some standard information security work. A few months passed, and the county decided to go with one of the other six companies. RFPs are a funny animal, so we weren't too surprised or concerned.

A few days later, the county sent out the list of companies who had responded, along with their bids. This is a little uncommon, but we just figured it was a government transparency practice. We reviewed the list:

- Company A: $172,800
- Company B: $112,000
- Company C: $67,000
- Us: $62,000
- Company D: $59,600
- Company E: $28,000

The county chose Company E. We were surprised by two things. One was the fact that there was such a wide range of prices, and two, that they chose the lowest cost when it was so far out of range of the others. It would make more sense if the county made attempts to reconcile why the costs were so widely disparate.

Some information security work is commodity work, but most of it isn't. A low price doesn't mean it's the best fit for you. You get what you pay for.

SOLUTION #3: BUY WHAT YOU NEED

Would you rather spend $100 on something that fits a specific need, or set of needs, or spend $10 on something for the sake of spending $10 on something? The answer should be obvious.

There are three ways to justify information security expenditures:

1. They make us more money.
2. They offset losses.
3. They further the corporate mission.

They Make Us More Money

Some information security expenditures can make us more money by opening new opportunities for business, and/or they could become a market differentiator, setting us apart from our competition. An example could be an agreement from a large customer that if we implement certain controls, or if we earn a specific certification, we will win their business. These justifications for information security expenditures are the easiest to budget and get approval for.

They Offset Losses

The most common justification for information security investment is likely to be one where the expense is used to offset loss. The most significant losses (impact) should be joined with the most likely events (likelihood), meaning that our justification should be risk. The way to determine our most significant risks would be through conducting an information security risk assessment. If we've done things correctly, then our risk-treatment plan has been approved by the organization's executives, and it contains the disposition of all identified significant information security risks.

> Justify budget through a portrayal of how the investments will make the information security program better.

The risk decisions are to accept, mitigate/remediate, transfer (commonly via insurance), or avoid. The budget starts with all the risks that require mitigation/remediation. Remediation requires either re-engineering an existing control or implementing a new control. Ideally, our risks have been prioritized and ranked according to their riskiness.

Grouping risks according to their kind allows us to identify one potential control (or product or service) that could address multiple risks. For instance, one risk might be associated with the lack of mobile-device encryption and another risk might be associated

Figure: Credibility behind our scoring comes from objective criteria, things like yes/no, zero/one, and so on. This prevents gaming of the system and makes the score more representative of actual change.

with the lack of mobile-device remote wipe capabilities. One potential control, maybe a mobile-device management (MDM) solution, could address both risks.

When your mitigation efforts lower the likelihood of a risk, the risk score changes. For example, let's say the risk score was 602.17 on a scale of 300 to 850 before the budget year begins. If our budget is approved, the revised risk score could be 675.42 at the end of the year. Some organizations use a scale of 1 to 5, or a grading system of A to F. The use of these scales enables executive management and the board of directors to visualize and better understand the value of our risk-mitigation efforts.

They Further the Corporate Mission

This type of justification is more subjective and hard to quantify. One could argue that an information security investment that protects corporate assets will enable the organization to further the corporate mission; however, this is a vague justification that would be harder to defend. Any use of this type of justification is likely to be challenged (or it should be).

These five steps should keep us honest:

1. Establish an information security budget.

2. Justify every expense item in the budget.

3. Use the risks that require remediation for the best justifications.

4. Express the changes that are expected to be made in the security program, given an approved budget, in a manner that resonates with stakeholders.

5. Buy the things that are in our budget.

If it costs $100 to mitigate a risk (by purchasing, re-engineering, or replacing a control), then spend the $100 to mitigate the risk. If it costs $100 to mitigate the risk, don't spend $10 or $1,000 to mitigate the risk.

Simple, right?

10

Too ~~Many~~ Few Experts

Need an expert but can't find an expert. Found an expert but can't afford 'em.

The information security industry is broken because we have too many "experts" but not enough experts. We're confused as an industry. We're confused about what we're looking for in talent, what we need for talent, and what we even call ourselves. All this is happening amid a severe talent shortage.

The global talent problem in our industry is urgent. We're not in panic mode yet, but if we don't do something now, we will be. Unfortunately, some people in our industry don't see the talent shortage as a problem at all. They may think it feels good to be in high demand and command higher wages in return. This is a very selfish view, in my opinion. If you are one of these people, and your justification of the value you provide is based upon nothing more than the fact that there are so few of us, then you are part of the problem. The value we provide should be based upon what we can do for our employer, not how many of us there are.

232

Problems covered in this chapter include:

- Problem #1: We need more good people, but we don't know who they are.
- Problem #2: The severe talent shortage is painful and getting worse.

Here are some of the potential solutions we'll explore:

- Solution #1: Define what makes a good security person.
- Solution #2: Commit to the cause.

PROBLEM #1: WE NEED MORE GOOD PEOPLE, BUT WE DON'T KNOW WHO

Before we can search for good security talent, we need to determine what it means to be "good" security talent. If you're in the market for information security talent, you've got your work cut out for you. Job titles don't mean much, as evidenced from the eight hundred–plus job titles in our industry. What do matter are job responsibilities.

What specifically do we expect from a new information security hire? I posed a similar

Identity Crisis

Here are samples from 822 information security job titles, compiled by Lenny Zeltser and John Hoyt. (Source: https://zeltser.com/information-security-job-titles-popularity/)

These are the least common job titles:

- Senior Information Security Assurance Consultant
- Senior IT Security Operations Specialist
- Regional Information Security Analyst
- Principal Cyber Security Manager
- Chief Information Security Consultant
- Principal Information Assurance Officer
- Senior Information Security Risk Officer
- Information Security Assurance Analyst

These are the most common job titles:

- Chief Information Security Officer
- IT Security Engineer
- Information Assurance Analyst
- Security Systems Administrator
- Senior IT Security Consultant

question to CEOs when I asked them what their expectations are for a CISO or the person who leads their information security program. The most popular answer was "I expect them to keep us out of the news." Another popular answer was "I expect them to keep us safe." Answers like these aren't good enough.

Hire a good security person, assuming you know what one looks like.

This is a subject of much debate in our industry. Some people think that an information security or technology degree is mandatory. Others think that education doesn't really matter that much. Some require one or more certifications; some don't. Some even think that security-related certifications are a bad idea.

In the fallout from the Equifax breach, as we mentioned earlier, critics wagged their finger at the company's chief security officer, Susan Mauldin, for having a master's degree in—*gasp!*—music composition. Others rushed to her defense by stating that certain college degrees don't qualify or disqualify people for CISO roles.

So, do we as an industry know or not know what makes a good information security expert? If we don't know, then this is a problem.

Certification

There's been plenty of debate over the years about the value of information security certification. Some companies mandate certification, while others don't. I know there are many well-respected information security experts in our industry who have no certification whatsoever, and there are those with multiple certifications who are pure information novices posing as experts.

Most certifications require a specific number of study hours and a passing score on an exam. Some exams are an hour or so, and some can take as long as twenty-four hours (OSCP). Students learn through books, hands-on

A Partial List of Popular Certifications

- Certified Information Systems Security Professional (CISSP)
- Certified Information Security Manager (CISM)
- CompTIA Security+
- Certified Ethical Hacker (CEH)
- SANS GIAC Security Essentials Certification (GSEC)
- Systems Security Certified Practitioner (SSCP)
- Certified Information Systems Auditor (CISA)
- EC-Council Certified Security Analyst (ECSA)
- Cisco Certified Network Administrator Security (CCNA Security)
- CompTIA Advanced Security Practitioner (CASP)
- Offensive Security Certified Professional (OSCP)

exercises and labs, instructor-led lectures, and online recorded lectures.

Students need to choose their certification wisely, because it can get pretty expensive. It's not uncommon for people to foot the bill themselves because their company won't pay for it. The CISSP is the most common information certification in our industry, and the hard cost for attaining it can be $5,000 or more when you consider training, practice exams, and the certification itself.

The fact that there is still so much disagreement about the value of information security certification, and the fact that it's so expensive, are problems, especially when we consider our overall talent shortage.

Education

We are still feeling our way around how to properly educate information security professionals, but we intrinsically know that education is important. There are many ways to educate oneself, and an ever more popular course of action is to complete a college or university degree program.

The number of information security or cybersecurity degree programs has exploded in recent years. The options are seemingly endless for bachelor's degrees and master's degrees in this field. Some programs undoubtedly prepare people for a rewarding career in this industry, but not all of them are created equally.

I was curious about some of these issues, so I sat down with a professor in a well-respected cybersecurity master's program. My first question was straightforward: "What is your definition of information security?" "Well, Evan," the professor said, "I like to think of information security in terms of policy, authentication, and vulnerability management."

OK. The definition may be reasonable, but it isn't one that I've heard anywhere else in my twenty-five years of working in this industry. This was the beginning of our discussion, and it was obvious that we weren't on the same page throughout our visit. I couldn't help but wonder what things his students would have to unlearn, assuming we would hire one in the first place.

How much value should we put on education in our industry? One professor claims that there are thousands of $80,000-per-year entry-level jobs available to applicants who have nothing more than an undergraduate degree in computer science or computer engineering.

At the company I work for, the starting pay is much less than this professor's quoted figure. Then again, we don't value education quite as much in the absence of information security experience. The problem isn't the cybersecurity degree programs, per se; the problem is that we don't know how to use them well in our industry.

SOLUTION #1: DEFINE WHAT MAKES A GOOD SECURITY PERSON

What makes a good information security professional? We all have our opinions, obviously, but there must be some things that we can all agree on. When I ask this question, most people answer, "It depends." This is a great answer, in my opinion. There are common traits that make a good information security professional, and then there's the "it depends" part of the equation. Maybe if we combine these factors, we'll have a better answer for what makes a good information security professional.

Making a good information security professional is like baking a cake. A good one depends on who we're baking the cake for. There are two primary parts in making many cakes: the basic ingredients and the flavors we add to make our cake more special.

Basic ingredients

Ever made a perfect cake? We've made good cakes and even great cakes, but nobody's made the perfect cake. The same is true with information security professionals. We'll make some good ones and some great ones, but we won't make a perfect one.

There are many possible ingredients that we could put into a cake. Let's assume for our example that all cakes require flour, eggs, and sugar. The basic ingredients are not negotiable. Likewise, for making a security professional, there are three mandatory ingredients: intangibles, education, and experience. Different proportions of ingredients create different types of cakes and different types of security professionals.

Intangibles

These are the things we can't teach. Either you have them or you don't. Intangibles are the things that a person has that match with your culture and core values. They're things like integrity, honesty, dependability, gifts, and responsibility. Some people are more gifted at one thing than another. If a person is not inherently gifted in a discipline, it's going to be difficult to make them gifted.

For us, intangibles are nonnegotiable. Like flour in our cake.

Education

Education is the second basic ingredient for a good information security professional. It's the "book smarts" part of the job. Information security professionals need a foundational level of knowledge from which to apply their skills in a manner that allows them to gain experience. Education—college, books, certification courses, blog posts, presentations/talks, and news articles—is beautiful and feeds the mind with other creative thoughts. Education is an essential ingredient.

Education is also nonnegotiable—like the eggs in our cake. There are different types of education, and there are different types of eggs. College degree—free-range egg. Certification course—standard brown egg. You get the point. The type of education is not as important as the education itself. An egg is an egg, and education is education.

Experience

Experience is like the sugar in the cake.

Experience is the street smarts. We gain experience only by applying our knowledge. Some could argue that experience can also come through others, but I chalk that up to education. There's nothing like firsthand experience. We all start with zero experience and add more as we go. The cake just gets sweeter.

What makes a good information security professional is a combination of the intangibles, education, and experience. It's not one at the expense of the other. The basic ingredients work together.

The Flavor

Flavors like cocoa and vanilla help create a specialized cake. In information security, a specialist requires the same sort of special handling. Penetration testers are more technical and are great solvers of puzzles. Train them in these areas and get them some experience in these areas, and they'll excel. The same holds true for any specialization in any job.

Don't forget the basic ingredients, though! Adding vanilla to a crappy cake just makes a crappy cake that tastes like vanilla. Specializations in information security should be added to the basic ingredients. They're not replacements.

Figure: This graphic shows a map that helps organizations know they've got an optimal team.

Advice

We all have a role to play in information security, and we all have some assigned responsibilities. Instead of copying information security job postings, we should spend more time looking within our own environment and assignments. Develop job responsibilities that will improve the organization's risk in the best manner possible, given our resource constraints in alignment with the organization's mission. It's becoming more and more common to find organizations that have lost their way a little by hiring people who don't specifically fit the needs of the organization. This happens either because we hired the incorrect people to begin with, or because things have changed over time.

Occasionally, it makes sense to check where we're at. One way we can do this is through a security team optimization or security team alignment project in which we map things out, from the organization's mission down to the individual security professional, to reassure ourselves that we have the right butts in the right seats. The following diagram depicts what this looks like.

Job descriptions, roles, and responsibilities should be as specific as possible and should be tied to the organization's mission as directly as possible. These things help us justify our existence.

PROBLEM #2: THE SEVERE TALENT SHORTAGE IS PAINFUL AND GETTING WORSE

> " Unfortunately, the pipeline of security talent isn't where it needs to be to help curb the cybercrime epidemic. Until we can rectify the quality of education and training that our new cyberexperts receive, we will continue to be outpaced by the Black Hats. "
>
> –Robert Herjavec, CEO of the Herjavec Group, and star on the TV show *Shark Tank*

The talent shortage problem cannot be overstated. We simply don't have enough people to do our work. Our unemployment rate has been 0 percent since at least 2016, and it will be 0 percent well into the foreseeable future. There are more open seats than there are people to fill them. This is a significant problem for our industry.

The problem is expected to get much worse in the coming years. By 2021 we're expected to have between 1.9 million and 3.5 million empty information security seats. The talent shortage has led to an increased workload for all of us, and more than two-thirds of us claim that we're too busy to keep up with our own skills development and training. (Source: https://www.csoonline.com/article/3238745/security/cybersecurity-skills-shortage-creating-recruitment-chaos.html) Many of us are burning out. The problem affects each one of us personally, and it affects us all collectively, as an industry.

Supply and Demand

The demand for information security talent exceeds the supply of talent. The simple fix is to add to the supply by increasing training and experience, but we're not keeping up. Why is this? There doesn't seem to be any shortage of training options for people. The number of training, degree, and certification programs has exploded in recent years. Perhaps the problem is the availability of the *affordable* training.

Cybersecurity degree programs generate millions of dollars in tuition and fees for colleges and universities. A bachelor's degree in cybersecurity will cost somewhere between $20,000 and $60,000. (Source: https://www.onlineu.org/most-affordable-colleges/cyber-security-degrees) And this might get you an entry-level job.

Obviously, a master's degree will cost much more. But most people don't have $20,000 or more lying around, so students in these programs need to be funded through their employer, student loans, scholarships, or some other means. This is a significant financial investment for most people, and it is a hurdle that must be overcome. If we want the best possible chance of solving our talent shortage problem, we'll need to remove as many barriers as possible.

We need to increase the supply, because the demand is not going down anytime soon. On the contrary, we have an insatiable demand for information security talent. Increased automation could help reduce the demand for human interaction, but we've got a long way to go before that makes a dramatic effect.

Acquisition

Our talent shortage problem is making it more and more difficult for organizations to acquire good talent. This only makes sense. When supply doesn't keep pace with demand, price increases. Today, the average salary for one of us is about $94,000 a year. And that will rise significantly in the coming years. Our salaries are expected to increase by twice as much as normal people's salaries in 2018, 7 percent versus 3 percent. (Source: https://www.infosecurity-magazine.com/news/cybersecurity-salaries-to-increase/) This is good news for those of us who work in this industry, but not good news for the people trying to employ us.

Despite our arguably reasonable salaries today, some organizations are struggling with information security costs. The expected increase in talent acquisition costs just makes problems worse. We can't afford to increase costs at a rate that exceeds what organizations can afford and expect the trend to be sustainable over the long term.

"URGENT!" was the first word in a recent recruiting email I received. The head of a well-known information security consultancy was looking for a "Senior Cyber Security Executive." This executive would be operating at the Partner/Managing Director level, so it was truly a senior role. The salary? Wait for it. As much as $550,000 per year, plus bonus, equity stock, and benefits.

That's an example of how far salaries are rising in our industry. There are many companies that could benefit from the services provided by a resource like the one being recruited, but there are few who could afford it.

Retention

This voracious demand for information security professionals means that many of us are solicited by recruiters for other jobs almost constantly. In fact, more than 60 percent of information security leaders are being recruited at least once per week. (Source: https://www.csoon-line.com/article/3238745/security/cybersecurity-skills-shortage-creating-recruitment-chaos.html) The presence of so many tempting offers means that it is harder to retain information security professionals. Tick us off, and we might just decide to take one of these interviews and entertain the idea of leaving. There are numerous factors at play with respect to talent retention, including market factors, lack of a clearly defined career path, burnout, and our mental health.

Make a "Unicorn"

If we need someone to run our information security program, we have three options: hire an experienced professional in-house, grow someone to become our in-house information security professional, or outsource to an independent consultant. Let's assume that outsourcing seems less appealing to us for some reason, and hiring an experienced professional is too expensive, so we decide to grow someone in-house. We call this "making unicorns" where I come from.

The process isn't simple. We'll need to discuss our strategy with other business executives in our company, identify a potential candidate, reach an agreement with the candidate, define our growth strategy for the candidate, announce the transition, and execute the growth strategy. This assumes that we've thought this all out and formalized our process.

We've made it through the first steps in our strategy, and the person we identified is flourishing in the new role. The execution of the growth strategy is thus far flawless. The new security guy is taking classes, actively participating in peer groups/associations, and regularly attending conferences. He's a sponge, and he's learning from the experiences of others. He's making a real impact in our organization too, which was the point all along. We decide to reward the awesome performance with a slight raise and a new title: Information Security Officer. What could be better?

In two years' time, we've grown a solid information security professional. It wasn't easy, but together we did it. It worked out better than we expected.

Unfortunately, we're not the only one who's noticed how great our Information Security Officer is. Recruiters are contacting him for new opportunities they need to fill, his peers are bragging about their new opportunities, and he begins listening to what was once only noise. Before long, he's entertaining offers from other organizations.

Suddenly, he gives us his two-week notice.

We're shocked, though we shouldn't be. This is the information security job market today. An information security professional with some education, a certification, and two years of experience can demand a compensation package of $200,000 or more. I know this because a very similar story has played out in front of me more than once.

Information security employee retention is a serious issue in our industry. It is compounded by the importance of continuity within an information security program design, implementation, and maintenance. A disruption in key personnel can derail progress.

When we leave a company, we leave what we've built for the next person to inherit. The next person won't have the same education, experiences, or context that we had, so they may not understand or like what we've left for them. We don't necessarily suffer, but the next person does, and more importantly, the organization does.

Career Path

Almost two-thirds of us don't have well-defined career paths. Many of us who work in this industry are ambitious; we want progress. We invest and even sacrifice significant amounts of time and money into our careers. Personally, I've spent thousands of hours outside of work developing my skills. I've done this to serve my company better, but I've also done this to further my career. Many of you have done the same.

When we stop to think how much we invest in time, it can be shocking. It only makes sense that we should want or expect a return on our investment. A return isn't always about salary either. We want a clearly defined career path. Without a clear career path, job satisfaction suffers, and employee retention drops.

Most of us want to grow and move forward. We want to know where we're heading. The future gives us hope for a better tomorrow. The thought of doing the same thing five years from now that we're doing today is depressing and maybe even a little scary. We want certainty (or at least probability) of a better tomorrow. We need to define career paths, as much as possible, for all information security talent. It gives us something to shoot for and it keeps us interested.

Burnout

When there are too few people to do the job, we either get new talent, let work go undone, or have everyone

> "Six Sources of Burnout at Work" by Paula Davis-Laack, JD, MAPP:
>
> 1. lack of control
> 2. values conflict
> 3. insufficient reward
> 4. work overload
> 5. unfairness
> 6. breakdown of community
>
> (Source: https://www.psychologytoday.com/us/blog/pressure-proof/201308/six-sources-burnout-work)

carry an extra load. Organizations can't ignore information security, and they can't find professionals that they can afford, so all the work falls upon existing employees. This extra burden creates stress, and ultimately burnout. When employees feel they've had enough, they leave. We work so hard to develop talented information security professionals, and then we drive them out. This is not a sustainable model.

Work overload is one of the six causes of burnout, according to Paula Davis-Laack, JD, MAPP (see sidebar). The challenge is determining how to get the most out of our talent without getting out of balance in one of these six areas. Burnout isn't a choice; it just happens, affecting both your mental and your physical health. Everyone has different thresholds, so be careful not to project your thresholds for balance onto other people.

Mental and Physical Health

Our jobs are stressful enough without adding extra work. This can start to affect our mental and physical well-being. If we don't keep things in check, we hit a breaking point. Stress levels rise, our body reacts, and we lose mental energy. Burnout ensues, if we don't catch things in time.

Burnout can lead to depression, which, in turn, has been linked to a variety of other health concerns, from eating disorders to heart disease. (Source: http://www.apa.org/helpcenter/job-stress.aspx) Securing information is not worth losing our physical and mental health.

National Security

A primary function of the US federal government is to protect its citizens. This means not only protecting us from physical threats like war and terrorism, but also protecting us against cyberthreats. Despite what we may read in the news, the US government is doing what it can, but there are some serious challenges associated with protecting our national interests online. The talent shortage is just one of those challenges.

Federal, state, and county agencies are competing with every organization in the private sector for the same information security talent. In many cases, government agencies can't afford the same quality of talent that private entities can. However, the potential impact could be significantly more severe. When a private company is breached, there may be private information leaked and financial damages. When a government agency is breached, the implications could be far worse, even including physical harm and death.

Government Defense

Many people agree that the next global war will be fought online; it will be a cyberwar. Assuming this is possible, some experts believe that the United States would lose such a conflict. One very well-respected expert, Kevin Mandia, FireEye CEO, said, "The reality is if all of Russia's cyber weapons went against us and all of our cyber weapons went against Russia, they would win." (Source: https://www.cnbc.com/2018/03/15/fireeye-ceo-if-the-us-and-russia-had-a-cyber-war-russia-would-win.html)

How many people can even fathom what this means? It means that we're in deep doo-doo, should this ever materialize. Take politics out of the conversation for a second or two. The fact that the Russian intelligence and/or attackers could interfere with the elections in the United States is a new threat that we've never seriously considered before. We'd better get our act together, and we'd better do it quickly.

President Obama's Commission on Enhancing National Cybersecurity issued its final report in December 2016. (Source: https://www.nist.gov/sites/default/files/documents/2016/12/02/cybersecurity-commission-report-final-post.pdf) The report's recommendations are focused on initiatives that can be undertaken over the next decade to improve our security. The report contains fifty-three action items, organized into sixteen recommendations, within six major imperatives:

1.   Protect, defend, and secure today's information infrastructure and digital networks.

2. Innovate and accelerate investment for the security and growth of digital networks and the digital economy.

3. Prepare consumers to thrive in a digital age.

4. Build cybersecurity workforce capabilities.

5. Better equip government to function effectively and securely in the digital age.

6. Ensure an open, fair, competitive, and secure global digital economy.

The focus for us here is the fourth imperative, "Build cybersecurity workforce capabilities." The report notes that "1.5 million more cybersecurity professionals will be needed globally by 2020," and says, "a sizable gap between open positions and qualified applicants has persisted for almost a decade." The report makes a key recommendation for addressing the imperative: "The nation should proactively address workforce gaps through capacity building, while simultaneously investing in innovations—such as automation, machine learning, and artificial intelligence—that will redistribute the future required workforce."

The recommendation is supported by eight action items:

1. The next President should initiate a national cybersecurity workforce program to train one hundred thousand new cybersecurity practitioners by 2020. (SHORT TERM)

2. The next President should initiate a national cybersecurity apprenticeship program to train fifty thousand new cybersecurity practitioners by 2020. (MEDIUM TERM)

3. To better prepare students as individuals and future employees, federal programs supporting education at all levels should incorporate cybersecurity awareness for students as they are introduced to and provided with Internet-based devices. (SHORT TERM)

4. The federal government should develop a mandatory training program to introduce managers and executives to cybersecurity risk management topics—even if their role is not focused on a cybersecurity mission area—so that they can create a culture of cybersecurity in their organizations. (SHORT TERM)

5. The federal government, SLTT governments, and private-sector organizations should create an exchange program aimed at increasing the cybersecurity experience and capabilities of mid-level and senior-level employees. (SHORT TERM)

6. The Office of Personnel Management (OPM) should establish a Presidential Cybersecurity Fellows program for federal civilian agencies with the goal of bringing on two hundred cybersecurity specialists by 2020. (SHORT TERM)

7. The National Science Foundation (NSF), the National Security Agency (NSA), and the Department of Education should work with private-sector organizations, universities, and professional societies to develop standardized interdisciplinary cybersecurity curricula that integrate with and expand existing efforts and programs. (MEDIUM TERM)

8. In order to attract more students to pursue cybersecurity degree programs and enter the cybersecurity workforce in both the public and private sectors, incentives should be offered to reduce student debt or subsidize the cost of education through a public–private partnership. (MEDIUM TERM)

These are good ideas, but the solutions aren't so simple. We certainly need the government's help in solving our talent shortage problem, but we can't expect the government to solve this on its own.

Global Problem

The talent shortage is much worse in other parts of the world. The United States and Canada are the only two countries where supply exceeds 50 percent of the demand. We think we have it bad, but there are much more severe information security talent shortages in countries like Israel, Ireland, and the United Kingdom. The United States ranks fourth in terms of the gap between demand and job seeker interest, followed by Germany, Australia, Canada, France, Italy, and Brazil.

This is a global information security talent shortage, and we're all in it together.

Economic Security

Our talent shortage has a negative impact on our collective economic security, although the exact amount is difficult to quantify. We know that our adversaries (nation-state and criminal enterprises) covet our financial assets, and that we don't have enough information security professionals to protect them. We are more vulnerable than ever.

We could also argue that the number of threats (adversaries) has increased in recent years. An increased number of vulnerabilities coupled with an increased number of applicable threats leads to an increased risk.

The global economic loss estimates from cybercrime range from more than $2 trillion by the year 2019 to as much as $6 trillion annually by 2021. (Source: https://www.juniperresearch.com/press/press-releases/cyber-crime-cost-businesses-over-2trillion) These estimates represent some serious economic security issues, and our talent shortage doesn't help matters.

Our Culture

Our information security culture is unique, to say the least, but we embrace it. We may wear the geek badge with honor or take pride in being different. We deserve to feel proud about the good things we have accomplished over the years. Our culture emphasizes outside-the-box thinking, innovation, close-knit friendships, and a strong sense of camaraderie. These good things about our culture are awesome! I love the excitement I feel when I travel to a security conference like Black Hat, and I love working on serious challenges that nobody else in the world can relate to except for my security brothers and sisters.

The good things about our culture help us attract new talent and keep them with us through thick and thin.

Cultures often have a dark side too, and our culture is no different. Much of our dark side comes from an exaggerated sense of self-worth and pride. Not the good sort of pride, but the bad sort of pride where instead of building each other up, we put each other down. The sort of pride that makes us feel good when we put someone in their place.

In some cases, our sense of pride grows into arrogance and exclusivity. We know that we are cyberwarriors and should be treated with respect. Not just anyone can be one us; you must earn your stripes first. Our arrogance and exclusivity prevent people from interacting with us and from wanting to join our ranks. Some people feel intimidated by our arrogance and bloated brilliance.

Here's one recent example. Our company hosted an online discussion on information security that was open to everyone, even normal people. The purpose was to facilitate open communication among all of us. The invites went out, and the response rate was awesome, but there was one response that led me to wonder about our culture:

Mr. Francen,

Can I just Audit? I am the office manager at a nonprofit and three years ago was asked to learn "some IT" to help out the people in the office. So I now work as the "help desk" for employees.

I am not qualified to join the hangout, but I love to learn, and am the only one to teach our employees about internet safety. So I watch these webinars, and I pay close attention to the current events. I would not be comfortable in a discussion with highly trained people in this field. But I would like to glean as much information as I can and pass it on to my employees, who are social workers mostly and not tech savvy at all.

If I don't hear back, I will assume that this is not the appropriate place for me to learn and will continue to learn in other places.

This email made me think deeply about how its writer must feel. For some reason, this person felt as though she was "not qualified." She "would not be comfortable," and felt that this was possibly "not the appropriate place" for her to learn. These feelings came from somewhere. How often do we make others feel unqualified, uncomfortable, and unwelcome?

The dark side of our culture contributes significantly to our talent problem. If we want to fix it, we need to change our culture. Some people won't consider entering our industry because of their perceived unworthiness and their false assumption that they don't have what it takes. We intimidate them.

We can pick any number of different things to focus on as problems in our culture, but I think the two ugliest are our gender inequity and our racial inequity.

Gender Inequity

There are so many incredibly talented women in our industry, and they stand out. They stand out because they are incredibly talented, and they stand out because they're so rare. We simply don't have enough talented women in our industry. I've heard all sorts of justifications and excuses, but facts are facts. Women make up half of the world's population, 45 percent of the overall workforce, but only 20 percent of the information security workforce. The good news is that we've improved. In 2013, the percentage was closer to 11. The not-so-good news is that we have a long way to go still. (Source: https://cybersecurityventures.com/women-in-cybersecurity/)

One problem is that our culture is not conducive to attracting and retaining women. Since our industry is so male dominated, it's a "bro culture." "It can be a little more crass, a little bit more rough and maybe some . . . females don't like that, and it is off-putting," says Ellison Anne Williams, PhD, founder and chief executive of Enveil, a data security company (Source: https://www.mcclatchydc.com/news/nation-world/national/national-security/article196363499.html).

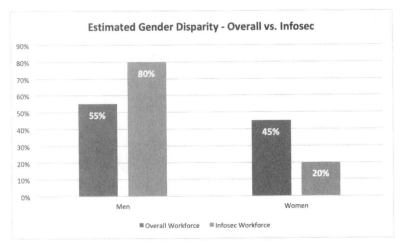

Figure: This provides an example of gender disparity in the field.

It's not just the people in our industry who contribute to the problem. Customers, clients, and other normal people also assume that information security is a male sport. "They have clients who won't speak directly to [female information security professionals]. It's the assumption that the woman is not the lead on the project. They just default to speaking to the men," says Leah Figueroa, lead data engineer at Gravwell, a data analytics company. (Source: http://www.govtech.com/workforce/Why-Are-So-Few-Women-in-Cybersecurity.html)

Recruiting women into our industry is one part of the problem. Our bro culture will have to go at some point, and we'll need to look for opportunities for women to advance. When I look at my own company, we only recently appointed the first female to our executive leadership team. This wasn't by accident, and it wasn't done just so we can say we have a woman in leadership. It was intentional, and she is absolutely, 100 percent the right person for the job.

Get involved, change what can be changed, and support those who can do more.

Each of the following programs advance the cause of recruiting more women into our industry. If we're committed to the cause ourselves, then we should look for ways to partner with these organizations, donate resources (money and/or volunteers), encourage women to get involved, and help where we can.

- **SANS CyberTalent Immersion Academy for Women:** This program, created by the SANS Institute, is meant to help fill the skills gap. The Academy is an intensive, accelerated training program that provides SANS world class training and GIAC certifications to quickly and effectively launch careers in cybersecurity. (https://www.sans.org/cybertalent/immersion-academy)

- **Computer Science for Cyber Security (CS4CS) Summer Program for High School Women:** This FREE, three-week, full-day summer program provides an introduction for high school women on the fundamentals of cybersecurity and computer science at the NYU Tandon School of Engineering. No background or experience in cybersecurity or computer programming is needed in order to apply, only your interest and enthusiasm. (http://engineering.nyu.edu/k12stem/cs4cs/)

- **Women's Society of Cyberjutsu (WSC):** This nonprofit organization is passionate about helping and empowering women to succeed in the cybersecurity field. (http://womenscyberjutsu.org/)

- **Women in CyberSecurity (WiCyS):** This initiative was launched in 2013 with support from a National Science Foundation grant for a collaborative project among several colleges. Thanks to support from various industry, government, and academic partners, WiCyS has led a continuing effort to recruit, retain, and advance women in cybersecurity. (https://www.wicys.net/)

A good book specifc to recruiting and retaining women in our industry is *InSecurity: Why a Failure to Attract and Retain Women in Cybersecurity Is Making Us All Less Safe*, written by Jane Frankland.

Racial Inequity

According to a survey by (ISC)², professionals of color are underrepresented in the industry, composing just 26 percent of our workforce. The bright side is that we're doing better than the overall US workforce, which stands at 21 percent. There is also a disparity in rank. Just 23 percent of cybersecurity professionals of color hold the role of director or above, compared to 30 percent for Caucasian people.

More information from the survey:

- *Yet people of color are more educated: 62 percent of them have obtained a master's degree or higher, compared to 50 percent of professionals who identify as Caucasian.*

- *On average, a cybersecurity professional of color earns $115,000, while the overall US cybersecurity workforce average is $122,000.*

- *Men of color are slightly behind their Caucasian male peers by $3,000, while women of color make an average of $10,000 less than Caucasian males and $6,000 less than Caucasian females.*

- *In addition to a higher average salary, Caucasian workers were more likely to have received a salary increase within the past year, as compared to other races and ethnicities.*

- *32 percent of cybersecurity professionals of color report that they have experienced some form of discrimination in the workplace.*

- *In the United States, 17 percent of the cybersecurity workforce who identify as a minority are female, proportionally exceeding overall female representation of 14 percent.*

- *To foster diversity in the workplace, 49 percent of minority cybersecurity professionals said mentorship programs are very important.*

  (Source: https://www.isc2.org/News-and-Events/Press-Room/ Posts/2018/03/15/ISC2-Study-Finds-US-Minority-Cyber security-Professionals-Underrepresented-in-Senior-Roles)

Most of us agree that we are short-staffed; however, most of us are not concerned by the underrepresentation of women and minorities in our industry, according to a survey conducted at the 2017 Black Hat conference. About 71 percent of respondents felt their companies lacked sufficient staff to defend itself against current cyberthreats. But less than half (45 percent) were concerned about the underrepresentation of women and people of color. The obvious thought is that if we need more people, why don't we recruit more women and people of color?

We need information security professionals from all ethnicities and all walks of life. Suprisingly, the employment disparity in information security doesn't vary much from employment disparity in the entire US workforce.

A Resource

One leader in this area is the International Consortium of Minority Cybersecurity Professionals (ICMCP). (Source: https://icmcp.org/) The nonprofit association is geared toward fostering the development and advancement of globally competitive minority cybersecurity practitioners. It is sponsored by powerful players in our industry, including ADP, Cisco, and Intel. If this is a cause that calls out to you, then get involved.

We Need More Unicorns

There are a lot of busted things related to our talent shortage problem: troubles with defining what a good security professional is, supply and demand problems, talent acquisition problems, talent retention problems, global and national security problems, cultural problems, gender inequity problems, and racial inequity problems. With all these challenges, who would want to join our ranks in the first place?

It all seems overwhelming, but I'm convinced that if we stay focused, we can make a positive difference. It's not an industry thing as much as it's a "you and me" thing—working not only individually, but also collectively. This is a cause that we can believe in and commit to. If each of us can convince one other person to join our cause, then we've created a movement.

Pointing out problems is the easy part. Solving them requires skill, commitment, and a lot of work.

SOLUTION #2: COMMIT TO THE CAUSE

Supply Problem Ideas

It's going to take a multifaceted approach to solve our supply-side problem, requiring the efforts of many different organizations and people. It will take a commitment on multiple fronts.

Mark van Zadelhoff, the General Manager of IBM Security, points out that the accounting industry went through the same sort of introspection in 1951, when it realized that there were only five hundred female certified public accountants in the country. After recognizing the problem, leaders across the accounting field teamed with industry associations and academic institutions to solve the issue through awareness campaigns and hiring initiatives. Today there are over eight hundred thousand female CPAs in the United States. Once the accounting industry recognized the problem and unified in its approach to fix the problem, the industry made great strides in solving it. (Source: https://hbr.org/2017/05/cybersecurity-has-a-serious-talent-shortage-heres-how-to-fix-it)

Security businesses need to follow this example. We need to take a hard look at ourselves to see what's holding us back. We need more unity in our industry if we're going to solve some of our industry-wide challenges, like this one. IBM is trying a "new collar" approach to hiring information security professionals. It puts a greater emphasis on skills, knowledge, and willingness to learn than on degrees. About 20 percent of IBM's information security hiring has reportedly come from this approach.

Early Education

Get them early. We need to educate our children and young adults better. Even if kids and young adults never enter the field, they'll be better off for having rudimentary information security education and skills in middle schools and high schools. Progress has been made on this front through President Obama's Commission on Enhancing National Cybersecurity, (Source: https://www.nist.gov/cybercommission) President Trump's Executive Order on Strengthening the Cybersecurity of Federal Networks and Critical Infrastructure, (Source: https://www.whitehouse.gov/presidential-actions/presidential-executive-order-strengthening-cybersecurity-federal-networks-critical-infrastructure/) and a planned new cybersecurity strategy. (Source: http://www.defenseone.com/technology/2017/10/trump-administration-plans-new-cybersecurity-strategy/142042/)

A few high schools in the United States are starting to integrate information security education into mandatory class offerings, though most schools do not offer any formal information security education beyond this.

While we wait for a national movement to take hold, there's nothing wrong with us working with our local school districts and their administrations. We could offer to assist the schools with the development of curriculum, or we could just request that they start teaching our children relevant information security skills. One resource that we can encourage them to use is the National Initiative for Cybersecurity Careers and Studies, where they can find resources and support for information security education. (Source: https://niccs.us-cert.gov/formal-education/integrating-cybersecurity-classroom)

Through funding from DHS, the CIC offers professional development opportunities for middle and high school teachers. STEM Explore, Discover, and Apply (EDA) workshops are available for middle school teachers and the Education Discovery Forum (EDF) for high school teachers. This professional development training allows teachers to bring new projects, technology, and curriculum into their classrooms.

We can encourage our administrators and teachers to follow the examples set by other teachers, such as Nicholas Coppolino at Parkville High School in Maryland. He's developed a curriculum using resources like Hacker Highschool and Cyber Aces to teach students basic information security skills. (Source: http://blogs.edweek.org/edweek/curriculum/2017/11/schools_are_training_students_to_be_cyber_sleuths.html)

Another program targeting young adults is the Pathways in Technology Early College High Schools (P-TECH) model. (Source: http://www. ptech.org/model) This model has expanded to at least twenty-seven schools in the United States.

Universities are also getting involved, such as the University of Rhode Island's Fundamentals of Cyber Security course. URI offers free curriculum material and teacher professional development training for high schools to implement this course. (Source: http://k12.cs.uri.edu/ cyber_fundamentals.php).

Even the Girl Scouts of America are getting in the game by offering eighteen new cybersecurity badges. All Girls Scouts can explore STEM opportunities and develop leadership skills. (Source: http://www. girlscouts.org/en/press-room/press-room/news-releases/2017/palo-alto-networks-girl-scouts-collaborate-cybersecurity-badges.html)

Information security education in our schools is still lagging far behind. There are great opportunities for improvement, but we need to get involved and act. Find a cause that hits home with you, and contribute your time and/or money to it.

Free Training

Some people can't afford training to get into our industry, or they can't afford to take the financial risk to pay for it. We need more free training opportunities for people who are considering our industry as a career option.

Mentorship

Imagine what would happen if each of us mentored just one person. This would make a tremendous difference. I get a lot of satisfaction from helping people learn the ropes in our business. People need mentors, whether they are people with no experience who are interested in the field or people new to the industry. There is no single way to mentor someone. Mentoring is just advising and training someone else from a position of experience and trust.

Free Training Resources for Information Security

FRSecure's Mentor Program (https://frsecure.com/cissp-mentor-program/): The program was established in 2010 to provide free information security training to those interested in taking the CISSP exam. The program is free; there is no obligation and no prerequisite, and it's offered both on-site and online.

SANS Cyber Aces Online (http://www.cyberaces.org/courses/): The global leader in cybersecurity training, SANS offers courses as open courseware to help grow the information security talent pool.

Cybrary (https://www.cybrary.it/catalog/): This excellent resource offers a full open-source library of high-quality information security training content.

Cyber Degrees (https://www.cyberdegrees.org/): These free MOOCS (Massive Open Online Courses) pertaining to cybersecurity are offered by universities and freely available to anyone interested in cybersecurity.

Personally, I think every information security professional with five or more years of experience should be mentoring someone. It can mean so much to people, and it's very rewarding. Find someone to mentor, or maybe find five people to mentor. The more the merrier.

Hire Intangibles

Set expectations appropriately when you are hiring information security talent. I prefer to hire someone for the intangibles and teach them as opposed to hiring someone with loads of education and experience. It's my preference, and it appears to work for us. We call it growing unicorns.

There are benefits to growing unicorns, such as teaching the way we want them to be taught (we don't have to unteach much) and building the bonds that come with mentorship. The downside is that we need to have much more patience in career development, but some of us are in this for the long haul anyway.

Apprenticeships

Reach out to local colleges and universities and offer apprenticeships. These are great opportunities to leverage inexpensive talent for tasks that are often a productivity drag for more senior information security talent. It gives the apprentice the opportunity to know your organization, and it gives you a chance to know the apprentice. These are usually short-term engagements (between college breaks), and there's very little risk.

We've had great experiences with apprentices. We end up hiring about half of them at some point.

Market Factors

We know that people want our information security talent, and in many cases, they're willing to pay top dollar to get it. We shouldn't feel threatened; we should feel motivated to do whatever it takes to keep our talent happy, engaged, inspired, and appreciated.

We've found that our information security professionals are often willing to take lower pay to work in a place where they have a strong sense of purpose, a flexible work schedule, and feel loved. They are part of the family, and we're on mission. We trust that they get their work done, so we don't have to micromanage them. They may be in the office every day, or they may work remotely. We trust them, so we don't always need to know where they are. Remember earlier when I told you that we hire for the intangibles? It's easy to trust our employees, because they're all trustworthy.

There's much more to keeping information security talent than a good salary. We could pay them 20 percent more, but if we have a crappy culture, we'd still lose them.

In addition to a strong, purposeful culture, we need to make sure—always—that our talent is relevant and well trained. We should look at the market factors that threaten our talent retention as opportunities for improvement. These factors keep us honest.

Experience Matters

We have a crop of information security professionals who are leaving our industry for one reason or another. Maybe they're burned out;

maybe they're retiring. No matter the reason, they are taking with them years and years of valuable experience. Some of us have been in this industry for more than twenty-five years, since even before what we do today was a formal thing. Use every opportunity at your disposal to spend time with our veterans and learn as much as you can. Once they're gone, so is all the wisdom they've built through their years in the trenches.

Acknowledgments

This is where I give credit where credit is due. I'll start from the top, and the top is Jesus. Jesus is the CEO of our business and he is the CEO of my life. I'm grateful for every opportunity that's been afforded me, and I'm most grateful for the presence of the Lord in my life.

My blessings are many, but arguably the greatest is my wife. My wife's name is Marlyce, and there could never be a way to reward her for what she's done in my life. Thank God we don't keep score, because she'd be kicking my ---. Always the encourager, always the selfless supporter, always everything a guy like me needs to get through life. To her, a "thank-you" doesn't express enough.

Somehow, and only by the grace of God, I have four amazing children. They inspire me to want to be a better father. Alyssa, Brenden, Joe, and Lydia, thank you. To my other children (it's complicated), Tyler, Ethan, and Ashleigh, also thank you. The inspiration you give me is an incredible gift.

Can't forget Mom. Thank you, Mom!

Then there's all the people I've met along the way.

Kevin Orth, my business partner, believed in my crazy ideas enough to risk almost everything. He's the one true friend that will always tell me the truth. Always. Everyone needs a "Kevin" in their life.

The leaders of FRSecure and SecurityStudio are a management dream team. Anyone who's had some success in business knows how important it is to work with a stellar management team. I think mine is the stellarest (my new word)! John Harmon, Renay Rutter, Drew Boeke, Brad Nigh, Ivan Peev, Andy Forsberg, and Peter Vinge are all pretty much the bomb. Did I miss anyone? Oh yeah, there's this guy named James Williams too. I don't think I would have written this book without his encouragement.

Thank you to Suzy Feine. She's a patient one, this Suzy. She coached me throughout the process and does a lot of the work behind the scenes. I'm grateful.

All the "unicorns" at FRSecure and SecurityStudio deserve more gratitude than I can give. These are the hard workers who day in and day out strive for 100 percent client satisfaction on every FRSecure project and for every SecurityStudio subscriber. To make matters more challenging, they do only projects that contribute to fixing the broken industry while walking away from those that don't. Amazing people, and I'm humbled to work alongside you.

Others? Oh yeah, there's more!

Thank you to my former coworkers who had more of an impact on my life than they may realize. People like Sean Seamans, Josh Quandt, Michelle Killian, and Greg Quale. We went through some difficult times, and I hope we're all better off for it.

Thank you to my endorsers. These are incredible people. Thank you, Tony Cole, Theresa Semmens, Nick Hernandez, Serge Suponitskiy, Tom Kieffer, and Dixon Gould. Special thanks to you, Dixon. You've always been a great friend and confidante.

Of course, I would be remiss if I didn't give a shout-out to the great people behind the scenes who make books like this happen. The publishing journey started with Cathy Paper. Thank you, Cathy! Before this, I had no idea how making a book happens. My publisher, Lily

Coyle, at Beaver's Pond Press, is a patient lady who knows what she's doing. Thank God for Lily! Other masters of their craft who brought this book to fruition include Steve LeBeau, editor (between you and me, think I almost killed him); Christine Zuchora-Walske, editor (she can edit anything); Laurie Buss Hermann, proofreader (she actually read this whole thing); and Athena Currier, designer (she makes stuff look good).

Thank you, too, to @M1ndFl4y (he doesn't like when I use his real name) for contributing the binary code for the secret message on the book cover.

Seriously, I could write for days about all the people who deserve acknowledgment. The problem is that you'd stop reading. Every person that I've ever met is another opportunity for learning something. If I neglected to mention you, please don't think that I'm not grateful! I simply ran out of paper.

About the Author

Evan Francen is the CEO and Founder of FRSecure®, a leading information security consulting company based in Minnesota. In 2017, he also founded SecurityStudio®, a software-as-a-service (SaaS) company dedicated to building a community of information security practitioners who speak the same security language. He coinvented FISASCORE®, the information security risk translation and assessment tool for companies.

Throughout his more than twenty-five-year career in information security, Evan has helped hundreds of businesses, small and large; has advised legal counsel in high-profile breaches, including Target and Blue Cross Blue Shield; and has served as an expert witness in several federal criminal cases.

Collectively, these accomplishments, and a few others, all lead to his mission: To fix the broken information security industry. This is a mission that requires the help of many like-minded people coming together as one, which is a central theme of this book.

Hidden in the binary code on the cover is a secret message that sums up the state of the information security industry. Can you decipher it? When you do, visit EvanFrancen.com/cover.